Economic Successes in South Asia

This book analyses economic successes in South Asia and the reasons why they emerge by offering an in-depth analysis of a few case studies against the backdrop of overall policy context and economic performance of these countries.

Offering a brief comparative review of South Asia in a global context, the book shows that the region remains economically and socially lagging. The author argues that within South Asia most countries demonstrate examples of economic or social success. This book explores such successes that provide lessons for other South Asian countries and beyond. Case studies include the textile industry and microcredit in Bangladesh, information technology in India, forestry management in Nepal, surgical and sports goods in Pakistan and human development in Sri Lanka. At the macro level, the book discusses India's catch-up growth first given the country's global importance and because of the prominence of the debate on its catch-up growth to development economics.

A novel addition to the literature with its focus on successful initiatives with broad policy implications, this book will be of interest to researchers in the field of development economics, development studies and South Asian Studies, in particular South Asian policy.

Shahrukh Rafi Khan is a research associate at Mount Holyoke College, USA. He formerly taught at Vassar College and served as the executive director of the Sustainable Development Policy Institute, Islamabad. He has published extensively in refereed journals and authored and edited numerous books. His most recent books are *Development Economics: A Critical Introduction* (2019) and *A Microcredit Alternative in South Asia* (with Natasha Ansari, 2018), also published by Routledge and *Spontaneous and Induced Collective Action in Pakistani Rural Development* (with Shaheen Rafi Khan, 2021).

Routledge Studies in the Growth Economies of Asia

141. Development Agenda and Donor Influence in South Asia
Bangladesh's Experiences in the PRSP Regime
Mohammad Mizanur Rahman

142. How China's Silk Road Initiative is Changing the Global Economic Landscape
Edited by Yuan Li and Markus Taube

143. Trade Unions and Labour Movements in the Asia-Pacific Region
Edited by Byoung-Hoon Lee, Sek-Hong Ng and Russell Lansbury

144. International Entrepreneurship: A Comparative Analysis
Susan Freeman, Ying Zhu and Malcolm Warner

145. Ritual and Economy in Metropolitan China
A Global Social Science Approach
Carsten Herrmann-Pillath, Guo Man and Feng Xingyuan

146. Cyber Risk, Intellectual Property Theft and Cyberwarfare
Asia, Europe and the USA
Ruth Taplin

147. Changing Labour Policies and Organization of Work in China
Impact on Firms and Workers
Ying Zhu, Michael Webber and John Benson

148. Vietnamese Labour Militancy
Capital-labour antagonisms and self-organised struggles
Joe Buckley

149. Economic Successes in South Asia
A Story of Partnerships
Shahrukh Rafi Khan

Economic Successes in South Asia

A Story of Partnerships

Shahrukh Rafi Khan

Routledge
Taylor & Francis Group
LONDON AND NEW YORK

First published 2022
by Routledge
2 Park Square, Milton Park, Abingdon, Oxon OX14 4RN

and by Routledge
605 Third Avenue, New York, NY 10158

Routledge is an imprint of the Taylor & Francis Group, an informa business

British Library Cataloguing-in-Publication Data
A catalogue record for this book is available from the British Library

Library of Congress Cataloging-in-Publication Data
Names: Rafi Khan, Shahrukh, author.
Title: Economic successes in South Asia : a story of partnerships / Shahrukh Rafi Khan.
Description: 1 Edition. | New York, NY : Routledge, 2022. | Series: Routledge studies in the growth economies of asia; 149 | Includes bibliographical references and index.
Identifiers: LCCN 2021045888 (print) | LCCN 2021045889 (ebook) | ISBN 9781032003108 (hardback) | ISBN 9781032009339 (paperback) | ISBN 9781003176411 (ebook)
Subjects: LCSH: Economic development--South Asia. | South Asia--Social conditions--21st century. | South Asia--Social policy--21st century. | South Asia--Economic conditions--21st century. | Partnership--South Asia.
Classification: LCC HC430.6 .R3364 2022 (print) | LCC HC430.6 (ebook) | DDC 338.95--dc23/eng/20220107
LC record available at https://lccn.loc.gov/2021045888
LC ebook record available at https://lccn.loc.gov/2021045889

ISBN: 978-1-032-00310-8 (hbk)
ISBN: 978-1-032-00933-9 (pbk)
ISBN: 978-1-003-17641-1 (ebk)

DOI: 10.4324/9781003176411

Typeset in Times New Roman
by Deanta Global Publishing Services, Chennai, India

Dedication

To my delightful grandchildren, Raja Subotai Mawaz Khan and Nami Enid Khan.

Contents

Tables

Preface

This book emerged from a seminar on South Asian economic development I led over a dozen years at Mount Holyoke College. In thinking about the course when I retired, I realized that there were two connecting themes in the seminar topics. First, the seminar highlighted South Asian success stories. There are lessons to be learned from failures, but there often is an overemphasis on failures. Academics are trained to be critical and for good reason since trial by fire is a good way to advance knowledge. However, learning from successes, without suspending a critical perspective, is also possible.

The second connecting theme of the book is one of partnerships for economic development. This book explores such partnerships between the state (local and foreign), private sector (local and foreign) and civil society (local and foreign) that can facilitate economic development. A simple calculation makes it evident that many partnership combinations are possible. In the context of partnerships, another theme of the book is collective action of various kinds. This book explores innovative types of rural (village /community/apex organizations) and urban (producer cooperatives, clusters) collective action as outcomes of various forms of partnerships between state, civil society and local and foreign capital.

In focusing on partnerships, this book reiterates or contends that many of the dichotomies in the economic development literature are false. For example, many scholars like Sen (1981), Amsden (1989) and Wade (2004) among others showed that the import substitution industrialization (ISI) vs. export promotion (EP) was a false dichotomy. They showed that ISI could provide a foundation for EP and indeed could be going on simultaneously with EP occurring in different industries.

Chapter 1 and 2 of Part 1 also suggest that market vs. state is another false dichotomy and that this represents a stale debate. In the development economics literature, the debate has played out as the neoliberal (structural reform) vs. developmentalist (industrial policy) dichotomy. The book supports the view that there are valuable insights forthcoming from all approaches and that eclecticism and developmental pragmatism trump hardened ideological positions.

This point on false dichotomies in the development economics literature gets play in Part 1 of this book in both the overview chapter and in the debate explaining the success of India's catch-up economic growth in Chapter 2. This point is also supported by case studies in Part 4 of the book that point out that export successes of Pakistan's soccer balls and surgical goods industries, Bangladeshi garment Industry and Indian information technology and vehicle and accessory industries represent various combinations of the success of industrial policy, structural reforms (liberalization and deregulation) and market dynamism. Alternatively, these successes can be viewed as a partnership of the state, local and foreign capital. The success of producer cooperatives in Kerala, India, a business venture with a difference, also represents the success of a partnership, this time between state and civil society.

Parts 2 and 3 focus on state and civil society partnerships but also on the nonprofit sectors. A number of poverty alleviation initiatives have been discussed in the development literature and South Asia has been an important venue for initiating them or experimenting with them. These include basic human needs/human development, microcredit, employment guarantee schemes and conditional cash transfers (CCT). In addition, there are mechanisms to deliver poverty alleviation, such as participatory development, using one or more of the poverty alleviation initiatives mentioned above. South Asian success stories include participatory development, microcredit (initiated in Bangladesh), employment guarantee schemes (initiated in India) and a graduation scheme (a variant on the CCT initiated in Bangladesh).

Part 2 has chapters on successful experiments with participatory development in Pakistan, human development in Sri Lanka, interest-free microcredit in Pakistan and employment guarantee schemes in India. While Bangladesh's CCT is very promising and has been judged to be a success by prominent economists (Banerjee et al., 2015), it is relatively recent compared to the track record established by the other success stories. The success stories in Part 3 are on the theme of population and the environment and include fertility reduction in Bangladesh and joint forest management in India and Nepal.

The success stories selected for this book do not represent an exhaustive list, but perhaps this work will inspire others to write about successes they consider more noteworthy. I thank the hundreds of South Asian economists and scholars whose work I synthesized to present the success stories. As ever, I thank Mount Holyoke College for continued research support in my capacity as a research associate and Professor Kavita Khory, who was very supportive throughout my years at Mount Holyoke College. I thank Suzanne Sherman Aboulfadl, who has constructed excellent indices for several of my books over the last two decades and who goes beyond the call of duty and provides very helpful text editing suggestions.

I thank Dorothea Schaefter of Routledge, who viewed the book proposal as innovative and of potential value and for providing speedy and valuable feedback as I updated her. Thanks are also due to the reviewer for also seeing value in the book and for the comments provided. Finally, I thank the many congenial students of Mount Holyoke College who attended my seminars over the years and contributed to them with their own superb case studies and lively discussions that I fondly remember.

References

Amsden, A. H. 1989. *Asia's Next Giant* (New York: Oxford University Press).

Banerjee, A. et. al. 2015. "A Multifaceted Program Causes Lasting Progress for the Very Poor: Evidence from Six Countries," *Science*, 348(6236), DOI:10.1126/science.1260799.

Sen, A. K. 1981. "Public Action and the Quality of Life in Developing Countries," *OxfordBulletin of Economics and Statistics*, 43(4), 287–319.

Wade, R. 2004. *Governing the Market: Economic Theory and the Role of Government in EastAsian Industrialization* (Princeton, New Jersey: Princeton University Press).

Part 1: Macro context

Developmentalism and neoliberalism

1 South Asia overview[1]

Introduction

The World Bank's World Development Indicators provide a valuable database spanning over half a century that enables an economic and social evaluation of South Asian economies. Using this database, this chapter first provides a descriptive comparative evaluation of South Asia with other regions.[2] Next, it provides a descriptive comparative evaluation within the South Asian region focusing on country successes and weaknesses. Finally, the results of simple empirical exercises that address policy questions emerging from different approaches to economic development are documented followed by a summary.

South Asian region in a comparative context

Comparing the South Asian region[3] with others (Appendix Table 1.1) indicates that, overall, it remains an economically and socially lagging region. Progress or success is defined in conventional economistic and social or human development terms. Thus, per capita GDP growth, while containing inequality, export growth, economic diversification (manufacturing as a percentage of GDP), poverty alleviation and human development are the variables used to define progress when comparing regions or countries within a region.

The average GDP growth rate in the decade of the 2010s in South Asia (SA) was a whole 2 percentage points higher at 6.7 percent than that of even the East Asia and the Pacific (EA&P) and higher than the other three regions of Latin America and the Caribbean (LA&C), Middle East and North Africa (ME&NA) and Sub-Saharan Africa (SSA), respectively. This lead over EA&P closes down to 1.3 percent when comparing per capita GDP growth rates over the decade but, even so, the recent economic progress is impressive.[4]

Despite recent progress, economic and social indicators over time were not as impressive in relative terms. By 2018, in per capita GDP terms, SA was 5.5, 4.8 and 4 times lower than EA&P, LA&C and ME&NA, respectively, and only slightly higher than SSA. The size of manufacturing, measured as a percentage of GDP, is a proxy for the diversification and sophistication of the economy. At 15.3 percent, SA was well behind the 23.6 percent for EA&P, though marginally

DOI: 10.4324/9781003176411-2

higher than the other three regions. Export success is critical to earning foreign exchange for catch-up growth and averting trade imbalances and in this regard its performance lagged behind all the other regions. The productivity gap was even greater. For example, productivity per worker in industry was 4.6 times lower in SA compared to EA&P and was less than half of SSA.[5] Similarly, the human development index in SA at .64 was 10 points lower than EA&P.[6]

Notwithstanding these lagging indicators, there are positive signs as reflected in the GDP growth statistics. Gross capital formation in the decade starting 2010 at 32.3 percent was virtually the same as EA&P and much higher than the other regions, suggesting that SA might be able to sustain its economic progress. It has been streamlining business procedures and so the time required to start a business (19 days) was the lowest across the board in 2018. If it converts economic progress to social progress, that could further buttress overall progress.

Economic and social progress within South Asia

Regional aggregations are helpful in a limited sense, but as expected generalizations miss out on important country differences that are captured in Appendix Table 1.2a–g. While the review of the comparative Appendix Tables 1.2a–g in this chapter is selective, the interested reader consulting this comparative data can glean important insights.

Data are provided in the tables in terms of decadal averages and also for the base and terminal years over five decades. While in some cases smoothing over variations with decadal averages is helpful, in other cases, when there is an evident trend, more information is conveyed by information about the base and terminal years. The numbers in these tables are used to focus on striking successes and also to highlight failures.

South Asian countries share commonalities in culture, histories and institutions, but nonetheless vary a great deal. For example, the population ranged from half a million in the Maldives to 1.35 billion in India in 2018. While all South Asian countries are vulnerable to the impacts of climate change, Bangladesh and the Maldives and coastal India, Pakistan and Sri Lanka are particularly vulnerable to sea level rises that cloud their future. While Afghanistan, Pakistan and Sri Lanka have experienced war or political turmoil over the decades, Bhutan, isolated from such tensions, has been relatively harmonious and experimented with a highly acclaimed social innovation (see below).

Afghanistan desperately needs peace. It ended the second decade of the twenty-first century with the lowest per capita GDP in the region, highest poverty rate, collapsed per capita GDP growth rates, collapsed domestic savings rate of virtually zero, a huge trade deficit, very low productivity in all the sectors and an incomplete structural change.[7] Compounding these problems are the highest fertility rates in the region (5.3 births per woman in 2017). The rays of hope are that in 2018 virtually the whole population of the country had access to electricity (98 percent), among the highest in SA, and the time required to start a business (8.5 days) was the lowest in South Asia. However, the withdrawal of coalition forces from the region, the Taliban takeover, and the continued threat of civil war represent ongoing challenges Afghanistan will have to confront.

Bangladesh (formerly East Pakistan) declared its independence from West Pakistan in March 1971. As a province, it had a larger population but lagged far behind West Pakistan on all economic and social indicators. However, soon after independence, economic and social indicators started to dramatically improve.

In the 1980s, it invested heavily in the textiles industry and within a decade became a world beater in garment exports despite growing no cotton (Chapter 10). While in 2018 Pakistan ranked fourth in raw cotton exports, in 2017–2018 its total textile exports were $12.5 billion, while Bangladesh apparel exports alone in the same period were $30.6 billion. By 2018, it had over taken Pakistan's per capita income by a small amount, but since it had a much higher per capita economic growth trajectory (5.4 percent between 2010 and 2018 compared to 1.8 percent for Pakistan) the gap is very likely to widen.[8]

Bangladesh also appears to be the only South Asian country to have bucked the premature deindustrialization trend (Dasgupta and Singh (2006), Rodrik (2015)). All other South Asian countries indicate a sharp or mild inverted U-shaped pattern in industry and manufacturing share in GDP over the decades covered. In 2018, Bangladesh indicates a linear positive trend with both manufacturing and industry share in GDP increasing threefold since its independence. Its manufacturing exports as a percentage of the total averaged 93 percent for 2010–2018, far higher than most other South Asian countries averaging at or close to 70 percent. Other positive economic indicators were a modest central government debt of about a third of GDP, the lowest in South Asia. Also, it was the only country, other than Nepal, with a positive average current account balance for 2010–2018.

Unlike other countries in the emerging world, Bangladesh's catch-up growth has not been accompanied by a rise in inequality. Its Gini coefficient of 32 in 2016 was the lowest in South Asia and its human development indicators made a great stride from 0.39 in 1970 to .61 in 2018.[9] However, the big challenge it faces now is containing absolute poverty. The World Bank estimate for 2016 showed that its poverty head count at a cut-off of $3.20 per day (in 2011 PPP$s) was 53 percent of the population, the highest in South Asia.

Bhutan is a small country which had three-quarters of a million people in 2018. It clocked robust growth rates between 1980 and 2017, resulting in the third highest per capita GDP in the region after the Maldives and Sri Lanka in 2017. As a very small country economies of scale, except for exports, are difficult to attain. Thus two-fifths of the economy is based on agriculture, forestry and fisheries and two-fifths on services. Industry is just over a tenth of the economy, but highly productive in that value added per worker is over twice that of Sri Lanka, which ranks the second highest in this regard in South Asia.

Bhutan increased its per capita GDP eightfold between 1980 and 2017, the highest increase in South Asia. Not surprisingly, it also attained the highest reduction in absolute poverty for a roughly equivalent period.[10] For example, between 2007 and 2017, the poverty head count ratio at $3.20 a day (2011 PPP $s) declined from 30.5 percent of the population to 12 percent.

It however manifests the usual weaknesses of a low/low middle-income country (L/LMIC). Between 2010 and 2018, it averaged a negative current account balance of close to a quarter of the GDP, the highest in South Asia, other than Afghanistan. Also, central government debt as a percentage of GDP in 2016 at 108 was the highest in South Asia.

Bhutan's notable social innovation is a focus on the happiness of ethnic Bhutanese people and it has famously in this regard contributed to the development of the Gross Happiness Index that it utilizes annually (Ura et. al., 2012). Its head count poverty and poverty gap estimates are the second lowest in South Asia after Sri Lanka and so do reflect this concern for well-being. However, surprisingly, its Gini estimate is the second highest in South Asia after Sri Lanka. Also, surprisingly, its human development index at 0.62 in 2018 matches that of Bangladesh and is lower than India (.65), the Maldives (.72) and Sri Lanka (.78).

The numbers count for the most in India as the dominant country in the South Asian regional grouping. Thus, while in relative terms the decline in poverty between 2004 and 2011 was the lowest in South Asia at 15 percent for a roughly equivalent period, the percentage decline between 1987 and 2011 is more impressive at 27 percent. However, the point is that in absolute terms this amounted to hundreds of millions of people moving above the poverty line.

The per capita GDP growth rate in India until the decade of the 1980s was very modest (0.6 percent in the 1970s). In the 1980s and 1990s, this growth rate increased to 3.3 percent and 3.7 percent, respectively. It subsequently picked up to 4.6 percent and 5.8 percent, respectively, in the next two decades. Per capita GDP increased fivefold in the almost four decades between 1980 and 2018. This evident catch-up growth sparked a debate in the development economics literature. Thus, while Panagariya (2004) and Bhagwati and Panagariya (2013) claimed that market-driven "pro-entry" (neoliberal) reforms explained the Indian takeoff, Rodrik and Subramanian (2004) claimed this to be based on pro-business and pro-incumbent developmentalist policies (see below).

The Maldives, a tropical islands nation with half a million population, is the most prosperous in South Asia measured in per capita GDP terms. In terms of productivity in industry, agriculture and services, it dwarfs all the other South Asian nations. Even so, between 2002 and 2009, almost two-fifth of the population fell below the $3.20 per day (2011 PPP $s) poverty line. This might be ameliorated by the modern pension system it instituted in 2009.[11] It has also used resources generated from tourism and marine-based exports to enhance the human development of its population (second highest in South Asia at .72).

Nepal's performance to date has not been remarkable and it remains a low-income country (LIC). It suffers from low productivity and high poverty in all sectors. Its industrial productivity per person in 2018 was even lower than that of Afghanistan. Over half the population in 2010 was below the $3.20 (2011 PPP $s) per day poverty line. However, unlike most other South Asian nations, it has managed a current account surplus in the first two decades of the twenty-first century.

In the 1960s, Pakistan was viewed as the "development model" to emulate for having initiated impressive catch-up growth (Papanek, 1967).[12] The growth momentum was sustained such that up into the 1980s and 1990s Pakistan had the second highest per capita GDP growth rate in South Asia. However, Pakistan lagged in social investments and the associated human development indicators, the lowest in South Asia in 2018 after Afghanistan. Experts warned that Pakistan would not be able to sustain its economic growth momentum without concomitant investment in its people but the latter remained a low priority for Pakistani policy makers, both military and civil. Nonetheless, Pakistan was able to maintain its lead over India in per capita GDP terms until the turn of the twentieth century. India overtook Pakistan with a much higher growth trajectory in 2006 (Khan, 2011) and by 2017 Pakistan's per capita GDP was less than three-fifths of India's.

Given the state of the economy in 2018, the future was not looking bright. It was highly indebted and acquiring more debt at a rapid rate, which closes off future fiscal space. Its rate of capital formation was the lowest in South Asia and gross domestic savings were the lowest after Afghanistan. Apart from a fiscal imbalance, it also had a trade imbalance that seemed likely to persist given that its exports as a percentage of GDP of 11.4 were the lowest in South Asia after Nepal.[13]

Sri Lanka is the South Asian front runner among the larger South Asian countries. It initially came into notice for its high social investments, high human development indicators, low poverty rates and then for being the first in the sub-continent to attain MIC status (Chapter 4). Its poverty rate of 10 percent (population living below $3.20 a day (2011 PPP $s)) in 2016 continued to be the lowest in South Asia. However, inequality picked up and its Gini coefficient of 39 was the highest in South Asia in 2009. It also faced the usual economic challenges of MICs of a high debt ratio (74 percent of GDP) and a balance of trade deficit.

The brief review above provides a descriptive narrative highlighting strengths and weaknesses. In the next analytic section, an attempt is made to infer causes.

Evaluating policy

Table 1.1 provides summary statistics to document the economic and social success of South Asian countries over about five decades.

Sri Lanka made the least progress in human development, but it started off with a high base. Indeed, its human development index in 1970 matched what was attained by most of the other South Asian countries in 2018. By the same token, Afghanistan showed the highest progress in human development, but it started with a very low base and remained the country with the lowest human development in 2018. Thus, it needs to continue with rapid progress to catch up with other South Asian countries in this regard. Pakistan is among the laggards in economic progress, and this calls for testing the hypothesis that the lack of social investment might be a cause for its lack of economic progress.

Table 1.1 South Asian country economic and social status and progress

Country	*GDP per capita (constant 2010 US$), 2018*	*Percentage growth in GDP per capita (constant 2010 US$), 1970–2018*	*Human Development Index, 2018*	*Percentage growth in Human Development Index, 1970–2018*
Afghanistan	563.8	171	.50	167
Bangladesh	1203.2	293	.61	156
Bhutan	3172.8@	782@	.62	122
India	2100.8	531	.65	151
Maldives	8033.3	174	.72	131
Nepal	698.6	250	.58	153
Pakistan	1197.8	254	.56	140
Sri Lanka	3936.4	553	.78	123

Sources: GDP per capita from World Development Indicators, update 12/20/2019
Human development data from http://hdr.undp.org/en/data#, downloaded 1/23/2020.
Notes: @= Terminal year is 2017

In the rest of this section, we document the results of such simple empirical exercises that address policy questions emerging from alternative approaches to economic development. Specifically, we explore policy lessons from the basic needs/human development, developmentalist and neoliberal approaches that have been given chapter-length treatment in Khan (2020).

Sen (2000) made a convincing and well-received case suggesting that investing in people (human development) is a source of human flourishing and therefore a worthy end. It also serves the instrumental purpose of stimulating productivity and growth. The more orthodox view is that economic growth should be prioritized and human development follows since there is a high correlation between the two variables.

We tested the hypotheses regarding the mutual association of per capita GDP (PCGDP) and the human development index (HDI) for the five larger South Asian economies for which full data sets were available from the World Development Indicators and the UNDP Human Development Index from 1970 to 2018.[14] In all cases the hypothesis that HDI Granger causes PCGDP is rejected. For Bangladesh, India and Nepal, the hypothesis that PCGDP Granger causes HDI is also rejected. For Pakistan and Sri Lanka, the hypothesis that PCGDP does not cause HDI Granger is rejected at 11 and 10 percent, respectively, at best a weak association. These findings suggest that there are no simplistic policy explanations for the complex mutual association of PCGDP and HDI.

Developmentalists, going back to the 1940s, have argued for the centrality of manufacturing in the development process. This was further theorized and operationalized by Kaldor (1967). We estimated a Kaldor equation to identify the centrality of manufacturing to the development process for the five large South Asian economies and the results are reported in Table 1.2.

Table 1.2 Kaldor equations showing sector contributions to GDP growth in South Asia (Dependent variable, growth in GDP)

Independent variable	*Constant*	*B*	*R bar Sq.*	*F stat.*
Growth in manufacturing value added	.74	.50 (3.89)	.39	15.15
Growth in agriculture value added	.70	.94 (2.70)	.22	7.32
Growth in services value added	.08	.90 (10.69)	.84	73.9

Source: World Development Indicators, update 12/20/2019
Note: Parentheses contain *t*-values suggesting that all coefficients are significant at least at the 1 percent level. The F stat indicates the same significance level for the equations.

Before reporting the results of Table 1.2, some explanation about the nature of the empirical exercise conducted is called for. Kaldor's theoretical model called for regressing the growth of the manufacturing sector on GDP growth. The rationale was that manufacturing results in dynamic efficiencies[15] (such as economies of scale and positive externalities) that are diffused within the sector and to the rest of the economy and that this was not true for the other sectors.

Both time series and cross-sectional data are problematic when testing Kaldor's hypotheses. Using time series data might result in a cyclical phenomenon interfering in the long-term association between the two identified variables. However, cross-country associations are problematic because the countries in the sample could be structurally very dissimilar. As a compromise, we constructed a South Asian cross-section time series panel data set where ten-year averages were used to abstract from a cyclical phenomenon.[16] We assumed that there is a reasonable amount of structural similarity across the larger South Asian economies.[17]

Another possible problem in Kaldor's specification is the possibility of spurious correlation. Since manufacturing is a part of GDP growth, regressing manufacturing sector growth on GDP growth could be problematic. Thus, scholars (e.g., Wells and Thirlwall, 2003) have recommended regressing growth of manufacturing on GDP growth net of manufacturing or on non-manufacturing growth. However, since dynamic efficiencies can also be diffused within manufacturing, Kaldor's original specification was used.

All the coefficients in Table 1.2 are highly significant, the F statistics reveal robust equations, and the R bar squares are reasonable for panel regressions. The coefficients are in line with Kaldor and developmentalist expectations of the centrality of manufacturing to economic growth even though there have been some second thoughts on this issue (Dasgupta and Singh, 2005). The coefficients however are not straightforward to interpret. The beta coefficient for manufacturing has a value of .5, considerably less than 1. In Kaldor's causal model, the greater the difference between sector growth and GDP growth, the greater is the contribution to GDP growth by the sector. By contrast to the .5 manufacturing coefficient, the coefficients of services and agriculture are both close to 1 suggesting support for the Kaldor hypothesis of the importance of manufacturing to GDP growth.

Neoclassical economics emphasizes efficient allocation of resources by removing distortions, and this can yield economic growth, probably at a diminishing rate, until such misallocation is removed.[18] Neoliberalism has neoclassical economics as its underpinning but has some prescriptions that can complement or induce growth. The idea of requiring macroeconomic stability and internal and external balance can in principle create a foundation for economic growth if it does not undermine it. Growth can then be delivered by economic openness, including trade liberalization, export promotion and capital flows (portfolio and foreign direct investment).

The attempt to estimate the impact of trade, fiscal and savings/investment imbalances on economic growth in a heuristic production function framework was impeded by the lack of an adequate number of observations for reasonable time series analysis. We tested for the association of economic growth and export growth for Bangladesh, India, Pakistan, for which we had 58 observations (1961–2018), and Sri Lanka, for which we had 57 observations (1962–2018). The export growth series for the other South Asian countries was much shorter and not adequate for time series analysis. Only for Bangladesh did we find an association but it was two way such that export growth Granger causing GDP growth was not rejected at the 2 percent level and GDP growth Granger causing export growth was not rejected at the 10 percent level. Thus, there is very weak evidence of export growth being a driver of GDP growth in South Asia.

Similarly, there is only weak support of Granger causality between FDI and GDP growth between 1970 and 2018.[19] There was no association either way for Bangladesh and Sri Lanka. Nepal showed a two-way association at the 1 percent level. For India, the hypothesis that a one-year lagged FDI Granger caused an increase in GDP was not rejected at the 1 percent level.[20] For Pakistan, the hypothesis that FDI Granger caused an increase in GDP was not rejected at the 5 percent level. Thus, only for India and Pakistan was there a one-way association of FDI and GDP growth.

Summary

The World Bank, World Development Indicators, now provides enough data for time series analysis on several issues. South Asian economies are first descriptively compared with other regions, using conventional indicators, and found to be lagging economically and socially. Within South Asia, the data revealed a number of interesting and unexpected insights regarding country strengths and weaknesses. Next, the basic human needs/human development, developmentalist and neoliberal approaches are utilized to test various hypotheses that could shed light on South Asian economic successes and weaknesses using time series analysis. In most cases, there was no conclusive evidence. By constructing a panel data set, there was support for the developmentalist prescription regarding the centrality of manufacturing to the economic development process.

Appendix Table 1.1 Comparative economic and social standing by region

Region	*EA&P*	*LA&C*	*ME&NA*	*SA*	*SSA*
GDP growth (annual %), average 2010–2018	4.7	1.8	3.3	6.7	3.6
GDP per capita growth (annual %), 2010–2018	4.0	0.7	1.3	5.3	0.9
GDP per capita, constant 2010 USA$, 2018	10262.5	9224.7	7839.7	1888.1	1660.0
GDP per capita, PPP (constant 2011 international $), 2018	17244.8	14428.2	18345.8	6286.4	3535.5
Industry (including construction), value added (% of GDP), 2010–2017	34.6	26.6	44.3	27.1	26.5
Manufacturing, value added (% of GDP), 2010–2018	23.6	13.4	13.4	15.3	10.0
Agriculture, forestry and fishing; value added (% of GDP) 2010–2017	5.2	4.7	4.8	16.9	15.6
Services, value added (% of GDP), 2010–2018	58.6*	58.4	49.4	48.3	51.3
Industry (including construction), value added per worker (constant 2010 US$), 2010–2018	23758.0	26996.9	42728.6	5126.3	11660.8
Agriculture, forestry and fishing; value added per worker (constant 2010 US$), 2010–2018	3125.7	6642.2	6523.5	1429.3	1353.7
Services, value added per worker (constant 2010 US$), 2010–2018	21054.7	18902.8	21261.6	6674.8	7288.1
Time required to start a business (days), 2018	23.4	28.8	20.4	18.9	31.6
Gross capital formation (% of GDP), 2010–2018	32.8	21.9	27.9	32.3	21.7
Gross domestic savings (% of GDP), 2010–2018	34.7	20.3	36.5	28.2	20.1
Exports of goods and services (% of GDP), 2010–2018	31.3	22.0	45.2	20.6	27.9
Manufactures exports (% of merchandise exports), 2010–2018	80.0	46.1	20.1	68.5	10.0
Access to electricity (% of population), 2017	97.8	98.1	97.8	90.0	44.6
Individuals using the Internet (% of population), 2017	55.1	63.2	56.2	30.1	25.4
Fertility rate, total (births per woman), 2017	1.8	2.0	2.8	2.4	4.8
Human development index, 2018	.74	.76	.70	.64	.54

Source: Data from database: World Development Indicators, update 12/20/2019
Human development data from http://hdr.undp.org/en/data#, downloaded 1/23/2020

Notes: * = Terminal year, 2017
na = Data not available
EA&P = East Asia and the Pacific
LA&C = Latin America and the Caribbean
ME&NA = Middle East and North Africa
SA = South Asia
SSA = Sub-Saharan Africa

Appendix Table 1.2a Afghanistan's average decadal and end years economic and social progress

	1970–1979	*1980–1989*	*1990–1999*	*2000–2009*	*2010–2018*	*1970*	*2018*
GDP growth (annual %)	na	na	na	9.4	4.8		
GDP per capita growth (annual %)	na	na	na	5.9[%]	1.7		
GDP per capita (constant 2010 US$)	na	na	na	379.4[$]	566.7	330.3[$]	563.8
Industry (including construction), value added per worker (constant 2010 US$)	na	na	na	2410.3[$]	2113.4	2164.7[$]	1842.9
Agriculture, forestry and fishing; value added per worker (constant 2010 US$)	na	na	na	693.0[$]	954.8	780.0[$]	843.9
Services, value added per worker (constant 2010 US$)	na	na	na	1833.0[$]	2117.3	1522.6[$]	2001.1
Industry (including construction), value added (% of GDP)	na	na	na	25.4[$]	21.6[&]	23.8[$]	22.1[&]
Manufacturing, value added (% of GDP)	na	na	na	16.9[$]	12.0[&]	18.8[$]	11.1[&]
Agriculture, forestry and fishing; value added (% of GDP)	na	na	na	31.2[$]	22.7[&]	38.6[$]	20.5[&]
Services, value added (% of GDP)	na	na	na	40.6[$]	51.7[&]	36.2[$]	52.7[&]
Time required to start a business (days)	na	na	na	9.8[+]	8.5	9.5[+]	8.5
Gross capital formation (% of GDP)	9.2[+]	na	na	18.9[$]	17.9[&]		
Gross domestic savings (% of GDP)	6.7[+]	na	na	−31.7[$]	0.2[&]		
Manufactures exports (% of merchandise exports)	na	na	na	na	14.6[@]		

Exports of goods and services (% of GDP)	na	na	na	28.8[$]	14.8[&]		
Current account balance (% of GDP)	−2.4	na	na	−0.1	−18.1		
Access to electricity (% of population)	na	na	na	34.1[^]	72.7[&]	23.0[^]	97.7[&]
Individuals using the Internet (% of population)	na	na		1.2[$]	7.5[&]	0.0[$]	13.5[&]
Human development index			0.32	0.40	0.48	0.30	0.50
				2007	2016		
Poverty headcount ratio at national poverty lines (% of population)	na	na	na	33.7	54.5		
Population, million							37.2

Sources: Data from database: World Development Indicators, update 12/20/2019
Human development data from http://hdr.undp.org/en/data#, downloaded 1/23/2020.

Notes: * = Starting year 1991
= Starting year 2001
$ = Starting year 2002
% = Starting year 2003
+ = Starting year 200
^ = Starting year 2005
+ = Terminal year is 1978
@ = Terminal year is 2016
& = Terminal year is 2017
x = Estimate for 1979–82
y = Estimate for 2008–09
! = Estimate for 2010
na = Not available

Appendix Table 1.2b Bangladesh's average decadal and end years economic and social progress

	1970–1979	*1980–1989*	*1990–1999*	*2000–2009*	*2010–2018*	*1970*	*2018*
GDP growth (annual %)	1.5	3.5	4.7	5.6	6.6		
GDP per capita growth (annual %)	–0.6	0.9	2.5	4.0	5.4		
GDP per capita (constant 2010 US$)	354.3	385.1	455.6	619.8	969.2	411.2	1203.2
GDP per capita, PPP (constant 2011 international $)	na	na	1469.0[&]	1998.2	3124.6	1325.6[&]	3879.2
Industry (including construction), value added per worker (constant 2010 US$)	na	na	2417.0[*]	2907.1	3646.32	1608.8[*]	4564.4
Agriculture, forestry and fishing; value added per worker (constant 2010 US$)	na	na	419.4[*]	582.2	866.9	416.9[*]	976.4
Services, value added per worker (constant 2010 US$)	na	na	3402.2[*]	2900.4	3603.9	4236.7[*]	3846.0
Industry (including construction), value added (% of GDP)	12.1	20.2	22.2	23.5	26.5	8.7	28.5
Manufacturing, value added (% of GDP)	8.0	14.2	14.6	14.9	16.7	5.8	18.0
Agriculture, forestry and fishing; value added (% of GDP)	54.8	32.2	26.6	19.3	15.1	54.6	13.1
Services, value added (% of GDP)	33.1	45.2	47.3	52.3	53.4	36.7	53.0
Time required to start a business (days)	na	na	na	na	19.8[+]	21.8[+]	19.5
Gross capital formation (% of GDP)	9.1	16.1	19.4	25.3	28.8		
Gross domestic savings (% of GDP)	1.9	12.3	15.4	20.6	22.5		
Exports of goods and services (% of GDP)	5.7	5.1	9.3	14.3	17.6[%]		
Manufactures exports (% of merchandise exports)	61.1[^]	67.1	84.4	91.3	92.7		
Current account balance (% of GDP)	–2.8[^]	–2.5	–0.4	0.7	0.2		
Access to electricity (% of population)	na	na	20.1[*]	43.5	67.3[@]	14.3[*]	88.0[@]

Individuals using the Internet (% of population)	na	na	na	0.9	10.1[@]	0.07	15.0[@]
Central government debt, total (% of GDP)	na	na	na	31.5[&]	na		
Human development index	na	na	0.42	0.50	0.58	0.39	0.61
		1988	1995	2005	2016		
Gini	na	28.8	32.9	33.2	32.1		
Poverty headcount ratio at $1.90 a day (2011 PPP) (% of population)	na	37.8	35.7	25.7	14.8		
Poverty headcount ratio at $3.20 a day (2011 PPP) (% of population)	na	79.5	75.3	66.3	52.9		
Poverty headcount ratio at national poverty lines (% of population)	na	na	na	40.0	24.3		
Poverty gap at $1.90 a day (2011 PPP) (%)	na	9.1	8.2	5.1	2.7		
Poverty gap at $3.20 a day (2011 PPP) (%)	na	23.1	28.9	22.7	15.6		
Poverty gap at national poverty lines (%)	na	na	na	9.0	6.5[!]		
Population, millions							161.4

Source: Data from database: World Development Indicators, update 12/20/2019
Human development data from http://hdr.undp.org/en/data#, downloaded 1/23/2020.

Notes: * = Starting year 1991
^ = Starting year 1997
+ = Starting year 2013
% = Terminal year is 2013
@ = Terminal year is 2017
& = Estimate for 2001–2003
! = Estimate for 2010
na = Not available

Appendix Table 1.2c Bhutan's average decadal and end years economic and social progress

	1980–1989	*1990–1999*	*2000–2009*	*2010–2018*	*1980*	*2017*
GDP growth (annual %)	10.0[!]	5.4	8.3	6.0		
GDP per capita growth (annual %)	7.0[!]	4.3	6.6	4.8		
GDP per capita (constant 2010 US$)	547.8	927.6	1580.2	2757.5[@]	405.9	3172.8[@]
GDP per capita, PPP (constant 2011 international $)	na	2733.0[$]	4655.6	8124.4	2353.6[$]	9347.8
Industry (including construction), value added per worker (constant 2010 US$)	na	13015.7[z]	19364.8	25802.5[@]	10275.3[z]	27443.2[@]
Agriculture, forestry and fishing; value added per worker (constant 2010 US$)	na	1379.3[z]	1390.1	1525.8[@]	1320.7[z]	1602.7[@]
Services, value added per worker (constant 2010 US$)	na	3402.2[z]	2900.4	3846.0	4236.7[z]	3603.9
Industry (including construction), value added (% of GDP)	20.1	29.8	38.7	41.5[@]	11.5	40.6[@]
Manufacturing, value added (% of GDP)	5.6	9.2	7.8	8.1[@]	2.8	7.3[@]
Agriculture, forestry and fishing; value added (% of GDP)	40.1	31.1	22.5	17.4[@]	42.9	16.6[@]
Services, value added (% of GDP)	37.9	35.9	35.8	37.0[@]	43.9	37.2[@]
Time required to start a business (days)	na	na	55.4[y]	23.9	62[y]	12
Gross capital formation (% of GDP)	na	36.6	50.8	56.9[@]		
Gross domestic savings (% of GDP)	na	na	32.6	32.3@		
Exports of goods and services (% of GDP)	18.0	32.5	37.7	36.1		
Manufactures exports (% of merchandise exports)	na	40.6[%]	43.9[&]	62.0[#]		
Current account balance (% of GDP)	na	na	−2.8[^]	−24.1		
Access to electricity (% of population)	na	na	53.8[*]	89.8	31.2[*]	97.7
Individuals using the Internet (% of population)	na	na	3.7	28.2	0.4	48.1

Central government debt, total (% of GDP)	na	37.5	64.4	82.1^{+}	51.2	107.7^{+}
Human development index	na	na	0.54^{Q}	0.60	0.51^{Q}	0.62
			2007	2012	2017	
Gini	na	na	40.9	38.1	37.4	
Poverty headcount ratio at $1.90 a day (2011 PPP) (% of population) na	na	na	8.0	2.2	1.5	
Poverty headcount ratio at $3.20 a day (2011 PPP) (% of population)	na	na	30.5	14.5	12.0	
Poverty headcount ratio at national poverty lines (% of population)	na	na	23.2	12.0	8.2	
Poverty gap at $1.90 a day (2011 PPP) (%)	na	na	1.6	0.4	0.2	
Poverty gap at $3.20 a day (2011 PPP) (%)	na	na	8.7	3.3	2.5	
Poverty gap at national poverty lines (%)	na	na	6.1	2.6	na	
Population, million						0.75

Source: Data from database: World Development Indicators, update 12/20/2019
Human development data from http://hdr.undp.org/en/data#, downloaded 1/23/2020

Notes: ! = Starting year is 1981
$ = Starting year is 1990
z = Starting year is 1991
* = Starting year is 2000
x = Starting year is 2001
y = Starting year is 2003
Q = Starting year is 2005
^ = Starting year is 2006
+ = Terminal year is 2016
@ = Terminal year is 2017
% = Average over 1991–94
& = Average over 2005–09
# = Average over 2010–12
na = Not available

Appendix Table 1.2d India's average decadal and end years economic and social progress

	1970–1979	*1980–1989*	*1990–1999*	*2000–2009*	*2010–2018*	*1970*	*2018*
GDP growth (annual %)	2.9	5.7	8.8	6.3	7.0		
GDP per capita growth (annual %)	0.6	3.3	3.7	4.6	5.8		
GDP per capita (constant 2010 US$)	401.8	483.0	668.4	1023.0	1681.8	396.0	2100.8
GDP per capita, PPP (constant 2011 international $)	na	na	2191.5[&]	3354.5	5514.3	1905.7[&]	6888.2
Industry (including construction), value added per worker (constant 2010 US$)	na	na	3369.6[+]	4235.2	5616.4	2957.3[+]	6634.8
Agriculture, forestry and fishing; value added per worker (constant 2010 US$)	na	na	882.5[+]	1013.1	1507.2	803.6[+]	1712.6
Services, value added per worker (constant 2010 US$)	na	na	3179.7[+]	4750.0	7492.2[+]	2732.2	8985.0
Industry (including construction), value added (% of GDP)	23.4	26.5	27.3	29.2	28.2	21.7	26.7
Manufacturing, value added (% of GDP)	15.9	16.5	16.4	16.3	15.5	16.9	14.8
Agriculture, forestry and fishing; value added (% of GDP)	36.4	29.5	25.6	18.5	16.4	39.9	14.6
Services, value added (% of GDP)	34.9	35.7	38.5	44.4	47.2	35.0	49.1
Cost of business start-up procedures (% of GNI per capita)	na	na	na	314.9[!]	145.2[$]	428.0[!]	111.2[$]
Time required to start a business (days)	na	na	na	na	28.8[%]	32.7[x]	16.5
Gross capital formation (% of GDP)	19.2	22.4	26.7	34.3	34.6	16.7	31.3
Gross domestic savings (% of GDP)	12.5	15.7	23.9	29.9	31.5	11.4	29.4
Exports of goods and services (% of GDP)	5.2	5.9	9.9	17.9	21.9		
Manufactures exports (% of merchandise exports)	53.6	60.1	74.2	71.0	66.8		
Current account balance (% of GDP)	0.7	−1.6	−1.3	−0.5	−2.3		
Access to electricity (% of population)	na	na	53.7[*]	65.8	82.3[@]	50.9[*]	92.6[@]

Individuals using the Internet (% of population)	na	na	0.1*	2.5	17.5@	0.0*	3.5@
Central government debt, total (% of GDP)	na	na	49.7	59.3	51.0#	50.8	50.3#
Human development index	na	na	0.46	0.53	0.62	0.43	0.65
		1987	1993	2004	2011		
Gini		32.6	31.7	34.4	35.7		
Poverty headcount ratio at $1.90 a day (2011 PPP) (% of population)		48.9	45.9	38.2	21.2		
Poverty headcount ratio at $3.20 a day (2011 PPP) (% of population)		82.8	81.1	72.5	60.4		
Poverty headcount ratio at national poverty lines (% of population)		na	45.3	37.2	21.9		
Poverty gap at $1.90 a day (2011 PPP) (%)		13.8	12.0	9.2	4.3		
Poverty gap at $3.20 a day (2011 PPP) (%)		36.3	3.3	29.7	19.7		
Poverty gap at national poverty lines (%)		na	na	8.4	4.0		
Population, millions							1, 352.6

Source: Data from database: World Development Indicators, update 12/20/2019
Human development data from http://hdr.undp.org/en/data#, downloaded 1/23/2020

Notes: ^ = Starting year is 1975
& = Starting year is 1990
+ = Starting year is 1991
* = Starting year is 1993
! = Starting year is 2003
x = Starting year is 2013
# = Terminal year is 2013
$ = Terminal year is 201
@ = Terminal year is 2017
% = Estimate for 2013–2018
na = Not available

Appendix Table 1.2e Maldives's average decadal and end years economic and social progress

	1980–1989	*1990–1999*	*2000–2009*	*2010–2018*	*1970*	*2018*
GDP growth (annual %)	na	7.5[&]	5.0	6.2		
GDP per capita growth (annual %)	na	5.5[&]	2.3	1.8		
GDP per capita (constant 2010 US$)	na	5163.9[^]	6334.0	7527.6	4599.6[^]	8033.3
GDP per capita, PPP (constant 2011 international $)	na	8731.2[^]	10710.0	12727.7	7777.2[^]	13582.9
Industry (including construction), value added per worker (constant 2010 US$)	na	8754.6[^]	8700.9	7166.7	8899.7[^]	7828.6
Agriculture, forestry and fishing; value added per worker (constant 2010 US$)	na	4741.8[^]	8700.9	7166.7	4108.7[^]	7828.6
Services, value added per worker (constant 2010 US$)	na	23960.5[^]	20478.6	17221.1	22923.6[^]	17285.8
Industry (including construction), value added (% of GDP)	na	13.5[^]	11.4	10.2	14.1[^]	12.9
Manufacturing, value added (% of GDP)	na	7.7[^]	4.6	2.2	7.9[^]	2.1
Agriculture, forestry and fishing; value added (% of GDP)	na	10.2[^]	6.5	5.5	11.5[^]	5.6
Services, value added (% of GDP)	na	na	73.3[%]	67.9	73.1[%]	73.2
Time required to start a business (days)	na	na	31[%]	22.5	31[%]	21.7
Exports of goods and services (% of GDP)	106.3	77.1[!]	76.4[#]	79.6		
Manufactures exports (% of merchandise exports)	na	25.3	20.7	0.2[#]		
Current account balance (% of GDP)	−18.2	−5.6	−12.5	−12.6		
Access to electricity (% of population)			90.9[*]	99.8[@]	83.8[*]	99.8[@]
Individuals using the Internet (% of population)	na	0.6[&]	10.6	46.2[@]	0.2[&]	63.2[@]
Central government debt, total (% of GDP)		40.9	33.3	56.1[#]	30.8	57.3[#]
Fertility rate, total (births per woman)	7.1	7.0	4.5	2.4[@]	7.2	1.9[@]

Human development index	na	0.57^	0.64	0.70	0.55^	0.72
			2002	2009		
Gini			41.3	38.4		
Poverty headcount ratio at $1.90 a day (2011 PPP) (% of population)			10	7.3		
Poverty headcount ratio at $3.20 a day (2011 PPP) (% of population)			39.2	24.4		
Poverty headcount ratio at national poverty lines (% of population)				8.2+		
Poverty gap at $1.90 a day (2011 PPP) (%)			2.6	1.5		
Poverty gap at $3.20 a day (2011 PPP) (%)			11.1	7.3		
Population, millions						0.5

Source: Data from database: World Development Indicators, update 12/20/2019
Human development data from http://hdr.undp.org/en/data#, downloaded 1/23/2020

Notes: ^ = Starting year is 1995
& = Starting year is 1996
* = Starting year is 2000
% = Starting year is 2003
! = Terminal year is 1994
= Terminal year is 2011
@ = Terminal year is 2017
+ = Estimate for 2016
na = Not available

The decline from the earlier decade seems inaccurate but the numbers were double-checked and show a sudden drop to a negligible amount in 2004 that persisted.

Appendix Table 1.2f Nepal's average decadal and end years economic and social progress

	1970–1979	*198019–89*	*1990–1999*	*2000–2009*	*2010–2018*	*1970*	*2018*
GDP growth (annual %)	2.6	4.1	4.8	4.1	4.7		
GDP per capita growth (annual %)	0.4	1.7	2.3	2.7	4.1		
GDP per capita (constant 2010 US$)	283.3	312.5	396.2	499.9	817.4	284.4	698.6
GDP per capita, PPP (constant 2011 international $)	na	na	1328.6&	1676.4	2342.9	1188.0&	2741.4
Industry (including construction), value added per worker (constant 2010 US$)	na	na	2444.1+	1460.9	1445.6	3617.8+	1445.6
Agriculture, forestry and fishing; value added per worker (constant 2010 US$)	na	na	391.7+	470.0	599.1	396.6+	571.5
Services, value added per worker (constant 2010 US$)	na	na	2346.9+	2940.6	3761.4	1988.2+	4140.0
Industry (including construction), value added (% of GDP)	9.7	13.4	19.7	16.7	13.8	11.5	13.5
Manufacturing, value added (% of GDP)	4.0	4.9	8.2	7.7	5.6	3.7	5.0
Agriculture, forestry and fishing; value added (% of GDP)	65.0	52.7	40.9	33.8	30.4	66.9	25.3
Services, value added (% of GDP)	21.6	28.0	33.5	45.2	48.5	21.0	51.4
Time required to start a business (days)	na	na	na	31.0x	21.6	31.0x	18.5
Gross capital formation (% of GDP)	11.0	19.9	22.7	25.7	40.5		
Gross domestic savings (% of GDP)	12.1!	11.0	12.0	10.6	11.5		
Exports of goods and services (% of GDP)	8.2	11.4	19.5	16.2	10.0		
Manufactures exports (% of merchandise exports)	31.7^	48.6	81.1	na	69.7		
Current account balance (% of GDP)	−0.3	−4.4	−6.2	1.2	1.0		

Access to electricity (% of population)	na	na	19.0*	43.2	80.3$^{@}$	17.9*	95.5$^{@}$
Individuals using the Internet (% of population)	na	na	0.5*	0.9	16.0$^{@}$	0.0*	34.0$^{@}$
Central government debt, total (% of GDP)	na	na	63.1	55.3$^{\#}$	na	52.6	33.9$^{\#}$
Fertility rate, total (births per woman)	5.8	5.5	4.7	3.2	2.0$^{@}$	5.9	2.0$^{@}$
Human development index	na	na	0.43	0.41	0.58	0.38	0.58
			1995	2003	2010		
Gini	na	na	35.2	43.2	32.8		
Poverty headcount ratio at $1.90 a day (2011 PPP) (% of population)	na	na	61.9	46.1	15.0		
Poverty headcount ratio at $3.20 a day (2011 PPP) (% of population)	na	na	86.6	75.5	50.8		
Poverty headcount ratio at national poverty lines (% of population)	na	na	na	na	25.2		
Poverty gap at $1.90 a day (2011 PPP) (%)	na	na	21.2	14.5	3.1		
Poverty gap at $3.20 a day (2011 PPP) (%)	na	na	86.6	75.5	58.0		
Poverty gap at national poverty lines (%)	na	na	na	na	25.2		
Population, millions							28.1

Source: Data from database: World Development Indicators, update 12/20/2019
Human development data from http://hdr.undp.org/en/data#, downloaded 1/23/2020
Notes: ! = Starting year is 1975
^ = Starting year is 1976
& = Starting year is 1990
+ = Starting year is 1991
* = Starting year is 1996
$ = Starting year is 2002
x = Starting year is 2003
# = Terminal year is 2008
@ = Terminal year is 2017
% = Estimate for 2010
na = Not available

Appendix Table 1.2g Pakistan's average decadal and end years economic and social progress

	1970–1979	*1980–1989*	*1990–1999*	*2000–2009*	*2010–2018*	*1970*	*2018*
GDP growth (annual %)	4.8	6.9	4.0	4.5	4.3		
GDP per capita growth (annual %)	1.9	3.5	1.1	2.1	2.1		
GDP per capita (constant 2010 US$)	483.8	643.3	792.3	908.4	1096.0	472.0	1197.8
GDP per capita, PPP (constant 2011 international $)	na	na	3267.5[&]	3746.3	4408.5	3055.8[&]	4939.8
Industry (including construction), value added per worker (constant 2010 US$)	na	na	2286.8[+]	2716.1	2770.4	2100.2[+]	2864.3
Agriculture, forestry and fishing; value added per worker (constant 2010 US$)	na	na	1690.1[+]	1703.2	1683.0	1557.0[+]	1683.8
Services, value added per worker (constant 2010 US$)	na	na	3799.6[+]	4209.5	5096.1	3582.3[+]	5653.0
Industry (including construction), value added (% of GDP)	20.8	20.9	22.0	22.0	19.4	20.3	18.0
Manufacturing, value added (% of GDP)	14.5	14.3	14.9	14.5	13.0	14.6	12.2
Agriculture, forestry and fishing; value added (% of GDP)	30.9	25.6	23.6	22.0	23.6	33.4	22.9
Services, value added (% of GDP)	39.7	43.2	44.7	50.1	52.2	37.1	52.7
Time required to start a business (days)	na	na	na	na	18.9[x]	20[y]	16.5
Gross capital formation (% of GDP)	16.0	18.7	18.7	17.8	15.4		
Gross domestic savings (% of GDP)	8.2	8.3	15.1	14.1	8.1		
Exports of goods and services (% of GDP)	10.5	12.1	16.4	14.4	11.4		
Manufactures exports (% of merchandise exports)	29.1[^]	48.6	81.1	na	69.7		
Current account balance (% of GDP)	−5.0[^]	−2.7	−4.0	−1.4	−2.4		
Access to electricity (% of population)	na	Na	70.4[*]	70.4	70.8[@]	70.5[*]	70.8[@]
Individuals using the Internet (% of population)	na	Na	0.03[!]	5.5	11.5[@]	0.0	15.5[@]
Central government debt, total (% of GDP)	na	Na	77.4[$]	na	na	78.8	74.0[%]

Fertility rate, total (births per woman)	6.6	6.4	5.7	4.5	3.7@	6.6	3.6@
Human development index	na	Na	0.43	0.43	0.54	0.40	0.56
		1987	1998	2007	2015		
Gini		33.3	33.1	31.6	33.5		
Poverty headcount ratio at $1.90 a day (2011 PPP) (% of population)		62.2	23.4	13.2	3.9		
Poverty headcount ratio at $3.20 a day (2011 PPP) (% of population)		87.9	66.0	55.4	34.7		
Poverty headcount ratio at national poverty lines (% of population)		Na	57.9	44.1	24.3		
Poverty gap at $1.90 a day (2011 PPP) (%)		20.6	4.8	2.1	0.5		
Poverty gap at $3.20 a day (2011 PPP) (%)		43.8	21.8	15.5	7.6		
Poverty gap at national poverty lines (%)		Na	na	na	5.8#		
Population, millions							212.2

Source: Data from database: World Development Indicators, update 12/20/2019
Human development data from http://hdr.undp.org/en/data#, downloaded 1/23/2020
Notes: ^ = Starting year is 1976
& = Starting year is 1990
+ = Starting year is 1991
! = Starting year is 1995
* = Starting year is 1998
y = Starting year is 2013
@ = Terminal year is 2017
$ = Estimate for 1990–93
% = Estimate for 2010
# = Estimate for 2015
x = Estimate for 2013–2018
na = Not available

Appendix Table 1.2h Sri Lanka's average decadal and end years economic and social progress

	1970–1979	*1980–1989*	*1990–1999*	*2000–2009*	*2010–2018*	*1970*	*2018*
GDP growth (annual %)	4.2	4.1	5.3	5.0	5.6		
GDP per capita growth (annual %)	2.3	2.6	4.3	4.2	4.7		
GDP per capita (constant 2010 US$)	763.4	101.7	1410.2	2100.3	3464.9	711.8	3936.4
GDP per capita, PPP (constant 2011 international $)	na	Na	4380.8[&]	6490.5	10523.4	3613.2[&]	11955.5
Industry (including construction), value added per worker (constant 2010 US$)	na	Na	4602.7[+]	5770.0	8934.3	3139.5[+]	9539.0
Agriculture, forestry and fishing; value added per worker (constant 2010 US$)	na	Na	1233.2[+]	1418.0	2368.9	1183.8[+]	2788.6
Services, value added per worker (constant 2010 US$)	na	Na	5850.0[+]	7624.3	11414.8	5717.2[+]	13035.0
Industry (including construction), value added (% of GDP)	26.4	27.3	26.6	28.9	27.9	24.2	27.0
Manufacturing, value added (% of GDP)	18.3	14.2	14.2	17.9	17.3	16.1	16.2
Agriculture, forestry and fishing; value added (% of GDP)	29.3	27.5	23.8	14.1	8.0	28.8	7.9
Services, value added (% of GDP)	44.3	45.2	49.6	57.0	56.1	47.1	56.8
Time required to start a business (days)	na	Na	na	46.3[y]	15.9	56[y]	9
Gross capital formation (% of GDP)	17.5	26.2	24.9	25.5	31.6		
Gross domestic savings (% of GDP)	15.2	17.8	18.0	16.9	22.9		
Exports of goods and services (% of GDP)	28.2	27.3	33.7	30.8	21.1		
Manufactures exports (% of merchandise exports)	8.7[^]	34.4	65.9[%]	71.7	68.7[@]		
Current account balance (% of GDP)	−1.7[^]	−7.7	−4.4	−3.5	−3.4		

Access to electricity (% of population)	na	Na	na	77.5[*]	91.5[@]	63.6[*]	97.5[@]
Individuals using the Internet (% of population)	na	Na	0.1[!]	2.8	19.4[@]	0.0[!]	34.1[@]
Central government debt, total (% of GDP)			93.9	95.6[$]	71.9[#]	96.6	77.7[#]
Human development index	na	Na	0.65	0.66	0.77	0.63	0.78
		1985	1995	2009	2016		
Gini		Na	na	38.4	na		
Poverty headcount ratio at $1.90 a day (2011 PPP) (% of population)		13.3	8.8	2.4	0.8		
Poverty headcount ratio at $3.20 a day (2011 PPP) (% of population)		45.4	41.5	18.3	10.1		
Poverty headcount ratio at national poverty lines (% of population)		Na	na	8.9	4.1		
Poverty gap at $1.90 a day (2011 PPP) (%)		2.6	1.6	0.4	0.1		
Poverty gap at $3.20 a day (2011 PPP) (%)		13.3	10.9	3.9	3.4		
Poverty gap at national poverty lines (%)		Na	na	1.2	na		
Population, millions							21.7

Source: Data from database: World Development Indicators, update 12/20/2019
Human development data from http://hdr.undp.org/en/data#, downloaded 1/23/2020
Notes: ^ = Starting year is 1976
& = Starting year is 1990
+ = Starting year is 1991
! = Starting year is 1994
* = Starting year is 2001
y = Starting year is 2003
# = Terminal year is 2015
@ = Terminal year is 2017
% = Estimate for 1990–94
$ = Data for 2008 missing
na = Not available

Notes

1 For a complementary overview, refer to Osmani (2018).
2 The data have several shortcomings as is true for most secondary data and secondary data compendiums. This issue is discussed in detail in Khan (2020, Chapter 2). However, notwithstanding this qualification, the trends identified in the paper in a comparative context are viewed as meaningful.
3 The definition of South Asia varies and the World Bank definition has been adopted for this book.
4 India's economic slowdown in 2019 and early 2020, if it persists, and an uneven fall out of the COVID-19, may change this positive scenario.
5 Capital-intensive mining in SSA probably accounts for some of the difference.
6 The index is a composite of literacy, mean education, life expectancy and income and compiled each year by the UNDP. The index range varies from the hypothetical low of zero to a high of 1.
7 Structural change is defined in terms of the change in the relative size of the three main economic sectors, agriculture, industry and services as identified by Chenery, Robinson and Syrquin1(1986). As the economy matures to middle-income status, initially agriculture is expected to cede its share to industry and the move to high-income status is accompanied by the rising share of professional services.
8 Bangladesh is considered one of the most climate vulnerable countries of the world, and it has already experienced sea level rise, salt water intrusion and extreme climate events, such as hurricanes (Hossain, Kathuria and Islam, 2010, chapter 12). It will need the sustained high growth rates to adapt to climate change.
9 The Gini coefficient is only available for selected years so the numbers for the latest years in a given decade are reported in Appendix Tables 2a–h for all countries.
10 For exact date ranges for the different countries, refer to Appendix Tables 2a–h.
11 https://www.worldbank.org/en/results/2013/04/10/maldives-development-success-story, consulted 2/9/20.
12 Unlike East Asian countries such as South Korea and Taiwan, it was unable to sustain the catch-up momentum. Why that was the case is discussed in Khan (2020, Chapter 9) in the context of what the East Asian countries did right compared to Latin American, South Asian and African countries.
13 The numbers for 2020 and the first two-quarters of 2021 looked more promising.
14 In this and all the other time series exercises we engaged in for this paper we first tested for unit roots to see if the series were stationary. If not, we re-tested after first difference. The analysis proceeded only if the Johansen tests indicated the series were cointegrated.
15 For details refer to Khan (2020, Chapter 6).
16 Each data point was generally a ten-year average. However, the last decade only runs to 2018 in the data and in that case the average is over eight years. Using this method yielded a total of 23 data points.
17 Maldives and Bhutan have tiny populations by comparison to the larger South Asian countries and are structurally very dissimilar. Afghanistan has been embroiled in military and civil conflict and also afforded only a couple of data points.
18 Banerjee and Duflo (2019, pp. 194–204) provide examples of growth dividends available from removing misallocations.
19 The starting year for Nepal was 1972 and for Bangladesh 1973, respectively.
20 FDI was not cointegrated with GDP or GDP growth but FDI lagged one year was.

List of References

Banerjee, A. V. and E. Duflo. 2019. *Good Economics for Hard Times* (New York: Public Affairs).

Bhagwati, J. and A. Panagariya. 2013. *Why Growth Matters: How Economic Growth in India Reduced Poverty and Lessons for Other Countries* (New York: Public Affairs).

Chenery, H., S. Robinson and M. Syrquin. 1986. *Industrialization and Growth: A Comparative Study* (New York: Oxford University Press).

Dasgupta, S. and A. Singh. 2005. "Will Services be the New Engine of Indian Economic Growth?" *Development and Change*, 36(6), 1035–1057.

Dasgupta, S. and A. Singh. 2006. "Manufacturing, Services and Premature Deindustrialization in Developing Countries," United Nations University - World Institute for Development Economics Research (UNU-WIDER) Research Paper No. 2006/49, Helsinki, Finland.

Hossain, M., R. Kathuria and I. Islam. 2010. *South Asian Economic Development*, 2nd ed. (New York, Routledge).

Kaldor, N. 1967. *Strategic Factors in Economic Development* (Ithaca: New York State School of Industrial and Labor Relations, Cornell University).

Khan, S. R. 2011. "Growth Diagnostics: Explaining Pakistan's Lagging Economic Growth," *Global Economy Journal*, 11(4), 1–17.

Khan, S. R. 2020. *Development Economics: A Critical Introduction* (New York: Routledge).

Osmani, S. R. 2018. "Socio-economic Development in South Asia: The Past 50 years," WIDER Working Paper 2018/105, Helsinki, Finland.

Panagariya, A. 2004. "India in the 1980s and 1990s: A Triumph of Reforms," International Monetary Fund Working Paper Series No. 04/43, Washington, D. C.

Papanek, G. F. 1967. *Pakistan's Development: Social Goals and Private Incentives* (Cambridge, Massachusetts: Harvard University Press).

Rodrik, D. 2015. "Premature Deindustrialization," *Journal of Economic Growth*, 21(1), 1–33.

Rodrik, D. and A. Subramanian. 2004. "From 'Hindu Growth' to Productivity Surge: The Mystery of the Indian Growth Transition," National Bureau Working Paper Series No. 10376, Cambridge, Massachusetts.

Sen, A. K. 2000. "What is Development About?" in eds., G. M. Meier and J. E. Stiglitz, *Frontiers of Development Economics: The Future in Perspective* (New York: Oxford University Press), 506–513.

Ura, K., S. Alkire, T. Zangmo and W. Karma. 2012. "A Short Guide to Gross National Happiness Index", https://opendocs.ids.ac.uk/opendocs/handle/20.500.12413/11807, Consulted 6/13/2021.

Wells, H. and A. P. Thirlwall. 2003. "Testing Kaldor's Growth Laws Across the Countries of Africa," *African Development Review*, 15(2/3), 89–105.

2 India's economic success

Introduction

Based on Appendix 1.2d, the narrative on India's economic and social progress is repeated here by way of introduction. The per capita GDP growth rate in India until the decade of the 1980s was very modest (0.6 percent in the 1970s). In the 1980s and 1990s, this growth rate increased to 3.3 percent and 3.7 percent, respectively. It subsequently picked up to 4.6 percent and 5.8 percent, respectively, in the next two decades. Per capita GDP increased fivefold in the almost four decades between 1980 and 2018.[1]

The social indicators also showed decent progress. Using a headcount ratio for extreme poverty at $1.90 a day (2011 PPP), the percentage of population in this state more than halved, from 48.9 percent to 21.2 percent between 1987 and 2010–2011, using World Bank estimates. A similar trend is evident using the national poverty line (from 45 to 22 percent). The human development index increased from an abysmal 0.43 in 1970 to a moderate 0.65 in 2018.

This evident catch-up growth and social progress sparked a debate in the development economics literature about the proximate causes. The main focus of this chapter is on exploring the literature to identify when the takeoff occurred and what might have triggered it. The chapter builds up to a discussion of this debate by first briefly summarizing India's early economic history post-independence, its early use of economic planning, exploring current policy options and where they fit into its reforms in the 1980s and early 1990s. However, framing the debate of India's economic success in terms of a couple of economic policy approaches is limiting and so other explanations that do not fit into this mold are also explored.

India's early postindependence economic history[2]

After independence, India's development model, which was very influential in the rest of South Asia, had several determining factors. Nehru's inclination toward British Fabian socialism promoted a welfare and reformist (e.g., land reform, minimum wages) rather than a revolutionary agenda. Mahalanobis's (the father of Indian planning) emphasized the need to produce machine goods and for the state

DOI: 10.4324/9781003176411-3

to be in charge of the "commanding heights" of the economy and this advice was well received by the founding politicians of India's democracy.

In the United States, given India's alliance with the Soviet Union, it was viewed to be a socialist economy by politicians. This was a misunderstanding. Most market capitalist countries engage in planning (for example, that is what an annual budget is). Unlike socialist economies, in India the means of production were mostly privately owned, except for some state-owned industries, and most economic activity was in the market domain. Thus, it was not a socialist economy but it was one in which the state was very interventionist.

The perception of the phenomenal industrialization and growth of the Soviet Union within a generation based on a planned system was certainly an inspiration for the founding politicians in India. Also, the negative colonial experience caused India to be suspicious of outside intervention embodied in foreign trade and foreign investment (Basu, 2004, pp. 11–12). This colonial experience, the alliance with the Soviet Union and the perception of its success led to a desire for a planned autarkic development model based on trade restrictions, foreign exchange controls and extensive use of licenses. In keeping with this desire for technological accomplishment, there was a heavy investment in higher education relative to primary education.

Gandhi's inclination toward a village and crafts-based self-sufficient full-employment economy was ignored based on the understanding that the prosperity of the nation and its economic success would need to be based on an industrialization drive. Nonetheless, there was some deference to the Gandhian vision on the need for self-sufficiency and encouragement of crafts. This included subsidized credit, tax concessions, including tax holidays, and reserved domains for small-scale industry.

Stringent labor laws were imposed on large-scale industries (> 300 workers (Industrial Disputes Act 1947, later reduced in 1982 to >100 workers), which included the requirement of state permission for firing a worker. There was also an aggressive monopoly control legislation using the Monopoly and Restrictive Trade Policies (MRTP) Act and the use of administered prices.

The international economic environment was one that was recovering from the Great Depression and the "beggar thy neighbor" policies that had induced. Thus, the pressure for openness was a long way off. The influential thinking of "developmentalists" (development economists of the late 1940s and 1950s, i.e., the pioneers of the field, Khan (2020, Chapter 5)) endorsed industrialization based initially on protection (this came to be called import substitution industrialization (ISI)).

Planning

At a macro-level, the simplest framework was to identify the target growth rate and then identify the target investment needed to realize it based on an aggregate economic growth model. The shortfall of the estimated savings relative to target investment would have to be made up with domestic resource mobilization or foreign aid.

More sophisticated models acknowledged that investment depended on the availability of savings but also on an adequate amount of foreign exchange being available to import the necessary machinery for the requisite industrialization effort. The macroeconomic accounting framework suggests that if there is a revenue and savings shortfall, a balance of payment deficit must follow. Foreign assistance could initially address the fiscal and balance of payment deficits. Simple macro exercises were complemented by dynamic growth models for forecasting.

Once the macro targets were determined and the budget finalized, the Planning Commission (PC) would plan for and very closely oversee the allocation of scarce capital and foreign exchange to different activities. The PC was responsible for the formulation and implementation of the five-year plans, and, within that framework, the Annual Development Plans (ADP). The PC determined priorities across sectors as implicit in the resource allocation in the ADP.

All projects had to be approved by the PC in the context of the ADP. Notwithstanding this planning, as earlier noted, this was not a command economy that suspended the market but a planned economy that directed market and non-market activities. This process became less important as the private sector grew relative to the state sector.[3]

Some of the problems of the planning process were that the finance ministry, under political leadership, controlled the funds and could be at odds with the priorities set by the PC. The focus was on the productive sectors and so the social sectors, particularly basic education, health, water supply and sanitation, were neglected. The colonial background and training of the economic bureaucrats stifled the economy via an authoritarian "rule by regulations". For example, there were regulations for investments (new capacity or expanding capacity), use of urban land, money transfers, opening bank accounts and foreign exchange use. Foreign exchange earnings had to be turned over to the State Bank and severe criminal penalties existed for not doing so. This not surprisingly encouraged the growth of a secondary market.

> Licensing created rent-seeking opportunities and corrupted the economic administration that quickly realized that the controls and hindrances created more bribing opportunities. From a business perspective, Fabian socialism meant support for the labor movement, unionization and progressive labor legislation that made it difficult for exports to be competitive.
>
> Business reluctance to undertake high-risk lumpy investments with long gestation periods meant the state initiated basic industries like steel and downstream industries like automobiles. However, inefficiency was induced by high external protection and the simultaneous lack of domestic competition.

As mentioned earlier, given India's colonial experience, the perceived success of the Soviet Union, development thinking at that time and the international climate that existed at the time of Indian independence, it was not unreasonable for India to adopt the model it did. With hindsight, this is now viewed as a big mistake by mainstream economists. Also, the colonial traditions colored the behavior of the bureaucracy and the implementation of planning and this too is not surprising since some path dependency is inevitable until the costs become apparent and a rethink becomes necessary.

> If, as in South Korea, the state was business friendly and had a service rather than a governing orientation, India could have excelled earlier. However, a self-interested autocratic economic bureaucracy and the lack of a competition policy held it back. Also, there was virtually a license for everything, and the Indian development model came to be called "license raj" that stifled enterprise and productivity.

While orthodox economists view India's performance during its state-led industrialization phase to be an abysmal failure, others have argued that this critique ignores successes. For example, Singh (1995) pointed out that the concept of technological self-reliance resulted in India having one of the largest pools of trained technical manpower in the world. Among Third World semi-industrial countries, India became a leading exporter of technology by the 1970s. Citing Lall (1984), he pointed out that India was the leading technology exporter among newly industrialized countries, followed at a large distance by Korea and Brazil. Citing earlier work, the author also argued that the decline in growth of manufacturing output prior to the 1980s was not due to the microeconomic inefficiencies associated with industrial and trade policies but rather due to the slow rate of growth of demand for industrial output and the low rate of investment in infrastructure.

Current key economic development policy approaches

There are currently two main competing policy approaches for attaining catch-up economic growth that are summarized in this section.[4] Neoliberalism, the mainstream market-oriented approach, follows the liberal tradition of the classical economists. The policy proposals have been encapsulated in the structural adjustment conditionality tied to loans provided by the IMF and the World Bank.

The IMF's main concern is the twin deficits (fiscal and balance of payments) that often result in countries requiring its support. Macro-management is expected to redress these problems. The associated conditionality includes controlling the money supply to rein in inflation and fiscal stringency. The latter includes cuts in government expenditures (e.g., subsidies, public sector wage and employment freezes) and higher taxes. The balance of payment deficit is addressed by exchange rate liberalization (often resulting in a major devaluation) and trade liberalization (reducing tariffs and eliminating export subsidies and import quotas). The reasoning is that market-determined exchange rate will make the exports more competitive and protection hurts the export sector as it makes inputs more expensive and prevents goods from becoming competitive.

Structural reforms are expected to deliver long-term growth. Price reforms include liberalization in the capital (interest rate liberalization), labor (often wage repression if there are institutional protections) and product (goods and services) markets.

To encourage the private sector and to enhance its scope, deregulation and privatization are encouraged. Sector reforms include making social sector delivery (education, health, water supply) more efficient partly with a larger private sector role. The World Bank has suggested user charges to recover expenses and even subsidies for the private sector (for profit) schools.

Developmentalism (or new developmentalism) is an approach based on the interventionist prescriptions of pioneering development economists. The approach has been crystallized by scholars like Robert Wade, John Toye, Gorden White, Ha-Joon Chang, Dani Rodrik and Alice Amsdem, who explored policies that led to the success of the East Asian economies. While there were differences in the catch-up growth policies of individual countries like Japan, South Korea and Taiwan, commonalities became the design principles of new developmentalism.[5]

The broad approach is eclectic rather than dogmatic or ideological and relies on evidence and commonsense reasoning. The market is used as an instrument for resource allocation when it works well. While they concede government failure and inefficiencies in various cases, the answer is not necessarily less or no government but rather effective government.[6]

Developmentalists emphasize the importance of institutions and organizations. Thus, along with incentives and markets should come the "soft infrastructure" provided by the government rather than large-scale planning. The most broad-based intervention is industrial policy and all the successful East Asian economies entrusted implementing this policy to a super agency. For example, in Japan the Ministry of International Trade and Industry (MITI) had the necessary backing and powers to execute this policy, while in Taiwan the Industrial Development Bureau played this role.

All policies that affect industrial development can be subsumed broadly speaking under the rubric of industrial policy and these can have significant trade implications. The Japanese experience with it has been the most extensive and Korea and Taiwan developed it further and it now has broad acceptance in low and middle-income countries (L/MICs) that annually announce their "industrial policy".

In fact, industrial policy is not confined to L/MICs only, but high-income countries (HICs) routinely engage in them, such as the support of Boeing and Airbus by the United States and EU, respectively, and the bailout of the auto industry by the Obama Administration. The current US administration (2020) passed a bipartisan industrial policy support bill to match China's competitive edge supposedly gained with industrial policy. It has gained acceptance in mainstream economics and has a classification code in the *Journal of Economic Literature*.

The HICs had already paved the way so catch-up growth entailed using "off the shelf technology", adapting it and creating industries. This is not "picking winners" as industrial policy is pejoratively referred to. The decision by MITI (Ministry of International Trade and Development) to promote domestic automobile manufacturing when it did in the 1970s is one of numerous examples of successful industrial policy.[7]

The market is not passively relied on to provide the signals concerning what a country is to specialize in based on neoclassical trade theory. The state encourages industries based on its priorities which could be high technological potential, high-income elasticity of demand, scale economies, positive externalities, low energy intensity and learning by doing potential. All this could be summed up as dynamic efficiencies.

Incentives are provided conditional on firm profit, local content and export potential. Exports are the easiest to observe for use as a performance criterion. The threat of competition is used as a disciplining factor. For example, if domestic products do not have reasonable price and quality, imports could be let in. Further, enough firms are encouraged to operate in a given market for competition while over competition is avoided to ensure economies of scale.

The basic point is that government is needed to nurture industry since factors of production are not deemed a sufficient basis to compete in extremely competitive international markets and left to itself, local industry would get wiped out. An export orientation for industrial policy has advantages because of economies of scale, competitive pressures, technological potential and foreign exchange earnings. However, the industrial and trade strategy is not exclusively ISI or export promotion (EP) but rather import substitution nurturing successful EP (Sen, 1981).

Other support policies include land reform as an initial condition to enhance equity and a larger market and source of materials for industry. Similarly, high mean literacy, education, health care and training are also critical for equity and industrial support. The financial system is controlled and subordinated to the needs of industrial capital. Adequate infrastructure is provided to enable industry to flourish.

The use of foreign exchange is initially prioritized and capital controls utilized as needed. Foreign direct investment is subordinated to the domestic economic agenda of technology acquisition, promoting EP and local purchases. Imports are sequentially liberalized as local industries strengthen to effectively compete.

Notwithstanding these commonalities, there are different models of success to learn from. Korea used corporatist policies of government–industry interaction and the reliance on national champions or Chaebols like Samsung, Daewoo or Goldstar. Taiwan utilized state-owned industries with hands off incentives for downstream competitive supply chains. Malaysia and China relied more on tapping FDI for technology acquisition among other strategies.

Indian reforms

As described by De Long (2003) and Rodrik and Subramanian (2004), the set of reforms begun in the early 1980s were pro-business and, in this regard, fit it more but not entirely with a developmentalist mold.[8] Restrictions (imposed as part of the 1969 antitrust legislation) and licensing constraints on large firms were eased, modest deregulation initiated, capacity restrictions (the number of industries subject to government capacity licensing reduced from 77 to 27) and price controls were eased, corporate profit tax reduced, export profit tax halved, import restrictions on capital and intermediate inputs removed, tariffs reduced and quotas converted to tariffs. There was more liberal access to credit and foreign exchange. Thus, license raj started being rolled back.

However, Basu (2018) suggests the high fiscal expenditures of the 1980s led to a fiscal crisis and this was compounded by high inflation and a balance of payment crisis; the latter was enhanced by the Gulf War that blocked worker remittances from the Middle East and resulted in higher oil prices.

The reforms that followed in the early 1990s, described among others by Klein and Thangavel (2001), Nayyar (2004), Agarwal and Whalley (2013), Nayyar (2017) and Ahluwalia (2002, 2005, 2019), to deal with these crises are regarded to fit in more closely with neoliberalism.

These reforms included partial liberalization of foreign investment (51 percent of foreign ownership for priority industries instead of 40 percent – with the possibility of a larger foreign stake), opening up to foreign technology agreements (as long as royalty payments to foreigners were kept at or below 5 percent of total sales), opening up to portfolio investments, continued delicensing and deregulation, quicker approval process for investments, limiting reservations for the public sector (initially to 18 and this was further reduced), a modest limiting of reservations for small-scale industries and the ending of investment scrutiny under the Monopolies and Restrictive Trade Practices Act (MRTP) for investments over a prespecified amount. Instead, the MRTP became an instrument for enforcing competition.

In addition, export subsidies were eliminated, imports were liberalized with tariffs cut (from an average of 85 percent to 25 percent of import value), import licensing was removed for capital and intermediate goods and there was a further move to abolish quotas and other nontariff barriers in keeping with commitments made to the World Trade Organization.[9]

The currency was devalued, and there was a move toward market-determined exchange rates. There was some liberalization of capital markets and market-based currency convertibility via registered currency dealers. Similarly, there was some deregulation and privatization (sale of up to 20 percent of equity of profit-making state-owned enterprises to private mutual funds) and removal of limits on investment. Financial sector reforms included interest rate liberalization with oversight, a reduction of directed credit, allowing private banking and insurance, decontrol of capital issues and prudential reforms.[10]

While the reforms were part of the conditionality of an IMF policy package, Ahluwalia (2019, p. 49) and others have argued that there was a broad discussion of and consensus on the need for such reforms prior to the crises – which were made good use of to introduce them. As such, these reforms are considered to be home grown. Also, the fact that these reforms continued beyond the end of the term of the IMF package in 1994 is viewed as providing further support for this contention. However, because senior economic staff and advisors had IMF/World Bank experience, the neoliberal stamp on the reforms is not surprising.

The Indian catch-up growth debate

India's economic success, as is the case for any country, is complex and partial understanding is possible drawing on many disciplines. Thus, an economic explanation trying to frame the debate in terms of neoliberal or developmentalist prescriptions is inherently limited. Nonetheless, once the limited effectiveness of economic prescriptions is conceded, it is still worth understanding what policies kick-started India's catch-up growth.

De Long (2003) used growth theory to demonstrate a greater boost to the economy's long-run steady-state growth path following the early 1980s reforms relative to the more comprehensive reforms initiated a decade later. While he conceded that the 1990s reforms were necessary to sustain economic growth, he conjectured that the 1980s takeoff could be attributed to three factors: A shift toward India's integration with the world economy; a positive shift in entrepreneurial attitudes; and an understanding that the intrusive economic order of the Nehru dynasty was over.

Rodrik and Subramanian (2004) analyzed the second of these factors in challenging the conventional wisdom that the start of India's catch-up growth can be dated to the structural adjustment type of reforms that followed the 1991 fiscal and balance of payment crises. They agreed with De Long that the trigger was the reforms that created a pro-business environment created in the late 1970s and early 1980s.[11] The authors cited evidence to show that one can date the takeoff to 1980 and this evidence also bore up for a state-level analysis.[12]

They argued that the takeoff followed reforms that reflect an attitudinal change in the Congress government that was pro-business, thus undoing the traditional hostility to business. This spurred "animal spirits" and per capita GDP tripled in the 1980s (3 percent) relative to the 1960s and 1970s (1.2 percent). This followed from an increase in productivity and other economic indicators like savings and capital accumulation. It was also in the 1980s that key industries like information technology emerged and flourished.

Their analysis showed that about three-fifths of total economic growth could be attributed to total factor productivity, which they found amazing. This is desirable economic growth on the intensive rather than extensive margin (i.e., via an increase in factor inputs) and hence parsimonious and sustainable. Their analysis showed that given its institutions (political, economic, legal and higher education), India was underperforming and the pro-business reforms unleashed its productive potential. Their analysis also ruled out other possible explanations for per capita GDP growth, such as trade, fiscal stimulus, public investment, agricultural productivity growth, structural adjustment reforms (instituted in the early 1990s), exchange rate policy or favorable external conditions.

Panagariya (2004) is among those who have disputed the developmentalist explanation for India's takeoff.[13] He argued that economic growth in the 1980s was overstated and the nature of reforms mischaracterized. The first part of this proposition is demonstrated by decomposing the 1980s into subperiods and arguing that the high growth could really be attributed to the 1988–1991 subperiod and the reforms at that time (export incentives, import liberalization and delicensing of investment) were more of the pro-market structural adjustment variety.[14] Panagariya also claimed that the economic growth in the 1980s was fragile and not sustainable because it was volatile.[15]

Agarwal and Whalley (2013) dispute the contention that corporate investment as a share of GDP rose in the 1980s and hence dispute the mechanism by which the more pro-business policies of the government could have translated into higher growth as claimed by Rodrik and Subramanian (2004). Whether or not corporate investment rose is an empirical issue on which consensus should be possible. However, another empirical issue that Rodrik and Subramanian claim as a mechanism for higher economic growth in the 1980s is the higher factor productivity, including that of investment, and, in that case, even if corporate investment did not rise, an accelerated economic growth would still be possible.[16]

Nayyar (2017) assessed the success of 25 years of economic liberalization in India beginning in 1991. While he conceded that the economy had been stabilized by neoliberal policies, he pointed to many emerging crises resulting from errors of omission and commission. Prominent among these were jobless growth, rise in unemployment and inequality, a collapse of agriculture, deindustrialization and neglect of the social sectors. This critique is in keeping with the broader critique of neoliberalism. Nayyar called for the end to ideological entrenched positions and the need for a developmentalist state that works in an evolving fashion with the private sector to accommodate changing needs of the economy.[17]

Other explanations of India's economic success

Basu (2018) viewed India's catch-up growth to be exceptional, driven as it was by the information technology enabled modern service sector.[18] Basu viewed a stifling economic bureaucracy and poor infrastructure (roads, railways, ports) as the two binding constraints to catch-up growth. IT had the advantage of being able to bypass both these constraints. IT faced low taxes, few intrusive regulations and no need of hard infrastructure. The state's role in protecting local technology (IBM thrown out in 1977, see Chapter 10)[19] and investment in higher education, which produced an abundance of IT engineering capacity, set the stage for a fortuitous and mutually beneficial partnership with Silicon Valley.

Other factors that were notable were the rise in savings rates in the 1970s due to the nationalization of banks in 1969 and the state's requirement of nationalized banks opening bank branches across the country. The higher savings then provided fuel to the growth boost due to pro-business reforms of the 1980s and liberalization reforms of the early 1990s. The 1990s reforms that enabled currency convertibility changed incentives and provided a massive boost to foreign currency reserves such that these reserves moved from extremely low to among the highest in the world. Along with these changed incentives with regard to foreign exchange ownership rights, IT and pharmaceutical exports also boosted reserves.

Nayyar (2006) argued that a search for single factor explanations is neither warranted nor sensible or accurate. He ruled out the 1991 liberalization as the cause for India's takeoff since, post-1952, the next substantive takeoff was 1980–1981. He argued that a rise in aggregate expenditure, private investment and some trade liberalization and deregulation in the late 1970s and early 1980s, all played a role. More important, while there was a qualitative leap in the early 1980s, much of the credit is due to the quantitative efforts of the past three decades in terms of an investment in higher education, science and technology, institutional and managerial capacity, entrepreneurial talents, social institutions and a legal framework for a market economy. Without these foundations, a takeoff would not have been possible.

Summary and conclusion

It appears that the 1980s pro-business reforms were critical in moving India to a higher economic growth trajectory. Scholars like Ahluwalia (2002) and Basu (2018) believe that the 1980s reforms were not sustainable since they led to high fiscal deficits. It is not evident that this was the case since there is nothing in the pro-business 1980 reforms cited above that called for high fiscal deficits, and in any case, such deficits were not contained post-1991 reforms (Ahluwalia (2002, Table 2)).

Other proximate causes of the Indian takeoff, outside the frame of the narrow neoliberal/developmentalist debate, also appear to credit developmentalist policies. For example, the IT boost to economic growth is attributed to state support for local industry both via higher education policy and protection for local industry. The higher savings/investment rate is attributed to the nationalization of banking in the 1970s and the boost to financial intermediation provided by the requirement of opening rural bank branches.

From a policy perspective, the lack of counterfactuals leaves unanswered questions. Would the 1990s reforms have worked without the strong base of economic growth provided by the 1980s reforms? If the 1990s reforms were the ones introduced in the 1980s, would they have moved India to a higher growth trajectory?

The recent history of L/LMICs is littered with examples of neoliberal reforms that went nowhere across Asia, Latin America and Africa. To argue that this was because of poor implementation, as is often done, is facile. India was famously known for its overweening and inefficient and corrupt economic bureaucracy and hence a lack of implementation capacity. Yet the evidence shows that the 1980s pro-business reforms made a difference.

Notes

1 Sustaining this success will be a challenge, and some policy missteps (demonetization in 2016) and COVID-19 will result in short-term set-backs. Even so, the catch-up growth up to 2018 has been remarkable.

2 This section draws on Singh (1994), Basu and Pattanaik (1997), Joshi and Little (1997) and Basu (2004).

3 The Planning Commission was dissolved in 2014 and replaced by NITI Aayog, a think tank, in 2015.
4 Various approaches are discussed in detail in Khan (2020). While this section summarizes only the neoliberal and developmentalist approaches, others include the human development approach (Sen, 1999), which focuses on investing in human capital, and which could complement either of the two approaches above, and the political economy of development approach that focuses on class and distributional issues.
5 While these design principles distinguish developmentalism from new developmentalism, the former is a more widely used term, and hence also used in this chapter.
6 Like neoliberals, developmentalists have no state theory. The state is viewed as working in the national interest, but this is obviously complex when the country in question is heterogenous and issues such as class and ethnicity are glossed over. Refer to Kapur (2020) regarding state performance in India.
7 For each success there can be several failures, but high failure rate among private sector firms also characterizes a "non-interventionist" market economy.
8 Nayyar (2004) pointed out there were two earlier attempts at reforms: the first was an attempt at economic liberalization in the mid-1960s following a devaluation, and the second in the late 1970s.
9 However, tariffs remained high even by L/MIC standards.
10 State-level action to complement central government liberalizations varied (Ahluwalia, 2002, p. 73).
11 Sen (2007) challenged the notion that a more pro-business attitudinal change was instrumental in the economic takeoff in the early 1980s. He tried to demonstrate that the takeoff occurred in the mid-1970s due largely to a jump in corporate equipment investment and empirically identified the proximate causes of why that occurred.
12 Others who have used statistical techniques to date the takeoff broadly support this contention. Balakrishnan and Parameswaran (2007) date the takeoff to 1979–1980, Nayyar (2006) to 1951–1952 and 1980–1981, Virmani (2004) to 1980–1981, Wallack (2003) to 1980. Basu (2008, pp. 398–99) is skeptical of such statistical techniques (since they miss out on underlying economic phenomenon) and based on his own economic intuition sided with the mainstream view of 1991 as the takeoff year.
13 Also refer to T. N. Srinivasan's scathing attack on Rodrik and Panagariya and the latter's reasoned response. Comments on "From 'Hindu Growth' to Productivity Surge: The Mystery of the Indian Growth Transition" T. N. Srinivasan, https://www.imf.org/external/pubs/ft/staffp/2005/02/srinivas.htm,
Reply to T. N. Srinivasan's comments by Dani Rodrik and Arvind Subramanian https://www.imf.org/external/pubs/ft/staffp/2005/02/rodrik2.htm.
14 Actually, these could be either pro-market or pro-business; Rodrik and Subramanian's point was about who they were targeted to.
15 However, first, there was no theoretical reason provided to indicate why volatility should per se mean nonsustainability, and second, the data provided to argue the point showed much greater volatility in the 1988–1991 subperiod.
16 Agarwal and Whalley (2013) suggest that the higher growth could have been caused by a fiscal stimulus (by inducing higher capacity utilization), but Rodrik and Panagariya showed that this could only account for a small rise in total factor productivity.
17 For an account of India's unique growth path and challenges ahead, refer to Lamba and Subramanian (2020).
18 Following Eichengreen and Gupta (2009), this includes financial, communication, computer, technical, legal, advertising and business services that, as they report, are receptive to the application of information technologies and increasingly tradable across borders.
19 IBM refused joint ownership of subsidiaries (Basu, 2008, p. 400).

List of References

Agarwal, M. and J. Whalley. 2013. "The 1991 Reforms, Indian Economic Growth and Social Progress," National Bureau of Economic Research Working Paper 119024, Cambridge, Massachusetts.

Ahluwalia, M. S. 2002. "Economic Reforms in India since 1991: Has Gradualism Worked?" *The Journal of Economic Perspectives*, 16(3), 67–88.

Ahluwalia, M. S. 2005. "Lessons from India's Economic Reforms," in eds., R. Zagha and T. Besley, *Development Challenges in the 1990s: Leading Policymakers Speak from Experience* (Washington, D. C.: World Bank), 189–202.

Ahluwalia, M. S. 2019. "India's Economic Reforms: Achievements and Next Steps," *Asian Economic Policy Review*, 14(1), 46–62.

Balakrishnan, P. and M. Parameswaran. 2007. "Understanding Economic Growth in India: A Pre requisite," *Economic and Political Weekly*, 42(27, 28), 2915–2922.

Basu, K. 2004. "The Indian Economy: Up to 1991 and Since," in ed., K. Basu, *India's Emerging Economy: Performance and Prospects in the 1990s and Beyond* (Cambridge, MA: MIT Press, and New Delhi: Oxford University Press).

Basu, K. 2008. "The Enigma of India," *Journal of Economic Literature*, 46(2), 396–406.

Basu, K. 2018. "A Short History of India's Economy: A chapter in the Asian Drama," World Institute for Development Economic Research (UNU-WIDER), WIDER Working Paper Series, 124, Helsinki.

Basu, K. and P. K. Pattanaik. 1997. "India's Economy and the Reforms of the 1990s: Genesis and Prospect," *Journal of International Trade and Economic Development*, 6(2), 123–133.

De Long, J. B. 2003. "India since Independence: An Analytic Growth Narrative," in ed., D. Rodrik, *In Search of Prosperity: Analytic Narratives on Economic Growth* (Princeton: Princeton University Press).

Eichengreen, B. and P. Gupta. 2009. "The Two Waves of Service Sector Growth," National Bureau of Economic Research Working Paper No. 14968, Cambridge, Massachusetts.

Joshi, V. and I. M. D. Little. 1997. "Reform on Hold," *Asian Development Review*, 15(2), 1–46.

Kapur, D. 2020. "Why Does the Indian State Both Fail and Succeed?" *Journal of Economic Perspectives*, 34(1), 31–54.

Khan, S. R. 2020. *Development Economics: A Critical Introduction*, (New York: Routledge).

Klein, L. R. and P. Thangavel. 2001. "Economic Reforms and Growth Prospects in India," Center for Asian Pacific Studies (CAPS) Working Paper Series No.116, Lingnan University, Hong Kong.

Lall, S. 1984. "Exports of Technology by Newly-industrializing Countries: An Overview," *World Development*, 12(5/6), 471–480.

Lamba, R. and A. Subramanian. 2020. "Dynamism with Incommensurate Development: The Distinctive Indian Model," *Journal of Economic Perspectives*, 34(1), 3–30.

Nayyar, D. 2004. "Economic Reforms in India: Understanding the Process and Learning from Experience," *International Journal of Development Issues*, 3(2), 31–55.

Nayyar, D. 2006. "India's Unfinished Journey: Transforming Growth into Development," *Modern Asian Studies*, 40(3), 797–832.

Nayyar, D. 2017. "Economic Liberalization in India Then and Now," *Economic and Political Weekly*, 52(2), 41–48.

Panagariya, A. 2004. "India in the 1980s and 1990s: A Triumph of Reforms," International Monetary Fund Working Paper Series No. 04/43, Washington, D. C.

Rodrik, D. and A. Subramanian. 2004. "From 'Hindu Growth' to Productivity Surge: The Mystery of the Indian Growth Transition," National Bureau Working Paper Series No. 10376, Cambridge, Massachusetts.

Sen, A. K. 1981. "Public Action and the Quality of Life in Developing Countries," *Oxford Bulletin of Economics and Statistics*, 43(4), 287–319.

Sen, A. K. 1999. *Development as Freedom* (New York: Anchor Books).

Sen, K. 2007. "Why Did the Elephant Start to Trot? India's Growth Acceleration Re-examined," *Economic and Political Weekly*, 42(43), 37–47.

Singh, A. 1994. "Openness and the Market Friendly Approach to Development: Learning the Right Lessons from Development Experience", *World Development*, 22(12), 1811–1823.

Singh, A. 1995. "The State and Industrialization in India: Successes and Failures and the Lessons for the Future; The role of the state in economic change", *World Institute for Development Economics Research, Studies in Development Economics* (New York: Oxford University Press, Clarendon Press), 170–186.

Virmani, A. 2004. "India's Economic Growth: From Socialist Rate of Growth to Bharatiya Rate of Growth," Working Paper No. 122, Indian Council for Research on International Economic Relations, New Delhi.

Wallack, J. S. 2003. "Structural Breaks in Indian Macroeconomic Data," *Economic and Political Weekly*, 38(41), 4312–15.

Part 2: Meso context

Poverty alleviation

State and civil society partnerships

3 Participatory development in Pakistan

Introduction

Participatory, grassroots or people-centered development gained prominence in the 1970s. It was a reaction to the mainstream top-down/trickle-down economic development approach focusing on capital accumulation and economic growth. Poverty and inequality were viewed to have increased in low-income countries (LICs), and the proponents of participatory development (PD) argued that to mitigate these problems one had to engage directly with the so-called subjects of development and empower them to engage in collective action to enhance their own well-being. Development NGOs became the agents of participatory development. The basic needs approach of the 1970s and the human development approach of the 1990s complemented each other and participation was viewed as the delivery mechanism to attain the objectives of these approaches.

This chapter starts by describing participatory development. Next, its practice by Rural Support Programs in Pakistan is described, followed by a review of why this poverty alleviation initiative is viewed on balance to be a success.

Participatory development

PD, in some form, took off in the 1970s and became development orthodoxy once adopted by donor agencies such as the World Bank.[1] According to critics, this co-option of the concept by development agencies also coincided with the neoliberal push to pare down the role of the state and privilege development NGOs in service delivery (Veltmeyer, 1997).

PD is associated with concepts of decentralization and collective action. Briefly, the idea is that if communities, via social mobilization and training (outside interventions), take full or partial responsibility for providing for their needs via collective action, the results will be sustainable.[2] The reasoning is that such participation can tap local knowledge. Further, it can give communities a sense of ownership and involvement and that therefore the construction, operation and maintenance are sound. This process is viewed as associated not only with greater efficiency but also with greater democratization and community empowerment.[3]

DOI: 10.4324/9781003176411-5

In 1990, the World Bank instituted a learning process, assisted by 30 studies, on the issue. Adams and Rietbergen-McCracken (1994) summarized some of the lessons learned. On the positive side, stakeholder (earlier referred to as beneficiaries) participation in projects could result in an increased uptake of project services, decreased operational costs, increased income and an increased rate of return. By the same token, the lack of participation could result in a lack of support that could impede the use of services, reduce the sustainability of the intended benefits and limit the cost recovery of the projects. All this could result from a sense of indifference and dependency on the state by citizens who saw they had little or no say in projects intended to benefit them. The subsequent resentment could result in willful obstruction of imposed projects or policies.

For example, in the context of rural water supply scheme delivery (Khan, 1999), participation refers to the community selecting or electing a water committee and entrusting scheme operation and maintenance to the committee, participating in community meetings for collective decisions, collectively agreeing upon and paying the tariff in a timely manner and feeling a sense of ownership for the water scheme. This sense of ownership can result in the use of peer group pressure when others default and a reporting of leaks and malpractices, such as deliberate breakage, illegal connections and the use of suction pumps, to the water committee. Thus, participation and collective action is the broader framework that includes individual responsibility and effort harnessed to the provision of an individual and collective need.

Several possible motivations for participation and collective action could be identified. There could be a social motivation that includes altruism and a sense of well-being that comes from the social affirmation of performing a community role.[4] There could be an individual motivation, to be part of a collective effort, driven by personal and household needs.

In the literature on participation and collective action, among the major early contributions are those of Olson (1971), who could be viewed as a collective action pessimist, and Wade (1988), who could be viewed as guardedly optimistic about collective action. In Olson's derivation, collective action would occur if the benefit to any one individual exceeds the total project cost. In this case, the individual would essentially provide the public good, and the probability of this happening is inversely associated with the size of the community. Wade pointed out that community collective action could result from economic compulsions and externalities that require communities to work together. Both these views are based on a self-interested view of the world.

In the PD framework, the catalyst for collective action is the social mobilization and community organization (CO) formation by development NGOs. Social mobilization needs to be viewed from a dynamic perspective. There may be community resistance to social mobilization based on an innate suspicion of outsiders and on scams that they may have been subjected to.[5] Winning trust is a slow and painstaking process. However, once an organization is formed and the benefits of collective action demonstrated, the skeptical may join in. In the section that follows, PD as practiced by Rural Support Programs in Pakistan is reviewed.

Pakistan: Rural Support Programs (RSPs)[6]

The Aga Khan Rural Support Program is credited with initiating the RSP participatory development mechanism in Pakistan in 1982. Its initiation in Pakistan was backed by the Aga Khan who has a large Ismaili community following in Northern Pakistan. One interpretation is that the communities across the border in Afghanistan were experiencing much more social development with Soviet investments in health and education. Thus, the battle of the Cold War ideologies might have played out in Northern Pakistan. The AKRSP project had donor support and the backing of the government of Pakistan.[7]

Northern Pakistan was relatively suited for participatory rural development since high mountain villages had a culture of cooperation. Also, limited arable land meant fewer very large landholdings, compared to the plains down South.[8] One early criticism of this development mechanism was that it could not be replicated in the southern plains of the country where feudalism was much more entrenched and hence elite capture was a high probability for any development intervention. AKRSP proved its detractors wrong by helping with the initiation of a number of organizations to diffuse its RSP approach across the country in partnership with the government and donors (see below).

The AKRSP method, adopted with variations by other RSPs in Pakistan, first identifies village social activists and then engages, with their assistance and that of trained field staff, in intensive social mobilization via a process of dialogues with villagers. If the community accepts what is on offer,[9] a contract is entered by them to engage in assisted collective action. A village organization (VO) is formed and a chairperson, treasurer and secretary to record meeting minutes elected. The community undertakes to engage in regular meetings and regular savings. The VO is sovereign, and while the ARKSP is willing to backstop, it does not interfere in VO decision making.

The general body meeting in which the office holders report on accounts, savings and all matters relevant for the general body is considered critical to the vibrancy of the organization. It is also viewed as a key mechanism to prevent hijacking of the village organization by vested interests. The general body could expel the leadership by a three-fourth majority. The leadership thus serves at the pleasure of the general body but performs the de facto functions of community government such as nominating members for trainings (book keeping, natural resource management, agricultural extension, animal husbandry, poultry keeping), securing loans, disbursing agricultural inputs, allocating labor for road and irrigation channel construction and maintenance and mediating inter- and intra-village disputes.

The activities the AKRSP engages in comprise the full gamut of integrated rural development. These include agriculture, livestock, commercial marketing, forestry, human resource development and technical training, appropriate technology, rural credit and women-in-development components. It also supports a small-scale (village level) civil engineering section. In addition, via head office support, the AKRSP provides infrastructure (roads, bridges, irrigation systems and rural electrification), human capital development (agricultural and livestock extension training and primary and secondary education, in conjunction with the Aga Khan Education Services) and basic health care (in conjunction with the Aga Khan Health Services).

The community identifies an infrastructure project considered as a high priority for well-being and one that would provide benefit to most members of the community. This first infrastructure project is referred to as PPI (productive physical infrastructure structure), and viewed as a means of strengthening social capital. The community is expected to engage in other development work on their own by tapping their enhanced social capital and financial capital.[10] The AKRSP provides technical support and financial support – one-time subsidy for the PPI. The wages are below market rates since the labor is building a community asset and a quarter of the wages are expected to be saved and the community asset maintained.

Training and capacity building are part of the ongoing interaction of the AKRSP with the VO after the initial infrastructure interventions. Other interventions have been in natural resource management, social sector delivery, livestock, microcredit and small enterprise development. Ultimately, the package depends on expressed community needs and willingness to engage in collective action.

AKRSP also developed the concept of partnership or linkage with government line or service delivery departments. The idea was that mobilized communities with social capital embodied in VOs and with the development NGO often as an influential intermediary will be more effective in soliciting services than the communities could on their own.

Overall, AKRSP has been very effective in working with the government and in tapping into, leveraging and extending government resources for community benefit. For example, village or community organizations act as a platform able to leverage support from government line department technical personnel located in the area for trainings in say veterinary medicine or livestock management. The organization is able to provide transport, a key bottleneck, for the government personnel to deliver the trainings and provide them with an honorarium. Village specialists selected for skills training are compensated for time spent in the trainings, and a condition for being provided the training to a VO member is the willingness of other members to pay for the future services of the trainees.

The government also facilitated the organization via tailored research inputs from government research organizations (e.g., in output processing), duty-free capital imports, such as jeeps, office equipment, a helicopter for the rugged mountain terrain with poor roads and access to donor support. Early partnerships with the private sector included provision of agricultural inputs and marketing of outputs. The collective action by village and community organizations enabled economies of scale and market leverage in the form of reducing overheads and securing better prices.

Initially, the AKRSP viewed the sustainability of the VO to be dependent on its own organizational strength that facilitated maintaining the PPI and also in engaging in self-directed initiatives to reinforce this strength. However, to nurture the organizations along in the initial period until the village attained significant prosperity, it developed packages by drawing on scientific and technical expertise within and outside the organization for training. The packages are then implemented by the VO through its cadre of village specialists trained in activities such as livestock, plant protection, poultry, forestry, nursery and marketing.

Even so, AKRSP looked for an exit strategy and came up with an institutional innovation in this regard, which has been replicated across the country (Khan and Khan, 2012). The innovation has taken the form of a cluster organization referred to as Local Support Organizations (LSOs).[11] These are multitier apex organizations with community organizations (COs) as the lowest tier, Village Development Organizations (VDOs) as an intermediate tier (for villages with more than one CO) and LSO as the apex organization operating at the union council level.[12] LSOs are intended to be self-sustaining to enable the RSPs to exit[13] and focus on other roles (capacity building) or move to other communities. They also are a handy innovation when a need extends beyond one community or village such as in infrastructure or marketing.

One of AKRSP's major strengths has been its willingness to be flexible and to learn from experience and continue to adapt. It has welcomed new ideas no matter the source (VO, staff, external observers/advisors) and been willing to learn from them and innovate. The first managing director's willingness and insistence of being in the field and his open-mindedness set the stage for such practice, which subsequently became embodied in the organizational culture. It won the grudging respect of suspicious villagers and local government functionaries based on hard work and results achieved and therefore goodwill for future endeavors.

The AKRSP model was successfully replicated and now operates on a national scale (see below). Because RSPs have government backing, they are less likely to be blocked by the rich, who are threatened by social mobilization, or attacked by fundamentalists. They have for the most part averted elite capture by making it clear that they are operating on a very small scale and in a very accountable way and so there are no rents to distribute.[14] Because they operate on a national scale, they are also able to attract talent. It helps that they offer salary scales higher than other civil society or government organizations. They also invest heavily in the training of their staff in their own training institutes.

The National Rural Support Program (NRSP), an RSPN (Rural Support Program Network) member, provides an example of how the RSP model developed by the AKRSP was adapted to local conditions during its inception. Instead of a VO, there could be several COs in a village based on sect, *beraderi* (clan) or *quom* (caste), i.e., the expressed preferences of a cohesive group. This was a wise strategy given the greater heterogeneity in the plains.[15]

The entry point to addressing community needs and hence mobilizing communities into a community organization did not have to be a PPI but could also be a training, natural resource management, microenterprises or a social sector initiative like a primary school. This enabled NRSP to be more responsive to community needs since they vary a great deal in the plains compared to the mountainous regions AKRSP mobilizes. Credit was used across the board as an instrument for meeting a social need and for sustaining community interest in the CO for collective action. While there was a special focus on the poor, the nonpoor are not excluded.

The NRSP got a foundational grant from the government (Rs. 500 million) and wisely converted it into an endowment. It used the endowment resources sparingly and strategically to preserve its financial sustainability and leveraged its funds to draw on government and donor funds to operate on a much larger scale than its recurrent income from the endowment would have permitted.[16]

Many of the microcredit loans it gave were for encouraging individual enterprise and so, in character with its flexibility, NRSP was not solely wedded to collective action to enhance the rural standard of living. Recognizing the importance of personal incentives, it tapped into them to sustain interest in the COs, which then became a platform for collective activity.

In the context of the discussion of participation above, the RSP approach is an umbrella rather than a sectoral approach, i.e., participation is the mechanism which is utilized in all service delivery no matter the sector or subsector such as agriculture, forestry or finance.

In terms of an early conceptual distinction made by Oakley (1991), it represents participatory development rather than participation in development. The former is development-oriented and focused on participation as a mechanism for delivering efficiency in outcomes, while the latter is process-oriented with a focus on social change.[17] In a lecture presented at the Sustainable Development Policy Institute, Islamabad, in 1995, Shoaib Sultan Khan suggested that the RSP model was about building the social, human, financial and physical capital of the community in an integrated fashion.

RSPs as a success story

Some development practitioners in Pakistan scathingly criticized RSPs as introducing a cookie-cutter approach to rural development whereby forming the organizations, rather than inducing authentic development, became the yardstick for assessing success. Unfortunately, despite the scale they have attained, rigorous empirical evaluation of these organizations is limited. Part of the problem has been RSP organizations' reluctance in opening themselves to potentially hostile evaluation. This is to some extent understandable. Donor funding depends on good evaluations and RSP s have faced their share of doubt and hostility at least among the smaller development NGOs and others in civil society.

Even so, this author was invited to evaluate RSP work twice and in both cases the research was aborted, once on the night before the fieldwork was to begin. A sticking point in the first aborted study was the author's insistence on independent evaluation with free, open and unaccompanied access based on representative sampling. The top management of the RSP to be reviewed insisted that they be given authorship of the study, which would have completely compromised the actual or perceived validity of the research. A sticking point in the second study was the author's desire to randomly select community organizations that were dormant. This would have highlighted why some COs did not mature but would have highlighted failure and hence met with resistance among RSP staff; even though the stated objective was to learn from failure.

Given the limited empirical evaluation, other than the studies reviewed below, the case for the success of RSPs is premised on factors in addition to empirical evaluations. First, their ability to attain scale within the country. Second, the fact that the model has been replicated abroad. Finally, while there has been criticism, for the most part this seems to be misdirected.

Scale and replication

As indicated earlier, the RSP model has spread rapidly throughout the country. The RSPN was formed in 2000 and its ten members collectively operated in 149 of 154 districts of Pakistan in 2020 and had a total outreach of 58 million people, over a fourth of Pakistan's population.[18]

International replications

Another way to assess the success of the model is through its widespread adoption outside the country. With UNDP assistance, the model has been replicated in India, Bangladeshi, Sri Lanka, Nepal and the Maldives. In addition, it has been replicated in Kenya, Mozambique and Tajikistan via the Aga Khan Foundation (World Bank, 2002). Thus, if going to scale and exporting the model abroad is a measure of success, by this yardstick RSPs are a success story. However, one needs to go beyond numbers to outcomes and cost effectiveness.

Empirical evaluation

The World Bank, a minor donor, reviewed the AKRSP four times (1987, 1990, 1995, 2002) and all evaluations were positive. The first three reports relied primarily on the program's own monitoring and evaluation documents and were similarly structured. The fourth evaluation went beyond the first three in that it engaged in independent analysis based on case studies of 24 purposely selected villages, four semiformal village questionnaires, an institutional survey of staff members and an analysis of socioeconomic data collected in 1991 and 1997.

The first two reports were highly positive and concluded that the Aga Khan Rural Support Program continues to be remarkably successful. The third viewed the AKRSP to be an effective instrument for enhancing rural productivity and viewed it as an innovative initiative and a successful program with substantive accomplishments. The fourth evaluation also concluded that the achievements of the AKRSP over its 18 years had been highly satisfactory and the results remarkable. It noted that while weaknesses emerged, they were matched by strengths rarely found in rural development interventions. The program also appeared to have been very successful in enhancing beneficiary capacity and in building social capital.

The fourth report noted that between 1991 and 1997, farm incomes more than doubled in all except the most remote and challenging Astore area and that about one-third of this increase could be attributed to the AKRSP (with some methodological caveats). The estimated low-end economic rate of return (without accounting for many positive externalities due to the program but with caveats on method) was 16 percent, which compared favorably with the opportunity cost of capital of 12 percent during that period. The higher end estimates varied between 24 and 33 percent, respectively.

Earnings in project villages were estimated to be about a third higher than nonproject villages. Many of the VOs were active and thriving organizations 18 years after their creation although others did not need to be and were dormant (i.e., they had served their purpose). The World Bank (2002) also concluded that the efficacy of the microfinance program has been substantial, the NRM (natural resource management) had a significant beneficial impact and the PPIs had provided substantial benefits.

UNDP (1998) engaged in a qualitative interim evaluation of the NRSP. Echoing the World Bank's evaluations of the AKRSP, it referred to NRSP's overall performance over five years as remarkably successful. Based on a partnership with Pakistan's largest commercial bank (Habib), a virtual unlimited line of credit became available in a rural context and NRSP skillfully converted its program into an entrepreneurial model driven by individual initiative as noted above. Along with this, its success was premised on excellent relations with government line departments and therefore the ability to leverage the latter's resources to benefit community organization members and the rural sector more broadly. In so doing, the objectives of both NRSP and the state are served.

The author indirectly evaluated RSP work via several research projects. When studying rural water supply schemes for a World Bank-initiated research project (Khan, 1999, Chapter 2), the World Bank was persuaded to include an RSP in a comparative evaluation and NRSP agreed to the inclusion. Our research showed it clearly outperformed government agencies in delivering rural water supply. In two other studies of RSPs, Khan and Khan (2012a, 2015) found that they enhanced overall well-being and that of women in particular via their various programs.

Mansuri (2012) compared RSP projects to government projects based on constructing a sampling base of 8,000 projects and selecting 280 matched projects. The results were that RSP projects were better designed and constructed and had better records, completion dates and maintenance. This better record was attributed to maintenance being built into RSP contracts with the communities and RSP continued technical assistance in project maintenance. Similarly, Khwaja (2001) in exploring 132 AKRSP projects found that they were better maintained than local government projects.

Critique[19]

Critics of participatory development (PD) have picked holes in all aspects of the practice (e.g., Cleaver, 1999). They think there is an overemphasis on formal constructed organizations and a neglect of local "informal" institutions. A neglect of group social dynamics that complicate what participation really means. The motivation of participation as derived from rationality is not considered in accord with existing norms and cultural practices of social networks.[20] Since much of the funding comes from donor agencies, the accountability they claim is vertical rather than to the grassroots.

Participation is engendered within an external framework and on an external agenda and based on an external vision and values. Thus, there is no real shaping of the project by local needs and local knowledge but merely lip service to these concepts and indeed to local empowerment. There is no check on elite capture at the local level and little consideration of context (Platteau and Abraham, 2002; O'Meally, 2014). Participation can mean different things to different actors (e.g., donors, development NGO, state tiers), and there is little clarity on who is to be empowered and how and how much empowerment one project can deliver (Cleaver, 2001, p. 35).

Their more fundamental criticism is that PD is a cover for social injustice at the micro and macro levels. This conclusion is unsatisfactory for two reasons. First, it appears that the fundamental critique of PD is really a critique of the system it is introduced into and not a critique of PD per se. Hence, the fundamental critique amounts to a Marxist critique, i.e., private property and accumulation are the cause of social injustice wherever manifested. Many of these specific criticisms, such as elite capture and lack of community voice, do not apply to the RSP model for reasons discussed above. The systemic criticism however needs to be addressed.

In L/LMICs, a hybrid semifeudal/semi-capitalist/statist system usually prevails. This system, based predominantly on the private ownership of the means of production, gives some play to market forces. A Marxist critique applies to this hybrid system also (i.e., it is based on accumulation and hence can be extractive, predatory and oppressive). The outcomes of this hybrid system are more deleterious to the public good because effective legal and social protections, like those that were instituted in high-income countries (HICs) to counter the spread of Marxist ideology, are limited. To expect poverty alleviation initiatives to somehow address system shortcomings is a big ask.

The critics are right that the concept of empowerment should be associated with structural transformation of existing power structures at the societal level, i.e., in terms of a transformation of law, property rights and social and governance institutions. However, arguing that PD is blameworthy because it depoliticizes the concept of empowerment misses the point. The point of course is that the system and not PD deserves the blame.

Second, the critics provide no alternative to PD, or for that matter other poverty alleviation initiatives. A defense of PD and other poverty alleviation initiatives emerges from a clearer understanding of their limitations. Thus, while they are not the first best option, they are a pragmatic way to improve human well-being until say social movements successfully build a social democracy.

Settle (2011) launched a fundamental critique of the AKRSP based on a series of interviews with staff, community leaders and members and development experts. She argued that the evidence showed that the success of AKRSP was premised on the religious following of the Aga Khan. The Ismaili community venerates the Aga Khan and hence followed an approach that had his endorsement. She argued that the sustainability of VOs in the non-Ismaili communities was negligible.[21]

In fact, she argued that even the AKRSP lost its sheen and was far removed from the dedication and commitment of the early leadership. It appeared rife with corruption and nepotism, issues on which the positive World Bank evaluations were silent. The monitoring and evaluation systems were deficient since they had a technical bias and ignored social dynamics.

She argued that as the AKRSP expanded and corporatized, it lost its Gandhiesque culture inculcated by the founding advisor, Akhtar Hameed Khan. While the founding managing director Shoaib Sultan Khan continued to be well regarded, villagers were suspicious of the grandiose benefits and privileges of a self-serving AKRSP bureaucracy.

The other criticisms are familiar and echo the broader critical literature. The accountability is to donors rather than the communities. There is no mechanism to prevent elite capture (elite status and power is reinforced by the packages) or to address the needs of the poorest in the communities. It is consistent with the neoliberal approach of minimizing the role of the state and endorsing private enterprise. Thus, the social, financial and human capital building is very consistent with the neoliberalism and the state seems happy to abdicate its responsibility decapitated as it is by structural adjustment-induced austerity. AKRSP ignores the political process, since it is avowedly apolitical, and in this regard undermines the strengthening of democracy.

Seattle is skeptical of positive evaluations, which she views to have been facilitated by AKRSP, and she argued that since the World Bank was a donor, it had a conflict of interest (i.e., why undermine a well-regarding project absorbing funds). The World Bank evaluations she claimed also suffered from the same "one-size-fits-all technocratic frameworks for evaluation" that ignore social dynamics as is true of the internal monitoring and evaluation department.

Once again, the specific criticisms do not apply to RSPs due to reasons discussed above. Further, Campos, Khan and Tessendorf (2004, p. 57) pointed out that between 1982 and 2000, the World Bank's contribution to total donor funding was 0.13 percent.

The AKRSP has provided many examples in its annual reports of working with the government, and ignoring these is a weakness if the narrative is that AKRSP is playing to a neoliberal undermining of the government. In fact, AKRSP's ability to work with government was noted by the World Bank (1987) as one of its most impressive features.

World Bank (1987) stated that AKRSP's work complemented virtually all government programs, and that based on its congenial and extensive contacts with government, it had managed to enhance effectiveness of government without making the VOs dependent on it.

Finally, another weakness in Settle's analysis is ignoring how the model has been replicated throughout the country and abroad, and so suggesting that it works only in Ismaili areas is at best an overstatement. Her main recommendation is the strengthening of representative politics as the best hope for communities for a "rights-based" approach to development is not one this author would want to refute. However, as with the fundamental critique of PD, expecting RSPs to be a vehicle to attain this objective is misplaced. Attaining this objective is the very worthy goal of social movements. Thus, while critical scholarship, such as that Settle's, needs to be encouraged by RSPs for their own credibility, at the moment the balance of evidence appears to be in their favor in their claim to be a success story. While this author is sympathetic to Settle's perspective, dismissing the effectiveness of a large program on the strength of one case study based on a series of interviews does not seem plausible and more evidence is needed.

Conclusion

The RSP model of participatory development has gained significant traction in Pakistan and beyond. The ability of this model to go to scale and touch the lives of almost a quarter of the population of a large low middle-income country and also to be replicated in other countries is a measure of the success of the model. Beyond this, it has garnered positive evaluations both from donor organizations like the World Bank and academics.

The balance of RSP evaluations suggests the model to be promising. RSPs do not question the imperfections of the existing system they operate in, and a key feature of the model is working with the state. Thus, the criticism that it is a cover for the neoliberal pushing back the role of the state does not apply. In fact, RSPs attempt to use state power to their advantage in order to sideline elites so that they can directly address the needs of the most marginalized, including women. Further, they see one of their roles as addressing bottlenecks so that they can leverage state resources to benefit community organizations.

Critics who seek to go beyond mere technocratic and methodological criticism to more fundamental criticism view it as a cover for social injustice at both the micro and macro levels. My contention is that this fundamental criticism of PD really amounts to a criticism of the system that PD is introduced into and not necessarily of PD per se. To expect PD introduced into a flawed system to somehow address system shortcomings is a tall ask. The fault is that of the system and not that of PD. Given an acceptance of this limitation, PD can deliver as shown in this chapter.

Notes

1 See Narayan (1995) for empirical tests of this concept in the context of rural water supply and for other references to the literature. In one of many works, Ostrom (1996) reviewed examples and drew generalizations from cases across countries where participation and collective action was successful in different situations.

2 Refer to Mansuri and Rao (2013, Chapter 5) for an extensive review of the empirical literature in this regard. With qualifications, they conclude that community involvement does result in better quality infrastructure and resource sustainability.

3 As Mayoux (1995) pointed out, the efficiency argument is associated with right of center orthodox economists, while left of center social scientists, including sociologists and anthropologists, focus on empowerment.

4 This would be the case, for example, if an individual activist makes a social contribution to a scheme that exceeds the individual benefit from such an effort.

5 The Taj cooperative scandal in Pakistan that bilked unsuspecting rural households is a case in point, https://www.dawn.com/news/372009/aziz-warns-against-fraudulent-schemes-taj-company-scam-victims-compensated, consulted 5/23/2020.

6 The description of AKRSP's conceptual model is drawn from the writings of the first managing director, Sohaib Sultan Khan, in particular S. S. Khan (1992). Other sources are M. H. Khan (1992, 2009). Sohaib Sultan Khan credits the inspiration for AKRSP to the Raiffeisen model of cooperation. The model was developed by Friedrich Wilhelm Raiffeisen, who founded a cooperative credit union in 1864 in Germany to help poor farmers. For details refer to https://en.wikipedia.org/wiki/Friedrich_Wilhelm_Raiffeisen, consulted 5/25/2020.

7 As noted by Campos, Khan and Tessendorf (2004), the accession of the princely states in Northern Pakistan resulted in a governance vacuum that AKRSP was able to fill in with the support of the state. The local government and Rural Development Department of the Government of Pakistan, subpar at best, was unable to deliver rural development in this far-flung area populated for the most part with extremely destitute people even for Pakistan, then a low-income country.

8 As reported by Campos, Khan and Tessendorf (2004, p. 54), 20 percent of the largest land owners owned 60 percent of the land and the bottom 20 percent owned 3 percent. The land ownership Gini of 55 percent suggested that land inequality was high. However, it was the 75 percent of the population that owned less than 5 acres that became the target and mainstay of the program.

9 This meant that three-fourths of the community accepted the terms of partnership and agreed to the formation of the village organization.

10 Some of the projects undertaken by villages on their own initiative with bank loans include land development, acquiring agricultural machinery, nursery development and fruit processing units. Commercial banks had little incentive to locate in the area prior to this collective saving that could provide collateral.

11 By mid-2020, there were 1,878 LSOs and 15 LSO networks across the country, http://www.rspn.org/index.php/work/social-mobilisation/, consulted 6/14/20.

12 Union Councils are the lowest rural administrative tier below the province, district and *tehsil*.

13 The formation of these indigenous apex organizations was partly to address the criticism that the RSPs had no exit strategy and partly to confront financial constraints as donor funding shrunk and moved to other priorities.

14 A managing director of one of the prominent RSPs informed the author in a personal interview that rural elites come to check us out, find little honey in the pot and leave. Also, government backing provides protective cover for the village and community organizations from these elites. See Kyamusugulwa and Hilhorst (2015) for a distinction between "bad" and "good" elite capture. Their case studies suggested that it is possible to work with elites to deliver development particularly when the context is right and the incentives are aligned.

15 AKRSP was open to having more than one village organization in a large village from its inception. Sub-village organizations came to be referred to as COs subsequently.

16 The current (2021) Chief Executive Officer of NRSP, Dr. Rashid Bajwa, informed the author in private conversation that during his tenure the endowment fund grew from the initial 500 million to Rs. 11.5 billion (a 21-fold increase), partly based on wise marshaling of resources and subcontracting service delivery mostly from the government.

17 RSPs could be compared with other early participatory development initiatives reviewed or mentioned in Oakley (1991) such as Six-S in Burkino Faso, PPP in Ghana, PIDER

in Mexico and Small Farmer Development Program (SFDP) in Nepal. Participatory Institute of Development Alternatives (PIDA) is an early example of trying to initiate process-oriented participation in development in Sri Lanka.

18 This includes 496,352 COs (53 percent women only), 28,174 VOs (66 percent women only) and 8.6 million members (56 percent women). Given a household size of 6.7, the outreach is about 58 million, http://www.rspn.org/index.php/about-us/our-achievements/, consulted 6/14/2020.

19 This section draws on Khan and Khan (2021, Chapter 2).

20 This is referred to as rational choice vs. social being dichotomy in the literature.

21 World Bank (1995, p. 26) noted that "although the Program was initiated in the dominantly Ismaili areas of Gilgit, as it developed there has been no evidence of discrimination by the Program between regions or between communities."

List of References

Adams, J. and J. Rietbergen-McCracken. 1994. Participatory Development: Getting the Key Players Involved," *Finance & Development*, 31(3), 36–38.

Campos, N., F. U. Khan and J. E. Tessendorf. 2004. "From Substitution to Complementarity: Some Econometric Evidence on the Evolving NGO State Relationship in Pakistan," *The Journal of Developing Areas*, 37(2), 49–72.

Cleaver, F. 2001. "Institutions, Agency and the Limitations of Participatory Development," in eds., B. Cooke and U. Kothari, *Participation: The New Tyranny?* (London: Zed Books).

Cleaver, F. 1999. "Paradoxes of Participation: Questioning Participatory Approaches to Development," *Journal of International Development*, 11(4), 597–612.

Khan, M. H. 2009. *Participatory Rural Development in Pakistan: Experience of Rural Support Programs* (Karachi: Oxford University Press).

Khan, M. H. et. al. 1992. *Rural Change in the Third World: Pakistan and the Aga Khan Rural Support Program* (New York: Greenwood Press).

Khan, S. R. and S. R. Khan. 2012. "Local Support Organizations: An Exit Strategy for Rural Development NGOs," *Development Policy Review*, 30(3), 347–367.

Khan, S. R. and S. R. Khan. 2012a. "Women Faring Well, Filling Vacated Spaces, and Excelling in Community Development," *Development in Practice*, 22(2), 154–163.

Khan, S. R. and S. R. Khan. 2015. "Microcredit in South Asia: Privileging Women's Perceptions and Voices," *Progress in Development Studies*, 16(1), 65–80.

Khan, S. R. and S. R. Khan. 2021. *Spontaneous and Induced Collective Action in Pakistani Rural Development* (New York: Palgrave Macmillan).

Khan, S. R. 1999. *Government, Communities and NGOs in Social Sector Delivery* (Brookfield, USA: Ashgate).

Khan, S. S. 1992. "Nongovernmental Organization Alternatives and Fresh Initiatives in Extension: The Aga Khan Rural Support Programme Experience," in *Public and Private Roles in Agricultural Development: Proceedings of the Twelfth Agricultural Sector Symposium* (Washington, D.C.: World Bank), 249–261.

Khwaja, A. I. 2001. "Can Good Projects Succeed in Bad Communities? Collective Action in the Himalayas," Harvard University, Department of Economics, Cambridge, Mass.

Kyamusugulwa, P. M. and D. Hilhorst. 2015. "Power Holders and Social Dynamics of Participatory Development and Reconstruction: Cases from The Democratic Republic of the Congo," *World Development*, 70, 249–259.

Mansuri, G. and V. Rao. 2013. *Localizing Development: Does Participation Work?* (Washington, D. C.: World Bank).

Mansuri, G. 2012. "Bottom up or Top Down: Participation and the Provision of Local Public Goods," World Bank, Pakistan Poverty Alleviation Fund Research Partnership on Participatory Development, Brief 6, Washington, D.C., http://www.ppaf.org.pk/doc/ResearchProjects/16.%20Bottom%20Up%20or%20Top%20Down%20Participation%20and%20the%20Provision%20of%20Local%20Public%20Goods%20(Mobilization%20for%20Empowerment-MORE).pdf, consulted 6/13/2020.

Mayoux, L. 1995. "Beyond Naivety: Women, Gender Inequality and ParticipatoryDevelopment," *Development and Change*, 26(2), 235–258.

Narayan, D. 1995. The Contribution of People's Participation: Evidence from 121 Rural Water Supply Projects. Environmentally Sustainable Development Occasional Paper Series No. 1, World Bank, Washington D. C.

Oakley, P. 1991. *Projects with People—The Practice of Participation in Rural Development* (Geneva: ILO).

Olson, M. 1971. *The Logic of Collective Action* (Cambridge, Massachusetts: Harvard University Press).

O'Meally, S. 2014. "The Contradictions of Pro-poor Participation and Empowerment: The World Bank in East Africa," *Development and Change*, 45(6), 1248–1283.

Ostrom, E. 1996. "Crossing the Great Divide: Co production, Synergy, and Development," *World Development*, 24(6), 1073–1087.

Platteau, J.-P. and Abraham, A. 2002. "Participatory Development in the Presence of Endogenous Community Imperfections," *Journal of Development Studies*, 39(2), 109–136.

Settle, A. C. 2011. "The New Development Paradigm Through the Lens of the Aga Khan Rural Support Program: Legitimacy, Accountability and the Political Sphere," *Community Development Journal*, 47(3), 386–404.

UNDP. 1998. "Interim Evaluation of The National Rural Support Programme," UNDP, Pakistan.

Veltmeyer, H. 1997. "Decentralisation as the Institutional Basis for Community-Based Participatory Development: The Latin American Experience," *Canadian Journal of Development Studies*, 18(2), 303–325.

World Bank. 1987. "The Aga Khan Rural Support Program Pakistan: The First Interim Evaluation," Operations Evaluation Department, Washington, D. C.

World Bank. 1990. "The Aga Khan Rural Support Program Pakistan: A Second Interim Evaluation," Operations Evaluation Department, PUB-8448, Washington, D. C.

World Bank. 1995. "The Aga Khan Rural Support Program Pakistan: A Third Evaluation," Operations Evaluation Department, Report No. 15157-PAK, Washington, D. C.

World Bank. 2002. "The Next Ascent: An Evaluation of the Aga Khan Rural Support Program, Pakistan," Operations Evaluation Department, Washington, D. C.

Wade, R. 1988. *Village Republics: Economic Conditions for Collective Action in South India* (Cambridge: Cambridge University Press).

4 Human development in Sri Lanka

Introduction

The basic human needs (BHN) approach is a precursor to the human development (HD) approach. Both can be viewed as heterodox responses from within the fold of a mainstream economics since neither fundamentally challenges the status quo as do radical approaches to economic development.[1] Sri Lanka has historically excelled in human development in South Asia and, as Table 4.1 indicates, it still leads the other South Asian countries by a comfortable margin. Its success in this regard has mostly been state-driven.

De Silva (2004) pointed out that by international standards Sri Lanka's level of health expenditure (both government and private) around the turn of the twentieth century was low at 3.53 percent of GDP. This is despite the fact that Sri Lanka has been subject to a double burden of dealing with the unfinished communicable disease burden, such as malaria and diarrheal disease morbidity, and the challenges posed by noncommunicable diseases such as diabetes and ischemic heart disease that are confronted by HIC with long life expectancy and an aging population. Similarly, Aturupane (2004) pointed out that Sri Lanka's educational expenditure represented a comparatively modest level of education investment relative to comparator countries internationally and even relative to other South Asian countries.[2] Sen (1981) pointed out that looking at comparable statistics of country rank relative to income, Sri Lanka's attainment in poverty alleviation was second only to South Korea.

De Silva (2004) noted that an infant mortality rate of 12.2 per 1,000 live births in 2001 and a maternal mortality rate of 2.3 per 10,000 live births in 1996 marked Sri Lanka as an outlier among developing countries. The World Health Organization (WHO) classified it as a low child and adult mortality country in the World Health Report of 2000.

Similarly, Aturupane (2004) noted that gross primary enrolment exceeded 100 percent in all provinces for which data were available among both males and females and gross secondary enrolment ranged between 85 and 98 percent in all areas at the turn of the twentieth century.[3] Internal efficiency in the primary and junior secondary levels was high, with low dropout and repetition rates. Adult

DOI: 10.4324/9781003176411-6

Table 4.1 Sri Lanka's human development attainment in a comparative context

Country	*1990–1999*	*2000–2009*	*2010–2018*	*1990*	*2018*
Afghanistan	0.32	0.40	0.48	0.30	0.50
Bangladesh	0.42	0.50	0.58	0.39	0.61
Bhutan	Na	0.54*	0.60	0.51*	0.62
India	0.46	0.53	0.62	0.43	0.65
Maldives	0.57^	0.64	0.70	0.55^	0.72
Nepal	0.43	0.41	0.58	0.38	0.58
Pakistan	0.43	0.43	0.54	0.40	0.56
Sri Lanka	0.65	0.66	0.77	0.63	0.78

Source: Human development data from http://hdr.undp.org/en/data#, downloaded 1/23/2020.
Notes: *= Starting year is 2005.
^= Starting year is 1995.

literacy rates for males and females were well above literacy rates in other South Asian countries and close to rates in countries at considerably higher economic levels.[4]

To summarize, apart from the statistics indicating its high human development attainment relative to comparators, the phenomenon of low health and educational expenditure and high achievements in health and educational status marks it out as a success story in social development. Its success in poverty alleviation similarly distinguishes it. So much so that Sen (1981) identified Sri Lanka as a special case for further exploration.

This chapter first reviews the BHN approach and then how the HD approach is a logical successor to it. The next brief section shows Sri Lanka's record in HD relative to the other South Asian countries. Following that, the reasons for this success are evaluated and the chapter ends with a brief conclusion.

Basic human needs and human development

The concern in the 1960s with poverty and income inequality was part of a heightened social conscience associated which several social movements (e.g., antiwar, antiracist, environmentalist, feminist). The growth of revolutionary movements in the "Third World" during the Cold War were however the real motivating factors. These movements were often supported by the Soviet Union and/or China. The Western response was the recognition that deprivation is the cause of radicalization. Robert S. McNamara, ex-Secretary of Defense in the United States, led this change in thinking as president of the World Bank (1968–1981) in the late 1960s by getting behind the BHN approach.

BHN as a comprehensive approach to development was first advocated in the 1970s by the ILO (1977). The starting point of this approach was challenging the prevailing mainstream economics view in the 1970s that higher growth would automatically lead to higher employment and improved living standards across the board. The ILO report also challenged the assumption that because growth required capital formation, therefore inequality should be expected to increase before the fruits of prosperity could be diffused (i.e., challenged trickle-down economics).

A well-known but controversial empirical regularity in the development economics literature is the inverted U-shaped Kuznets curve (1955).[5] This suggested that redistribution would eventually follow growth as the size of the pie increases. This is the classic trickle-down approach, although given the paucity of data available to him, Kuznets acknowledged that the implied trickle-down was a stretch. Many now view this approach to have been successfully demolished by the numerous studies that have questioned the method or found evidence to the contrary.[6]

In any case, the ILO argued that waiting for generations for the prosperity to trickle down, even if the Kuznets hypothesis was correct, was "unacceptable in human terms and irresponsible in political terms". Instead, it advocated a strategy for restructuring growth such that the volume and productivity of employment increased to meet the basic human needs of the population at large; all wanting and available for work should find adequately remunerative work. Unemployment was viewed as among the major causes of absolute poverty and inequality. From a narrow economistic perspective, the social objective function was maximizing employment, rather than economic growth, subject to resource constraints.

BHNs were defined as the minimum requirements in a particular climatic, social and cultural context for a family for personal consumption (food, clothing, shelter) and access to essential services (safe drinking water, sanitation, transportation, health and education). To achieve this, under- and unemployed workers would need to be utilized by a better allocation of capital and the redistribution of productive resources. The rural poor would need to be provided with inputs, including land, credit, physical infrastructure and extension service in agriculture. The general population would need better nutrition, health (including clean drinking water, sanitation) and education.

The issue boils down to how and where to start the development process. While advocates of BHN argued, and still do over half a century later, that the starting point should be investments in humans, mainstream economists argued, and basically still do, that a focus on capital accumulation and economic growth should be the starting point and the prosperity would then enable an investment in humans. Concessions to BHN are in the form of a safety net as evident in the case built by IMF and World Bank for their advocated structural reforms.

Sen (1999) extended the BHN approach and this was formalized into what is now widely referred to as the human development (HD) approach. For Sen, entitlements, including assets (land credit), livelihoods and public services (nutrition, education, health, shelter), build elementary capabilities so people can avoid starvation, undernourishment, premature mortality and morbidity that emanate from the lack of social services. Capabilities are the substantive freedoms that enable individuals to "enjoy the kind of life they have reason to value" and hence they have intrinsic merit. Capabilities refer to "alternative combinations of 'functionings' that are feasible to achieve", such as in participating in the life of a community or in attaining higher life expectancy and higher literacy.

The functioning vector identifies the actual achievements based on the choices exercised. This conceptualization suggested a multidimensional rather than an exclusively income-based measure of poverty. Sen argued that individuals or households may be above the income threshold of poverty but poor on other functionings (e.g., handicapped people). Alkire and her colleagues, following this advice, have developed a multidimensional poverty index and there are numerous case studies using this or a similar method to measure multidimensional poverty (Alkire et. al., 2011).

Mahboob ul Haq, who worked in the World Bank during McNamara's presidency and became a convert to the BHN approach, moved to the UNDP and embodied this thinking in the Human Development Index (HDI), currently the most commonly used method for measuring development across nations. The UNDP's flagship is the *Human Development Report* (HDR) that has been released each year starting in 1990.

Following Sen's conceptualization of development as freedom, development has been made operational for measurement as the extension of the range of choices available to humans. Choice is the central element in this conceptualization and so the specific indicators in the composite are selected because they were central to enhancing human choice.[7] Per capita GDP is included because it provides the wherewithal for choice, education because it enhances the quality of choice and life expectancy because it enables choice to be exercised over a longer period. The HDI recognizes that people are the "wealth of nations" and they are both the agents and beneficiaries of development. In this approach, economic growth is still prominent but decidedly as a means to the human development end. Over the decades, UNDP has innovated with regard to what needs to be measured and how to do it. Some examples are the human poverty index, the gender development index and regional human development indices.

While advocates for human development see it as an end in and of itself, there is a functional case for it that continues to be empirically explored. For example, female secondary education could induce positive externalities within the household in the form of reduced fertility, better child nutrition, lower infant mortality and hence higher life expectancy. Better health means a longer working life, higher productivity per hour, less work lost from sickness and better learning. Both the motivation and ability to learn can increase with better health.

Various mechanisms have been discussed in the literature for more effectively delivering BHN. The delivery mechanism for both goods and services should allow for participation in decision-making via a partnership with development NGOs (Chapter 3). If meaningful participation can be realized, this could be strengthened with politically and financially devolving authority for service delivery to the grassroots level if it is politically viable. Another mechanism, if administrative capacity is in place, is targeting to ensure services are directed to meeting the needs of the lower income groups.

Sri Lanka's human development success

Table 4.1 reports on Sri Lanka's human development attainment in a comparative context. What is particularly striking with regard to Sri Lanka's human development success is that, except for the Maldives, its level of attainment in 1990 exceeded or matched the human development index score of all the other South Asian countries in 2018. It started with a score of .63 (maximum is 1) in 1990, and attained a score of .78 in 2018, an increase of 15 points.

(Gunetilleke, 2000) cited the HDR (2000) to indicate that at .73, Sri Lanka's Gender Development Index was higher than the world average. As such, aggregate indicators showed no significant gender inequality in areas such as access to health and education services, and there was no significant difference in the prevalence of poverty between female- and male-headed households.[8] The question for this chapter is how Sri Lanka managed to get such an early start that gave it a momentum it has been able to sustain despite a debilitating civil war that it experienced between 1983 and 2009.

Explaining Sri Lanka's human development success

Gunatilleke (1994) uses a periodization for Sri Lanka's social and economic history that has been followed in this section. The first period is pre-independence, which includes British colonial rule. The second is post-independence 1948–1977. The third period is 1977 onward.[9]

The year 1977 is significant because it marks the adoption of an ostensible shift in economic governance from an interventionist to a liberalization approach. Since liberalization and structural adjustment can be associated with cuts in social expenditures and a fall in human development indicators, it makes sense to use 1977 as a cut off point for the first post-independence period.

As will be made evident below, Sri Lanka had adopted the human development approach a long time before it had been formally conceptualized as an approach.[10] In fact, Gunatilleke (1994) pointed out that the British administrators noted that the level of literacy that prevailed in the Kandyan kingdom in the beginning of the nineteenth century did not appear to be much lower than that of the United Kingdom.

Gunatilleke (1994) also pointed out that at the time of its independence from the British in 1948, Sri Lanka's population had already attained an enviable health status. In fact, it is one that has still not been attained by some of its lagging South Asian comparators. He noted that in 1953, Sri Lanka's crude death rate was 10.9 per 1,000, infant mortality rate was 71 per 1,000 live births, life expectancy at birth was 58 years and adult literacy was 69 percent. Given the emphasis of policy makers on basic human needs or human development, the indicators above continued to improve, as indicated in Table 4.1.

Gunatilleke (2000) documented that over the decades preceding independence, the government gradually developed the foundation for the infrastructure needed for a national health service. The state assumed the responsibility for providing medical care, and established a network of health care facilities throughout the country. For example, in 1928, the government budget for the health sector was about 8 percent of government expenditure. Medical care was provided by the state free of charge and the steady expansion of the system into the rural areas, particularly in the 1930s and early 1940s, ensured that the poor gained increasing access to health care.

A major focus of attention of the health services sector was on preventive care, including control of major infectious diseases such as smallpox and the plague via vaccination programs and other public health measures. Health education was designed to promote appropriate health behavior, sanitation and personal hygiene as essential components of a national health service. The government also established maternity homes and rural hospitals during the second half of the 1930s, and this effort had gathered momentum into the 1940s. Antenatal and postnatal care was provided through a network of clinics and a cadre of public health nurses and midwives. Since 80 percent of the population was rural in the 1950s, the demographic transition had a rural flavor and female literacy and labor force participation provided a growth impetus emanating from the rural sector.

Sri Lanka's wealth at the time of independence was generated by its plantation economy: Coffee, tea and rubber. This provided the revenue for welfare expenditures. The colonial authorities realized that the health of plantation workers was critical to the productivity and success of the plantations and accordingly invested in health practices (disease detection and control) and infrastructure that was subsequently built upon by the newly independent nation.[11]

The initial efforts to provide an education suited to the emerging needs of the colonial economy were undertaken by the Christian churches, motivated by humanitarian and missionary considerations. Post-independence, these denominational schools were managed by the religious organizations that had initially established them, and they received generous financial assistance from the state. Government schools provided education free of charge for the rest of the eligible population. The division between schools teaching in vernacular and English created a social duality: a problem that persists across the board in South Asia and is not one Sri Lanka, despite a stronger egalitarian ethic, escaped from.

The Tamil minority benefited from better education and performance, hence access to university and labor market opportunities. The educational reforms introduced post-1956, making Sinhalese the official language, enabled more social mobility for the less well-off Sinhalese relative to the English-medium privileged students but created resentment among the Tamil minority. The reforms also standardized marks in university admission exams to level the advantage of Tamil-medium students. Since the Tamil population was predominantly rural, reforms providing support to agriculture were partly designed to ameliorate this disaffection. The liberalization policies of the economy in 1977 did away with accommodations for the Tamil rural population, such as with the elimination of agricultural subsidies, and hence exacerbated ethnic tensions that welfare policies had contained (Jayasuriya, 2004).

Unlike political tensions and conflict in India, relations with the colonial authority were harmonious in what the British viewed as a model colony. The colonial government gradually ushered in representative institutions. As might be expected, the demand for social services – schools, hospitals, maternity homes, central dispensaries – and common amenities, such as roads and postal services, figured prominently in the agenda of the local politicians, whose records were judged by the success with which they procured these basic services for their constituencies.

Gunatilleke (2000) summarized the main components of a social welfare system established post-independence as follows: A national health system that provided health care free of charge to the whole population; free education from the primary to the tertiary levels, open to the entire school-age population in the primary and secondary levels and to students selected for tertiary education through an open competitive examination; a subsidized food ration available to the population as a whole; payment of allowances and public works programs for the benefit of the poor; the improvement of peasant agriculture, which provided livelihoods to the large majority of the population in the rural sector where poverty was widespread.

Sri Lanka also has two major interventions directed at the reduction of malnutrition. Nutritional supplements are provided to mothers and children and midday meals are provided to school children. These have been in operation from the pre-independence period and have been progressively enlarged and improved. The Triposha program supplies nutritional supplements to mothers during pregnancy and lactation and to children under five. It has countrywide coverage and reaches the majority of mothers in poor households.[12]

(Gunatilleke, 2000) also speculated on the causes of Sri Lanka's strong human development base at the time of independence. He attributed part of the success to the traditional value system that was highly receptive to and supportive of the welfare-oriented approach, particularly priority given to health and education. The Buddhist tradition and culture emphasized enlightenment of the individual through right knowledge and practice and supported a more broadly based access to learning and knowledge than, say, the Indian caste system. The decision to prioritize basic education (vernacular primary schools), which were able to raise literacy and life expectancy, rapidly followed from such a value system. Health services were similarly accorded a high place in a value system based on compassion toward all living creatures and the alleviation of pain and suffering. Once again, this value system gave birth to primary health care (preventive health services and child and maternal health care) for all. Finally, the influence of British Fabian social philosophy and the labor movement on some of the colonial officers, who wrote the influential government reports, was clearly evident in the social policy adopted in Sri Lanka (Jayasuriya, 2004).[13]

This strong political commitment to the expansion of health and education services to serve the population as a whole was endorsed by both local elites and the colonial rulers. The plantation economy in turn provided a revenue base sufficient to finance the delivery of such free services. As indicated above, the political process gradually promoted democratic institutions and empowered the people to a degree that enabled them to articulate their needs and demands and required elected representatives to be responsive to these needs. The newly created representative institutions placed the focus on peasant agriculture and on improving the livelihoods of the rural poor. This also meant that there was no urban bias in service delivery.[14]

The establishment of a solid infrastructure of primary and curative health care services generated a momentum for an improvement in health indicators that continued into the 1948–1977 period. A critical element in building the base for a continued momentum was the improvement in the status of women through education and child and maternal health care. In addition, the country had developed its physical and human capital over the preceding decades This then enabled it to take advantage of the improvements in medical technology such as antibiotics, vaccines and insecticides (a mixed blessing).

While the two main political parties varied in ideology from a right-wing pro-private enterprise orientation to a left-wing socialist orientation, both remained committed to the three main components of human development: Free health, free education and food subsidy. Another redistribution program was the promotion of import substitution for food crops in the smallholding agricultural sector. This program included a range of rural development interventions, including land reforms, access to credit, large-scale development of new land for rice cultivation and resettlement of the landless poor, which contributed to an increase in income in the peasant farming sector. The rural peasantry had access to social assistance measures and relief programs such as drought and flood relief (Jayasuriya, 2004). In addition, there were schemes for housing and settlements and potable water and sanitation (Gunetilleke, 2000).

The links between economic growth and the progress in human development are not necessarily straight forward. Gunatilleke (2000) posited that while economic growth fluctuated in subperiods within the periodization being explored, progress in human development continued apace.[15] This may be because gains in health and education have an internal momentum and hence can keep compounding even during periods of economic decline. He argued that institutions, knowledge base and attitudinal changes and the solid base referred to above are all conducive to further progress. Also, there is likely to be a time lag in the returns to investment in the social sectors and so an increase in human development indicators may show up during periods of slow economic growth.

Just as Sri Lanka was the first to pursue a basic human needs strategy, it was also the first to adopt a change in development strategy from developmentalism to liberalization. This was marked by market-oriented reforms that began in 1977 (with a change in government) to respond to slow economic growth. In food policy, this meant a move away from food subsidies and controlled prices to a trickle-down liberalization approach with the expectation that the subsequent economic growth will deliver the necessities even to the vulnerable. Targeting of food stamps based on a means test, rather than blanket subsidies, was provided to the lower half of the income distribution. This meant that there was a continued provision of food support. However, the targeting enabled a considerable decline in expenditures on food subsidies as the subsidy was fixed in nominal terms and eroded with inflation (Sahn and Edirisinghe, 1993; Anand and Kunbar, 1995).

Anand and Kunbar (1995) document that despite the liberalization, health expenditures were protected and statistics continued to show improvements on health-related indicators such as death rates and infant mortality rates.[16] The World Bank advocated user charges in the health sector but policy makers in Sri Lanka were adamant in their refusal to consider such charges. However, they allowed the private sector to provide an alternative treatment source and hence laid the basis for a duality in health provision as in education (de Silva, 2004).[17]

Anand and Kunbar (1995) also documented the protection of educational expenditures and this showed up in education statistics such as enrolment rates and more rapid improvements in literacy rates relative to the target of 100 percent literacy. However, the food policy change does seem to have resulted in a higher incidence of poverty and malnutrition for the poor. Using time series analysis, which does not suffer from the shortcomings of cross-sectional (cross-country) analysis, the authors establish a tentative association between policy intervention and human development.

A case study, as documented by Fernando (2005), showed how Sri Lanka attained high human development as evident from how the high maternal mortality rate was brought down. She deemed the availability of an organizational structure for the provision of maternal health services at the time of independence and the political commitment at the highest level for implementation of welfare measures as the two crucial factors in this regard.

The organization structure included a public health nurse (PHN), a public health inspector, and public health midwife and a medical officer of health. Maternity services are provided through a widespread network of institutions, including central dispensaries, rural hospitals, general hospitals/teaching hospitals and through a health unit system responsible for providing preventive and promotive health services at the community/domiciliary level. The PHN is responsible for antenatal, natal and postnatal services. The PHN is also responsible for provision of domiciliary maternity and child health services in the community and provides care to pregnant women through home visits and through field-based clinic services.

The institutions are broadly classified into three groups. Group one includes the primary-level rural hospitals and central dispensary and maternity homes for uncomplicated deliveries. Group two includes intermediate-level peripheral units and district hospitals that have more facilities for in-patient care in addition to facilities for natal care. Group three includes the higher-level institutions (base hospitals, general hospitals and teaching hospitals) where specialist services are available.

The emphasis at the turn of the twentieth century was on increasing the availability of specialist services and for improved provision of facilities for emergency obstetric care. The higher levels of hospitals serve as referral centers. This strategy of developing a wide network of institutions interlinked with a referral system enabled easier geographical access to services and provision of services free of charge to enable access. In addition, several local authorities, especially the municipalities, provided maternity homes, where deliveries were attended to by trained midwives.

Conclusion

Several reasons were discussed regarding why Sri Lanka inherited such a solid base of human development at independence in 1948.[18] These reasons included Buddhist culture of universal caregiving, British colonial policy of maintaining high productivity of migrant labor they imported for the plantation economy, the influence of Fabian socialism and the British labor movement embodied in colonial policy makers, and a subsequent post-independence commitment to human development on the part of Sri Lankan policy makers as evident from social sector expenditures. The latter partly resulted from the formation of democratic institutions that responded to constituency pressure.

In addition to political commitment of policy makers, this chapter documented the cost-effectiveness of expenditures in health and education. Thus, even though the Sri Lankan government spent relatively less than comparators in health and education, it demonstrated better targeting and higher achievement. Similarly, Sen (1981) pointed out that food availability in Sri Lanka in per capita terms was not higher than comparators and unemployment higher (and low wages especially in the estate sector), and so the relatively lower malnutrition could be attributed to a better delivery system based on active government policies, including food programs.

Even if this solid base of human development can be viewed partly as historical serendipity, Sri Lankan policy makers deserve credit for sustaining the lead they inherited in social indicators relative to South Asian comparators. For example, continued investment in health, education and nutrition ensured high human development and very likely ensured Sri Lanka's lead even in income level and growth relative to the rest of South Asia. Sri Lanka's human development progress also survived liberalizations and structural adjustment. There is much for other South Asian policy makers to learn from Sri Lanka's human development and economic successes despite facing challenging odds.

Notes

1 The focus of the BHN and HD approaches are on development more broadly rather than on economic development. The latter is one component of development and it has a two-way association with development as indicated in the text. One heterodox approach outside the mainstream fold is the political economy of development approach.
2 Aturupane (2004) cited comparatively lower teacher salaries, due to excess supply of educated personnel, and a smaller tertiary subsector as part of the explanation for low educational expenditures.
3 Sri Lanka encouraged enrolments with free school uniforms (one set per year), textbooks for grades 1–11, and subsidized public transport.

4 As high, for example, as Hong Kong and Singapore, which had per capita incomes of about US$25,000 and US$33,000, respectively, in contrast to Sri Lanka's per capita income of US$800.
5 With per capita GDP growth on the horizontal axis and some measure of inequality on the vertical axis, the inverted U-shaped empirical regularity, if it existed, would suggest that as countries prosper, inequality first increases and then decreases based on a number of endogenous and exogenous mechanisms posited by Kuznets.
6 For a brief review of this literature, refer to Keifer and Khan (2008).
7 Given Sen's very high regard for Adam Smith in his writings, the extension of choice from the economic to the social domain is clever and insightful and as one might expect from this eminent scholar.
8 Notwithstanding these remarkable achievements in a South Asian and even broader context, (Gunetilleke, 2000) noted that Sri Lanka's low Gender Empowerment Index (0.309) in 2000 suggested that female education has not translated very well into decision-making positions. Further, as in other South Asian countries, Sri Lankan women confront domestic violence and abuse, sexual harassment in the work place as well as in the community.
9 For a pre-independence historical periodization and an account of colonial social policy that laid the foundations of Sri Lanka's welfare state refer to Jayasuriya (2004).
10 This is much the same as Japan pursuing the practice of a developmentalist state long before the terms developmentalist state and developmentalism were coined. In both cases, the later conceptualization was based on the inductive method.
11 For a more detailed historical account of this issue, refer to Anand and Kunbar (1995). They document how employers were called upon to provide hospitals, schools, maternity arrangements, creches and other amenities. It was logical to shift the burden of this responsibility to the colonial government of Ceylon and this subsequently occurred.
12 (Gunatilleke, 2000) noted that despite the substantial income transfers through social welfare programs, poverty remained high (a headcount of 22 percent in 1990). According to the data obtained in the national nutrition survey of 1994, malnutrition among children and adults was high for both males and females. The point to keep in mind is that it was unusual and commendable for a LIC to put into place the much-needed welfare programs of the kind that only HICs institute and that without them matters would have been far worse.
13 This source examined in detail the challenges and policy options facing the health sector, and Aturupane (2004) did this for the education sector.
14 Urban bias was a term popularized by Lipton (1977), who observed the social expenditures being siphoned off into more well-off urban areas where elites resided.
15 As expected, as the indicator base is increased, the rate of improvement can diminish. However, as Sen (1981) pointed out, the closer a country comes to the upper bound for a particular indicator, say 100 percent literacy rate, the greater the achievement in closing the gap.
16 Ironically, as pointed out by Anand and Kunbar (1995) and others, the estate sector, that partly trigged the focus on human development, lagged or even showed declines in human development indicators after independence.
17 A legitimate concern of policy makers in encouraging the private sector and subsidizing private practice was that this might contain migration of medical practitioners.
18 Attributing the extent of contribution to the different reasons may be an impossible task.

List of References

Alkire, S., J. M. Roche, M. E. Santos and S. Seth. 2011. "Multidimensional Poverty Index 2011: Brief Methodological Note," OPHI (Oxford Poverty and Human Development Initiative) Briefing 07, University of Oxford.

Anand, S. and R. Kunbar. 1995. "Public Policy and Basic Needs Provision: Intervention and Achievement in Sri Lanka," in eds., J. Dreze, A. Sen and A. Hussain, *The Political Economy of Hunger: Selected Essays* (Oxford: Clarendon Press), 298–331.

Aturupane, H. 2004. "Public Investment in Education: Conceptual Foundations," in ed., S. Kelegama, *Economic policy in Sri Lanka: Issues and Debates* (Thousand Oaks: SAGE Publications), 445–466.

de Silva, A. 2004. "Overview of the Health Sector," in ed., S. Kelegama, *Economic Policy in Sri Lanka: Issues and Debates* (Thousand Oaks: SAGE Publications), 426–444.

Fernando, D. N. 2005. "Orienting Health Systems for Maternal Health – the Sri Lankan Experience," *Development*, 48(4), 127–136.

Gunatilleke, G. 1994. "Health Policies for Rural Areas: Sri Lanka," in ed., V. W. Ruttan, *Agriculture, Environment, and Health: Sustainable Development in the 21st Century* (Twin Cities: University of Minnesota Press), 208–234.

Gunatilleke, G. 2000. "Sri Lanka's Social Achievements and Challenges," in ed., S. Kelegama, *Economic Policy in Sri Lanka: Issues and Debates: A Festschrift in Honour of Gamani Corea* (New Delhi: Sage Publications), 139–189.

Gunetilleke, N. 2000. "A Note on the Sri Lankan Experience in Poverty Reduction," *The Pakistan Development Review*, 39(4), 1193–1204.

ILO (International Labor Organization). 1977. *Employment, Growth and Basic Needs: A One World Problem* (New York: Praeger).

Jayasuriya, L. 2004. "The Colonial Lineages of the Welfare State," in ed., S. Kelegama, *Economic Policy in Sri Lanka: Issues and Debates* (New Delhi: Sage Publications), 403–426.

Kiefer, D. and S. R. Khan. 2008. "Revealed Social Preferences for Equality and Growth," *Journal of Income Distribution*, 17(1), 21–33.

Kuznets, S. 1955. "Economic Growth and Income Inequality," *American Economic Review*, 45(1), 1–28.

Lipton, M. 1977. *Why Poor People Stay Poor: Urban Bias in World Development* (Cambridge, Massachusetts: Harvard University Press).

Sahn, D. E. and N. Edirisinghe. 1993. "The Political Economy of Food Policy in Sri Lanka: From Basic Human Needs to an Increased Market Orientation," in eds., P. Pinstrup-Andersen, *The Political Economy of Food and Nutrition Policies* (Baltimore: Johns Hopkins University Press), 34–49.

Sen, A. K. 1981. "Public Action and the Quality of Life in Developing Countries," *Oxford Bulletin of Economics and Statistics*, 43(4), 287–319.

Sen, A. K. 1999. *Development as Freedom* (New York: Anchor Books).

5 Employment Guarantee Schemes in India

Introduction

An Employment Guarantee Scheme (EGS) was initiated as a rural sector poverty alleviation initiative by the government of Maharashtra in India in 1979. The Congress government in India in 2005 scaled up the EGS to the national level and renamed it the National Rural Employment Guarantee Act (NREGA) of 2005.[1] This Act of Parliament effectively made employment a human right.

It was initiated first in the poorest districts and over a three-year period extended to all of India's (748 in November 2021) districts. In 2009, it was renamed the Mahatma Gandhi National Rural Employment Guarantee Act (MGNREGA), although for convenience it is referred to as the EGS in this chapter. Because of its association with the Congress Party, the current administration of the Bharatiya Janata Party (BJP, 2014-) was viewed as initially hostile to it. However, rural unrest resulted in a reversal of course in 2016 and a modest budget allocation of $5.6 billion (about 0.25 percent of GDP or 2 percent of the national budget expenditure) was made to support it.[2]

The EGS continues to be relevant since the World Bank, World Development Indicators, suggest that about two-thirds of India's population was rural in 2020. Roughly a third of the rural population were considered poor by the Indian National Statistical Office in 2017-2018 based on the headcount measure of poverty.

Unlike the other success stories selected for this book, the EGS is not considered an unqualified success. Nonetheless, it was selected as a success story for this book for being so far ahead of its time as an innovative poverty alleviation initiative and one that continues to remain relevant for India and the rest of South Asia and other L/LMICs. It is entirely consistent with the ILO's Basic Human Needs approach (Chapter 4) in its focus on guaranteeing employment.

The first section describes the features of the EGS to explain what makes it unique and interesting. Since the EGS has garnered both negative and positive evaluations, the next two sections review evidence on criticisms and the plaudits of the schemes.[3] The critique is important for policy guidance and suggests there is much scope for improvement.

DOI: 10.4324/9781003176411-7

Features and administration[4]

This section reveals broad principles since the schemes are implemented at the state level and there can be wide differences in implementation and even philosophy across states.

The original EGS in principle guaranteed that all adults who wanted work would be provided unskilled labor reasonably close to the area they were living in. However, those who participated in the scheme were required to accept what was on offer.

One important innovative feature of the original EGS in Maharashtra was "self-revelation" or self-selection. The wage for temporary work was kept a bit below the minimum market wage so that only the poorest "revealed" themselves for such jobs. This in principle limited leakages to those not entitled. The nature of the heavy manual work provided was also designed to limit such leakage. Setting the wage below the minimum market wage was also designed to avoid disrupting the rural labor market. Obviously, if the EGS wage rose above the market wage, self-selection would be undermined. Targeting is an alternative mechanism for reaching the poorest and self-selection is by comparison administratively much cheaper.

To maximize employment generation, schemes were expected to be labor-intensive with a labor/non-labor (materials but no capital) ratio of about 60:40. It was reduced to 51:49, with discretion allowed. Another important feature of EGS was project selection designed to build rural infrastructure. If this goal is attained, it can raise productivity and up to a point pay for itself. Examples of projects to combat climate change-induced drought, where this is a problem, and to enhance rural productivity include percolation storage tanks, dams, wells, water harvesting, irrigation, sanitation, soil conservation, forestation, horticulture, flood protection, land improvements, feeder roads and IT connectivity. Finally, it was expected that the wage bill would boost the rural economy and also contain out-migration from the rural areas beyond the coping capacity of urban municipalities. It would also avoid the harsh outcomes migrants often suffer.

Coordination of the scheme was vested in three tiers: State planning departments, the collector's office at the district level and local government or the *panchayat samiti – tehsildar*. The planning departments released credit lines to the collector, whose office maintained an account of the expenditures to be reported back. Weekly and monthly progress reports were passed back to the collector's office and onward to the planning departments. There was a high-level vigilance committee to minimize corruption.

One notable policy change was a High Court decision in 1988 that required the wage to be set at the market minimum daily wage. The budgetary implications meant the imposition of work rationing. Participation in the schemes had in any case been declining. Between 1980 and 1997, there was a decline in participation from 205 million days per year to 90 million days. While part of the reason could have been the work rationing after 1988, part of the reason could have been on the demand side as agricultural work increased.

The scaling up of the EGS to the national level in 2005 was accompanied by additional progressive features. A hundred days of guaranteed work in the lean/dry season was to be made available to anyone, 18 or older, wanting it at a state-determined living (minimum) wage (above daily national poverty line).[5] The working conditions are expected to be decent and, for working mothers, mobile crèches are to be provided. In principle, the adverse effects on young infants are to be minimized by providing better support to pregnant women and women with young children participating in the program. Other facilities more broadly applicable like shade for periods of rest, drinking water and first aid are also to be provided as part of decent work conditions.[6] The labor to materials ratio was moved back to 60:40 with machinery not part of the mix.

The central government pays all of the administrative expenses (6 percent by law), unskilled wage bill and three-fourths of the skilled and semiskilled wages and material expenses, with the remaining 25 percent covered by state governments. In principle, state governments are liable for paying unemployment insurance in case of delays in providing employment.

To reduce corruption and worker exploitation, private contractors are prohibited. The separation of payment and implementing agencies and the payment of wages through bank and post office accounts were introduced to combat wage theft. Gram sabhas (village assemblies) are responsible for identifying the projects and for socially auditing them via vigilance and monitoring committees (VMC). Gram panchayats (GP - Village Governing Council; specifically, the gram pradhan or mayor) provide household working members with job cards (with empty spaces for recording work and wages) and have a central role in the planning and implementation of the projects.

In principle, work is to be provided within 15 days of application at a minimum wage rate or else unemployment allowance is to be provided (rarely done in practice). Work is also to be provided within a radius of 5 miles from the village and if greater than that, a 10 percent premium added to the working wage for transportation is to be paid by the state government. The objective of enhancing rural productivity with productive assets to address drought, deforestation and soil erosion has been retained.

Scheduled castes and tribes as the poorest are to be privileged in work allocation and a third of all available work is to be allocated to women at the same wage provided to men. In each period, a predetermined randomly selected share of villages has the gram panchayat leadership position (pradhan) reserved for a woman. From 2000, under the Panchayat Extension to Scheduled Areas (PESA) Act, all chairperson positions in three tiers of local government councils, as well as at least half the seats on each of those councils, are reserved for individuals from the scheduled tribes in relevant areas.

Workers need to present themselves for assigned work within seven days and work a minimum of 30 days at the assigned site. There is a premium on physical strength based on the nature of the activities (e.g., digging, carrying heavy loads of soil) and in this regard the strong are privileged.[7] The less-able bodied earn less since work is often assessed based on piece rates and the total remuneration due is calculated based on the specified wage (Jha, Gaiha and Pandey, 2012).[8] Weekly payments were preferable, but under no circumstance are they to be more than biweekly.

As Marcesse (2019) documented, the central government sends funds to the block office,[9] the administrative unit above the gram panchayat and below the district, via the State Finance Commission. The projects prepared by the gram panchayats are vetted at the block level. An engineering team reviews the projects and the payment of wages is approved when the projects are initiated.

The panchayat *mitra* takes attendance for recording the number of days each beneficiary has worked on a muster roll. These muster rolls show total wages receivable per beneficiary. Upon completion of the projects, the Block Development Officer approves payment requests, and the funds are transferred to individual postal or bank accounts.

We turn now to evaluations of the EGS. When reviewing evaluations, it is important to keep in mind that it is viewed as the world's largest public works or workfare program ever[10] and that many evaluations look at a very small part of its performance in a very small part of a given state. Thus, studies would have to be replicated over time to get an accurate macro picture.

Negative evaluations

Notwithstanding the intent of the scheme to benefit the poor, critics charge that there have been leakages. A substantial share of the benefits to date have accrued to the relatively affluent via project selection and wage employment at the *panjayat* level. In horticulture projects, that substantially raise incomes, many of the benefits have accrued to the larger farmers. Similarly, a substantial share (about a third) of the wells benefited the larger farmers.

Lakha, Rajasekhar and Manjula (2015) conducted research in Chitradurga district of Karnataka. They purposively selected the taluk (as average) and then randomly selected five GPs from among those that had conducted a social audit during 2010–2011. They conducted a qualitative study to research the local dynamics of social audits and in this context interviewed members of the Vigilance and Monitoring Committees (VMC). VMC members were appointed based on family connections by elites controlling the GP, the implementing agency, as a clear conflict of interest. Female VMC members were often appointed as surrogates based on family connections and functionally bypassed in their roles by male relatives. Land holding was one marker of elite status, but business and political connections or a combination also conferred elite status.

Dominant political parties colluded at the local level and benefits were distributed to VMC members, who were sometimes contractors (against the rules), by the sanctioning of projects on private land (against the rules) and by appropriating considerable amounts of wage income by fiddling with the employment records to show members had worked when they had not. For this purpose, job cards of workers were retained via coercion by GP office holders or contractors. The use of machinery was also widespread, also contrary to the rules. The reports to the

GS were often not filed by the VMC as required and at times the contractors filed the reports indicating a total capture of the scheme.

For other VMC members, the training available was patchy at best so they were not cognizant of their roles. While many VMC members claimed they had checked the quality of some of the works, an overwhelming majority (78 percent) had not participated in scrutinizing the invoices and receipts of expenditure. Many VMC members avoided making waves due to peer pressure and fear of social ostracization. Social audits were conducted rarely.

Another qualitative study also revealed the mechanics of corruption. Based on data collected (structured, semi-structured and interviews) for Bahraich district of Uttar Pradesh, Marcesse (2019) explored the emergence of rent-seeking based on the interaction of grassroots representatives and the local bureaucracy. The GP exercised discretion and awarded work to ensure that beneficiaries were willing to provide commissions (10 percent) shared by the block and district bureaucracy. Also, those who did the actual work were not necessarily the clients and relatives on the job cards and they confronted considerable delays[11] in getting paid - if wages were not diverted. Wage diversion was possible since the job cards were retained and bank officials / post masters (for postal accounts) were willing to let the gram pradhan withdraw the cash.[12] Norms governed the enforcement of the rent-seeking and distribution "system" and an individual gram pradhan opting out was likely to face the ire of the constituents for delayed or denied work and wages. A politically connected pradhan could however be protected from the district and block bureaucracy.[13]

Gaiha, Shankar and Jha (2010) reported the findings of the Comptroller and Auditor General. While, as one might expect, results varied by state, the report noted that only 3.2 percent of the registered needy households in 200 of India's poorest districts received the guaranteed 100 days of employment in a year (suggesting major supply constraints). NGO social audits showed various irregularities with regard to job card distribution, work assignment, project selection, design and execution and asset (public goods) creation. Collusion between village assembly officials and banks resulted in wage theft via ghost work, days and persons (Banerjee et. al., 2014). These findings were confirmed by Dreze and Khera (2009) based on their survey of 100 randomly selected worksites spread over six states, in which they interviewed (unannounced) a random sample of about 1,000 workers employed at these worksites.

Gaiha, Shankar and Jha's (2010) findings, based on a total of 1,500 randomly selected households from Andhra Pradesh, Maharashtra and Rajasthan, showed that a higher EGS wage relative to the market wage undermined self-selection and enhanced the incentive of the non-poor to access the scheme. Gaiha, Shankar and Jha (2011) using the same data set indicated that the poor also had less capacity to access and benefit from information than the better off due to a lack of access to cell phones and media. The poor were less likely to participate in public meetings and therefore had less knowledge of provisions – such as the 15 day and 5-mile rules – and therefore were less likely to enroll or benefit from provisions if they did enroll. Less information dissemination also meant less effective monitoring and more corruption.[14] They also found that transfers from the EGS net of the opportunity cost of time were quite modest.

Using the National Sample Survey (NSS), Dutta et al. (2012) estimated that there was considerable unmet demand. For India as a whole (great variation by state), 45 percent of rural households wanted work on the scheme and of these 56 percent got work. This meant an effective rationing rate of 44 percent. Notwithstanding the stated design features of the scheme (see above), rationing is inevitable since legislation has ruled out the lower wage option and the allocated budget is fixed.

Das (2016) used two consecutive rounds of the NSS conducted in the 61st (pre-MGNEGA initiation round) and the 66th rounds and concluded that the EGS had not been successful in enhancing the consumption expenditure of treatment households compared to the control households. A similar trend was evident for monthly food and non-food expenditure. Only about 43 percent of those getting work in India were laboring households and only about 26 percent of treatment households were below the poverty line. Similarly, only about 41 percent of job card-holding households represented unskilled manual labor households. The author determined that while the offer of 100 days' work per financial year was insufficient to provide livelihood security, the scheme provided only 42 days on average.

While the income effect of female labor force participation (LFP) might improve child health outcomes, the nature of the work might have an adverse outcome. Chari et al. (2019) examined the effect of maternal employment on infant health. They used data from the 2007–2008 and other rounds of India's District Level Household and Facility Survey (DLHS), a nationally representative survey of urban and rural households spread across 601 districts and 30,028 villages and urban wards. The authors found that the EGS rollout had negative impacts on newborn infant survival, increasing newborn mortality among women who were eligible to participate in the program. They also found that mortality effects were concentrated among working women.

They found support for two possible mechanisms they explored that could explain the findings. These were the crowding out of health inputs during pregnancy, which are time-intensive to procure, and negative effects of work on fetal (and maternal) health. Evidence for the latter was the increase in the probability of premature births and stillbirths and newborn deaths were concentrated within the first 24 hours after birth, suggesting the influence of prenatal factors.

In the evaluations reported in the next section, one of the positive spillover effects is on schooling due in large part to higher mother's income. This positive result is contested by Shah and Steinberg (2015), Ajefu and Abiona (2019) and Li and Sekhri (2020).[15] The positive income effect and mother's predilections for more schooling for children might be offset by the income earning opportunities available for boys in the informal sector, as a substitute for men engaged in EGS work, and the need for girls to take up housework as substitutes for working mothers. This then is an example of an unforeseen consequence that may need to be addressed with policy.

Positive evaluations

While the critique above needs to be taken seriously for policy improvements, EGS has also delivered substantial benefits though implementation and outcomes vary widely across states. Even though there are leakages via corruption and administrative problems, research findings show that EGS has been an effective way of reducing poverty via promotional (moving people above the poverty line) and preventive (keeping them above the poverty line) effects. It has served as effective social insurance to cover for an annual income shortfall – enabling income and consumption smoothing. While, net of opportunity cost of time, transfers may be modest in absolute terms (see above), they are significant for those close to the margin of poverty. Dreze and Khera (2009) are very enlightening in just how much positive difference EGS work made to the lives of the poorest.

Dey (2010), in his study of one district, found that the EGS catered to the poor (those below the poverty line) to a greater extent relative to their numbers in the sample. Benefiting from the scheme was also inversely associated with land ownership. Similarly, more scheduled castes/scheduled tribe members benefited relative to their representation in the population, and there was increasing gender inclusion in the workforce notwithstanding rationing in favor of men.

This was confirmed for scheduled tribes (in terms of job cards issued and days of employment secured) by Mishra, Behera and Nayak (2010) based on national level information accessed from government sources. Once again, there is wide variation at the state level and the authors made recommendations for making the scheme more effective in this regard.

As Dutta et al. (2012) noted, in principle the EGS enables the assumption of more risk, and hence potentially higher return, since it represents a safety net. It also reduces dependency since it raises the bargaining power of the poor and provides them with a backup and in this regard reduces monopsony power. While rationing of jobs is inevitable due to budget constraints and wage legislation, the poor and scheduled castes and tribes do not appear to be discriminated against overall in the rationing. The rationing rate is higher for women, but they were nationally allocated an impressive half of the total jobs (48 percent) in 2009-2010. This is impressive since the rural female LFP rate is much lower than that of men. There is also greater participation rate among the poor and the participation rate in the study declined above the poverty line.

Dey and Imai (2014) utilized three rounds (2009, 2010 and 2012) of household-level longitudinal data based on their own primary survey. The data were collected for a sample of 500 households and 2,249 individuals, drawn from 49 villages of 13 rural municipalities in Birbhum district of West Bengal. They found that cumulative days of participation in the EGS acted as collateral and significantly increased informal access to credit for consumption smoothing when confronting adverse income spells. Overall, consumption expenditure (food expenditure in particular) and income increased and consumption variability decreased.

Klonner and Oldiges (2014) constructed a district pseudo panel using NSS data with consumption and EGS coverage data for 2006-2007. They concluded from their analysis that EGS increased SC/ST consumption during the lean season by as much as 30 percent and halved poverty. Further, consumption smoothing occurred such that lean season consumption for these households converged with that of the peak season.

Liu and Deininger (2013) reviewed the earlier literature and studied EGS impacts on key welfare indicators using a three-round panel (2004, 2006 and 2008) of about 4,000 households in the Indian state of Andhra Pradesh (AP). They found the scheme was reasonably well targeted and had significant impacts, the magnitude of which exceeded the value of direct transfers. In the short term, participants benefited from higher nutritional intake and in the medium term the accumulation of nonfinancial assets. Scheduled castes and tribes and those relying on casual labor benefited in particular. Land improvements, partly on participants' fields, were a channel for positive EGS impacts. They found little evidence of EGS crowding out other types of employment or investment. They noted that AP is considered one of the better performing states regarding positive EGS impacts.

Using the nationally representative NSS, Imbert and Papp (2015) found evidence of crowding out. They found that EGS hiring crowded out private sector work and increased private sector wages. However, their calculations also showed that the welfare gains to the poor from the increase in private sector wages were large in absolute terms and large relative to the gains received solely by program participants.

Ravi and Engler (2015) used panel data of 1,064 extremely poor rural households from 198 villages of the Medak district of Andhra Pradesh over a two-year period. They reported a number of positive findings attributed to the EGS, including a significant increase in monthly per capita expenditure on food and non-food consumables, a significant reduction in the number of meals foregone by households per week, increase in the probability of household savings and a reduced incidence of depression.

Bose (2015) used cross-sectional consumption data for 19 major Indian states from the Consumption Expenditure Survey conducted by the NSS for pre- and post-scheme roll-out years (for 2001-2002, 2003, 2004-2005, 2006-2007 and 2007-2008). The author found a significant and sizable increase in household per capita consumption, slightly more so for the marginalized caste group. The author also found that households consumption behavior changed toward higher caloric and more nutritional items like protein. Households with children spent significantly more on "child goods" like milk and there was also greater expenditure on education. There was also evidence of consumption smoothing in that consumption in the lean and peak seasons was similar.

One of the expected benefits of the EGS was a decline in rural out migration. Based on a field survey on 556 randomly selected households in the Cooch Behar district from four randomly selected GPs from purposely selected blocks, Das (2015) found that the number of days of work and annual income from the EGS had a significant negative impact on short duration migration decisions. However, participation in EGS as well as number of days of work and annual earnings had no significant impact on longer duration migration decisions. Based on qualitative responses, the author deemed such migrants to have long-term associations in cities or highly marketable skills and hence their decisions were not impacted by EGS remuneration.

Deininger, Nagarajan and Singh (2016) used national panel data from 1999-2000 and 2007-2008. They found that in the short term the EGS contributed to wage growth and employment diversification, especially for females and those with limited land endowments. While the demand for agricultural labor decreased, mainly in the pre-harvest period, this was more than outweighed by more intensive use of family labor. The program triggered more intensive use of agricultural inputs and a diversification toward high-value crops. They attributed short-term productivity impacts to be largely due to resource transfers rather than due to improvements in local productive infrastructure. Gehrke (2019) confirmed that the EGS acted as a risk insurance scheme in Andhra Pradesh and hence enabled farmers to diversify into higher-risk higher return crops, hence increasing their annual earnings.

Berg et al. (2018) utilized monthly data (2000-2011) on agricultural wages for a panel of over 200 Indian districts from 18 states. They found that, on average, the scheme enhanced the real daily agricultural wage rate for unskilled labor by 4.3 percent per year in the peak season. This effect did not vary by gender. By using data sets that go beyond a district focus, Merfeld (2019) suggested that studies focusing on the district level have resulted in almost a twofold underestimate of the true effect of the scheme on wages.

Muralidharan, Niehaus and Sukhtankar (2016) used a large-scale experiment that randomized the logistically challenging rollout of physical smart cards (with chips containing biometrically authenticated information) in over 157 subdistricts to 19 million people in Andhra Pradesh, naturally with state cooperation. This payment method makes it feasible for monies to flow directly from the state coffers to banks based on information flowing up from the GPs, *mandals* and districts. The banks in turn used intermediaries, selected based on stringent criteria, to make biometrically verified payments.[16]

The authors found that smart cards substantially improved the performance of EGS by reducing the leakage of funds, payment delays and the time required to collect payments. There was also increased program earnings and real and perceived access to work. All this was achieved within a two-year period in a highly cost-effective manner and without changing fiscal outlays on the scheme. Not surprisingly, the government and beneficiaries overwhelmingly preferred (90 percent) the smart card system to the traditional payments method where in person authentication was not required while vested interests overwhelmingly disapproved and almost got the project canceled.

Dasgupta (2017) utilized the Young Lives Survey from Andhra Pradesh, India, a longitudinal data set of information of children who were aged 6-18 months in 2002 through household surveys conducted over three waves (years 2002, 2007 and 2009-2010). The sample of 4,289 children represented the different regions and income levels within the state. The estimates indicated that while exposure to drought in the past year significantly reduced height for age (stunting), access to the EGS substantially mitigated the negative impact of drought. The author concluded that this effect was quite substantial since it bridged about half the rural-urban gap in nutritional outcomes for children. Also, the impacts were more pronounced for the lower-educated and the more vulnerable scheduled caste/scheduled tribe households.

Afridi, Mukhopadhyay and Sahoo (2016) utilized child- and household-level panel data for 2007 and 2009-2010 from the Young Lives Study in the state of Andhra Pradesh and found that a mother's labor force participation (LFP) increased the probability of her children being enrolled in school, time spent in school and improved grade progression. Further, their analysis suggested that a greater weight given to working mothers' preferences in household decision making, due to earnings, could be among the primary drivers of the improvements in educational attainment of their children.

Mani et al. (2020) used three waves of panel data from the Young Lives Survey administered in Andhra Pradesh and Telangana states and found that the EGS had large positive effects on grade progression, reading comprehension test scores, writing test scores, math test scores and Peabody Picture Vocabulary Test (PPVT) scores in both the short and medium run.

Using nationally representative data from Indian NSS Azam (2012) found that the EGS had a strong positive impact on female LFP and wages. Its impact on wages of male casual workers was marginal by comparison, hence contributing to reducing the gender wage gap for casual workers.

Similarly, using representative household-level employment data, Ghani, Mani and O'Connell (2013) found that a longer exposure to women's mandatory political representation on local bodies significantly increased women's LFP via the EGS. They found evidence that women political representatives directly allocated more employment to women in public works and also indirectly facilitated greater female LFP via the nature of the public goods they opted for. Mandatory female political representation in local bodies enabled the achievement of mandatory EGS female job allocations (one-third of total), which is one of the scheme's progressive features.[17]

These findings regarding female political representation were supported by Deininger et al. (2020). They used individual data from a complete enumeration in 2014-2015 of all adult residents in 163 villages in 12 states that were part of the National Council for Applied Economic Research's (NCAER) long-running Rural Economics and Demographic Survey (REDS) panel. Information was collected on about 213,000 individuals in 69,206 households, of which 17,948 had a job card that allowed household members listed on it to apply for EGS work. They traced individual-level outcomes, beyond the period in which the gram panchayat leadership position (pradhan) was reserved for a woman, by matching individual data from the village to reservation history.

They found that having a female leader imposed by reservation enabled women to more effectively benefit from the EGS. It reduced the demand for bribes and harassment they encountered and enhanced their participation in program governance (e.g., via social audits). Leadership reservation resulted in increases in women's demand for work, program participation and access to financial services (bank accounts) that were sustained beyond the period of female political leadership.

Gulzar, Haas and Pasquale (2020) constructed a data set of 217,000 individuals and found large gains for targeted minorities where political reservations had been made for scheduled tribes. They also found that these gains came at the cost of the relatively privileged rather than other minorities.

Tsaneva and Balakrishnan (2019) utilized data from WHO's study on global aging and adult health administered in 136 districts across six states (Assam, Karnataka, Maharashtra, Rajasthan, Uttar Pradesh and West Bengal) selected to be nationally representative. They found significant positive effects of the EGS on the mental health of women. They found suggestive evidence that the greater economic security and independence may have accounted for this result.

Summary, recommendations and conclusion

Given the many criticisms, the EGS can at the moment be viewed as a work in progress that is tremendously bold and ambitious. In fact, it is for the latter reason that it is included in this book since the negative evaluations cited above suggest it is not universally considered a success, although the positive evaluations seem to far exceed the negative ones in the literature. Researchers have identified shortcomings and, in this regard, provided valuable service for improving the scheme going forward.

Notwithstanding the critique, the positive evaluations suggest that the EGS enhanced unskilled labor rural wages in the peak season (indirect contribution). In addition, via higher earnings it directly contributed to higher per capita consumption of the poorest, including scheduled castes and tribes.[18] The scheme-related earnings contributed to consumption smoothing between the lean and peak agricultural seasons. The scheme acted as an insurance and enabled farmers to diversify into higher-risk higher-return crops to increase their earnings. It also enhanced savings and assets, female LFP and, substantially as a consequence, improved health and educational outcomes for children and women's mental health. It reduced outmigration from rural areas that might have mitigated wage increases to some extent.

While there is much that is positive, many of the results above have been contested and critics have identified many areas for policy attention. One area needing attention in particular is possible health impacts resulting from female LFP. Based on their findings, Chari et al. (2019) argued for additional strategies to help minimize adverse effects on young infants by providing better support to pregnant women and women with young children participating in the program. These could include flexibility of work schedules for pregnant women, which would minimize the crowding out of health care during pregnancy due to its time-intensive nature. In addition, sensible strategies for reducing work stress for pregnant women may include shifting them onto lighter tasks, and, beyond a medically recommended date, incentivizing households to delay pregnant household members from working until after the delivery. They also call for stricter implementation of regulations regarding facilities for women at EGS worksites. For example, they are supposed to be equipped with crèches to accommodate women with children and cite Nair et al. (2014) to indicate this is not the case. To the extent that the EGS-induced higher opportunity cost negatively impacts child schooling in some locations, policy makers may need to offset this unforeseen perverse effect with incentives.

Some specific suggestions for improvements include avoiding building private assets like wells on land not belonging to scheduled castes and tribes or those not below the poverty line, since this could be better done with alternative funding such as via microcredit. For public assets, participation could be used as a delivery mechanism (Chapter 3). This way, the projects could draw on local knowledge for conception, design and implementation.

Another suggestion is encouraging more participation of the poor in assemblies to ensure information diffusion. Fortunately, appropriate grassroots-level institutions are in place and have legislative backing, so the issue is making better use of them to avoid a misdirection of benefits of the scheme. Evidence on rent-seeking, both qualitative and quantitative, suggests that policy makers have not yet managed to break the rent-seeking opportunities produced by the interaction of grassroots institutions and the district and subdistrict bureaucracy. Separating implementation from assessment in practice, as is the case in the scheme conceptualization, would be an important step.

While these suggestions and many more like them in the literature are valuable, they are easier said than done. The hierarchies, power structures, political alliances and vested interests of particular locations provide the context for the scheme and its implementation and outcomes. While this reality might cause some to simply give up, others take heart from the many positive evaluations and seek to build on that and diffuse practice leading to positive outcomes.

For example, while corruption at the local level based on the collusion of district and subdistrict bureaucracy and grassroots institutions may be difficult to root out, smart cards requiring biometric information for receiving wage payments have been shown to attain this objective in Andhra Pradesh. This mechanism bypasses the need for vigilance committees and social audits that are impossible to attain when local elites hijack the social accountability process.

The main recurring theme of this book is partnerships. The EGS is a state initiative at the central, state and local levels. Some states and localities have performed better in terms of accountability and delivery, notably Andhra Pradesh and Rajasthan. This success has been attributed in the AP to the galvanization of female Self-Help Groups and in Rajasthan to public interest in making the most of the opportunity (Derze and Khera, 2009).[19] There is of course a broader lesson here for other states that have not performed as well. While technology holds promise, so does cultivating partnerships with civil society groups to enhance accountability and delivery (Afridi, 2008).[20]

Notes

1 Refer to Mishra, Behera and Nayak (2010, Table 1) for eight predecessors of the nationally scaled up EGS dating back to the government of Maharashtra scheme.

2 Liu and Deininger (2013) noted an allocation of US $8.9 billion for 2010–2011. Gupta and Mukhopadhyay (2016) explored how party politics could play a role in EGS funds allocation. Sheahan et al. (2018) found spending consistent with needs-based correlates in AP despite its adoption of a top-down administrative approach to facilitate complex scheme administration. They concluded that politically partisan allocations were very modest.

3 The reviews evaluating the criticisms and plaudits are of studies examining the schemes post its being taken to scale in 2005 mainly from an economic perspective. There is an extensive literature that reviewed the original Maharashtra EGS, and made policy suggestions, that is not reviewed in this chapter. Since states run their own schemes, many of the case studies reviewed are of individual states or a combination of state schemes. In general, studies published in well-known referred journals or reports of prominent academic institutions were selected for the review. However, given the limited focus on the economics literature, the review is far from exhaustive. Many of the studies reviewed used the phased rollout of the national EGS in 2005 as an identifying strategy for their estimation, though since the phase out was non-random, poorer districts first, some scholars pointed out that further adjustments are needed in the estimation strategy adopted by most studies (Chari et al., 2019).

4 The institutional details are drawn from the many authors cited in the references, most notably from Marcesse (2019).

5 Dreze and Khera (2017) pointed out that since 2009 the central government has been revising state wages upward based on state-specific price indices.

6 Refer to Dreze and Khera (2009) on beneficiary satisfaction with work conditions and a lack of harassment at worksites (only 10 percent complained of it), and this is a far cry from conditions in private sector casual labor employment or in EGS sites managed by contractors (about 28 percent), under loopholes, who are theoretically banned from participating in the scheme. Women, particularly widows, were very gratified with the opportunity EGS provided. However, other than Rajasthan, the other five states did very poorly in providing facilities at the time of their survey in 2009 (p. 12).

7 Ravi and Engler (2015) noted that about a quarter of those eligible in households who did not apply for work cited the difficult nature of the work as the reason. Once the welfare losses from the unpleasant nature of the work are accounted for, Alik-Lagrange and Ravallion (2015) posited that a basic income guarantee could dominate net workfare earnings in terms of the impact on poverty for a given budgetary outlay, unless there are substantial positive indirect benefits (higher productivity from rural assets or female empowerment) from the EGS.

8 Assessing remuneration due opens up the possibility of corruption and wage theft.

9 The intermediary rural administrative level below the district could be also be the *mandal* or *tehsil*, though they may vary in size across states.

10 Berg et al. (2018) noted that the number of households that obtain work under this scheme fluctuates around 50 million per year. This corresponds to about a fifth of all Indian households, and more than a quarter of rural households.

11 Dreze and Khera (2017) point out that there are many steps in the payment process, such as filing of attendance data, work measurement and preparation of payment advice, and so foot-dragging can cause long delays. Also, bank processes themselves often take time and add to the chain of delays.

12 The lack of computational capacity in one case resulted in outsourcing to a cyber-café and that created additional rent-seeking opportunities via collusion and data distortion.

13 Niehaus and Sukhtankar (2013 and 2013a) quantitatively established the existence of rent-seeking.

14 Dreze and Khera (2009) also documented the low level of awareness regarding rights during the inception of EGS among casual labor.

15 For example, using a longitudinal data set of 1.13 million primary and middle schools, Li and Sekhri (2020) attribute a drop in primary enrollment and a deterioration in performance of middle school children (grade 7), in lower-quality private schools, to the EGS-induced increase in child labor.

16 Banerjee et al. (2014) explored a financial reform in 69 blocks as a randomized experiment. The idea was that if village functionaries could directly access Central Planning Scheme Monitoring System funds, cutting out the role of district and block level officials in the funds flow process, there would be fewer agents who could impede financial flows to extract rents. The reform relied on a number of assumptions, including that village level functionaries could master the necessary IT skills and that they have an incentive to enhance employment to win local elections. The most positive result was that the reform reduced EGS spending by about a quarter, suggesting a reduction of rent-seeking. Also, the more efficient funds flow meant a reduction of funds parked at various administrative levels.

17 Higher female LFP could be a mixed blessing. Amaral, Bandyopadhyay and Sensarma (2015) found that increased female LFP as a result of the EGS increased violence against women. While dowry deaths decreased, perhaps due to the increased earnings, there were increases in kidnappings, sexual harassment and domestic violence.

18 Cook and Shah (2020) conducted research at the aggregate level and found evidence that EGS increased aggregate economic output by 1--2 percent per capita, as measured by nighttime lights, but only in the more prosperous districts. Heterogeneity in EGS impacts is another policy concern.

19 In the author's view, worker organizations should seize the opportunity that has been made available to ensure that the progressive agenda of the EGS is attained. This statement is based on observations in surveys on how much of a difference such worker mobilization makes.

20 Afridi (2008) documented how this process of social accountability via social audits, using the Right to Information (RTI), works in the AP (top-down) and Rajasthan (bottom-up) to bring corrupt local grassroots and bureaucrats to shame. In AP, state resource persons (SRP), belonging to nonprofit and civil society groups, are engaged to train district resource persons (DRP) and villager social auditors (VSA), usually from another village to minimize intimidation and ensure security. All auditors are paid an honorarium, including expenditures incurred on the conduct of audits, by the state government. In general, villages are intimidated by elites and without state/NGO support, unlikely to get the necessary documents or raise a voice. With civil society/NGO support and use of the RTI (as expected they face much resistance in procuring the necessary documentation), there is some chance of some redress (getting omitted payments) via public shaming. However, there seems much less likelihood to date that the local, block and district officials will be sanctioned, notwithstanding legislative support for such action.

List of References

Afridi, F. 2008. "Can Community Monitoring Improve the Accountability of Public Officials?," *Economic and Political Weekly*, 43(42), 35–40.

Afridi, F., A. Mukhopadhyay and S. Sahoo. 2016. "Female Labor Force Participation and Child Education in India: Evidence from the National Rural Employment Guarantee Scheme," *IZA Journal of Labor & Development*, 5(7), 1–27.

Ajefu, J. B. and O. Abiona. 2019. "Impact of Shocks on Labour and Schooling Outcomes and the Role of Public Work Programmes in Rural India," *The Journal of Development Studies*, 55(6), 1140–1157.

Alik-Lagrange, A. and M. Ravallion. 2015. "Inconsistent Policy Evaluation: A Case Study for a Large Workfare Program," National Bureau of Economic Research Working Paper 21041, Cambridge, Massachusetts.

Amaral, S., S. Bandyopadhyay and R. Sensarma. 2015. "Public Work Programs and Gender-Based Violence: The Case of NREGA in India," University of Birmingham Department of Economics Discussion Paper 15-09, Birmingham.

Azam, M. 2012. "The Impact of Indian Job Guarantee Scheme on Labor Market Outcomes: Evidence from a Natural Experiment," IZ Bonn

Banerjee, A., E. Duflo, C. Imbert, S. Mathew and R. Pande. 2014. "Can E-Governance Reduce Capture of Public Programs? Experimental Evidence from a Financial Reform of India's Employment Guarantee," https://www.3ieimpact.org/evidence-hub/publications/impact-evaluations/can-e-governance-reduce-capture-public-programmes, consulted 5/10/2021.

Berg, E., S. Bhattacharyya, D. Rajasekhar and R. Manjula. 2018. "Can Public Works Increase Equilibrium Wages? Evidence from India's National Rural Employment Guarantee," *World Development*, 103(November), 239–254.

Bose, N. 2015. "Raising Consumption Through India's National Rural Employment Guarantee Scheme," SSRN: https://ssrn.com/abstract=2635553 or http://dx.doi.org/10.2139/ssrn.2635553, consulted, 5/10/21.

Chari, A. V., P. Glick, E. Okeke and S. V. Srinivasan. 2019. "Workfare and Infant Health: Evidence from India's Public Works Program," *Journal of Development Economics*, 138(May), 116–134.

Cook, C. J. and M. Shah. 2020. "Aggregate Effects from Public Works: Evidence from India," National Bureau of Economic Research Working Paper No. 27395, Cambridge, Massachusetts.

Das, U. 2015. "Can the Rural Employment Guarantee Scheme Reduce Rural Out-migration: Evidence from West Bengal, India," *The Journal of Development Studies*, 51(6), 621–641.

Das, S. 2016. "Impact of MGNREGA on the Livelihood Security of Rural Poor in India: A Study Using National Sample Survey Data," *Oxford Development Studies*, 44(4), 420–440.

Dasgupta, A. 2017. "Can the Major Public Works Policy Buffer Negative Shocks in Early Childhood? Evidence from Andhra Pradesh, India," *Economic Development and Cultural Change*, 65(4), 768–804,

Deininger, K., H. K. Nagarajan, S. K. Singh and K. Sudhir. 2020. "Women's Political Leadership and Economic Empowerment: Evidence from Public Works in India," *Journal of Comparative Economics*, 48(2), 277–291.

Deininger, K., H. K. Nagarajan and S. K. Singh. 2016. "Short-Term Effects of India's Employment Guarantee Program on Labor Markets and Agricultural Productivity," World Bank Policy Research Working Paper 7665, Washington, D. C.

Dey, S. and K. S. Imai. 2014. "Workfare as "Collateral": The Case of the National Rural Employment Guarantee Scheme (NREGS) in India," University of Manchester Economics Discussion Paper Series EDP-1412, Manchester.

Dey, S. 2010. "Evaluating India's National Rural Employment Guarantee Scheme: The Case of Birbhum District, West Bengal," International Institute of Social Studies Working Paper No. 490, The Hague.

Dreze, J. and R. Khera. 2009. "The Battle for Employment Guarantee," *Frontline*, 26(1), 3–16.

Dreze, J. and R. Khera. 2017. "Recent Social Security Initiatives in India," *World Development*, 98 (June), 555–572.

Dutta, P., R. Murgai, M. Ravallion and D. van de Walle 2012. "Does India's Employment Guarantee Scheme Guarantee Employment?" World Bank Policy Research Working Paper 6003, Washington, D. C.

Gaiha, R., S. Shankar and R. Jha. 2010. "Targeting Accuracy of the NREG: Evidence from Rajasthan, Andhra Pradesh and Maharashtra," ASARC Working Paper 2010/03, Australian National University, Canberra.

Gaiha, R., S. Shankar and R. Jha. 2011. "Information, Access and Targeting: The National Rural Employment Guarantee Scheme in India," *Oxford Development Studies*, 39(1), 69–95.

Gehrke, E. 2019. "An Employment Guarantee as Risk Insurance? Assessing the Effects of the NREGS on Agricultural Production Decisions," *The World Bank Economic Review*, 33(2), 2019, 413–435

Ghani, E., A. Mani and S. D. O'Connell. 2013. "Can Political Empowerment Help Economic Empowerment? Women Leaders and Female Labor Force Participation in India," World Bank Policy Research Working Paper Series No. 6675, Washington, D. C.

Gulzar, S., N. Haas and B. Pasquale. 2020. "Does Political Affirmative Action Work, and for Whom? Theory and Evidence on India's Scheduled Areas," *American Political Science Review*, 114(4), 1230–1246.

Gupta, B. and A. Mukhopadhyay. 2016. "Local funds and political competition: Evidence from the National Rural Employment Guarantee Scheme in India," *European Journal of Political Economy*, 41(January), 14–30.

Imbert, C. and J. Papp. 2015. "Labor Market Effects of Social Programs: Evidence from India's Employment Guarantee," *American Economic Journal: Applied Economics*, 7(2), 233–263.

Jha, R., R. Gaiha and M. K. Pandey. 2012. "Net Transfer Benefit under National Rural Employment Guarantee Scheme," *Journal of Policy Modeling*, 34(2), 296–311.

Jha, R., S. Battachariyam, R. Gaiha and S. Shankar. 2009. ""Capture" of Anti-poverty Programs: An Analysis of National Rural Employment Guarantee Program in India," *Journal of Asian Economics*, 20(4), 456–464.

Klonner, S. and O. Christian. 2014. "Safety Net for India's Poor or Waste of Public Funds? Poverty and Welfare in the Wake of the World's Largest Job Guarantee Program", Discussion Paper Series No. 564, University of Heidelberg, Department of Economics, Heidelberg.

Lakha, S., D. Rajasekhar and R. Manjula. 2015. "Collusion, Co-option and Capture: Social Accountability and Social Audits in Karnataka, India," *Oxford Development Studies*, 43(3), 330–348.

Li, T. and S. Sekhri. 2020. "The Spillovers of Employment Guarantee Programs on Child Labor and Education," *The World Bank Economic Review*, 34(1), 164–178.

Liu, Y., and K. Deininger. 2013. "Economic and Social Impacts of an Innovative Self-Help Group Model in India", *World Development*, 43, 149–163.

Mani, J. R. Behrman, S. Galab, P. Reddy and Young Lives Determinants and Consequences of Child Growth Project Team. 2020. "Impact of the NREGS on Children's Intellectual Human Capital," *The Journal of Development Studies*, 56(5), 929–945.

Marcesse, T. 2019. "Public Policy Reform and Informal Institutions: The Political Articulation of the Demand for Work in Rural India," *World Development*, 103(March), 284–296.

Merfeld, J. M. 2019. "Spatially Heterogeneous Effects of a Public Works Program," *Journal of Development Economics*, 136(January), 151–167.

Mishra, P., B. Behera and N. C. Nayak. 2010. "A Development Delivery Institution for the Tribal Communities: Experience of the National Rural Employment Guarantee Scheme in India," *Development Policy Review*, 28(4), 457–479.

Muralidharan, K., P. Niehaus and S. Sukhtankar. 2016. "Building State Capacity: Evidence from Smartcards in Biometric India," *American Economic Review*, 106(10), 2895–2929.

Nair, M, P. and P. Ariana. "Impact of mothers' employment on infant feeding and care: a qualitative study of the experiences of mothers employed through the Mahatma Gandhi National Rural Employment Guarantee Act," *BMJ Open*, 4(4), e004434.

Niehaus, P. and S. Sukhtankar. 2013. "The Marginal Rate of Corruption in Public Programs: Evidence from India," *Journal of Public Economics*, 104(August), 52–64.

Niehaus, P. and S. Sukhtankar. 2013a. "Corruption Dynamics: The Golden Goose Effect," *American Economic Journal: Economic Policy*, 5(4), 230–269.

Ravi, S. and M. Engler. 2015. "Workfare as an Effective Way to Fight Poverty: The Case of India's NREGS," *World Development*, 67(March), 57–71.

Shah, M. and B. M. Steinberg. 2015. "Workfare and Human Capital Investment: Evidence from India," IZA Discussion Papers No. 9486, Bonn.

Sheahan, M., Y. Liu, C. B. Barrett and N. Sudha. 2018. "Preferential Resource Spending under an Employment Guarantee: The Political Economy of MGNREGS in Andhra Pradesh", *World Bank Economic Review*, 32(3), 551–569.

Tsaneva, M. and U. Balakrishnan. 2019. "The Effect of a Workfare Programme on Psychological Wellbeing in India," *The Journal of Development Studies*, 55(12), 2593–2609.

6 Akhuwat

Interest-free microcredit in Pakistan

Introduction

Yunus (2002, pp. 496-501) is widely credited to be the founder of modern microcredit – he established the Grameen (village) Bank in Bangladesh in 1983. The bank's website reported having 93.36 million members in 2020, of whom 97 percent were women. It had 2,568 branches that provided services in 81,678 villages, covering more than 93 percent of the total villages in Bangladesh.[1]

The perceived early success converted microcredit, and more broadly microfinance, into a global movement.[2] Corsi et al. (2006, p. 68) reported that by 1995, about 500 million economically active poor people worldwide were operating microenterprises and small businesses. World Microfinance Forum (2009, Figure 6.1) reported that between 2001 and 2007, microfinance assets increased more than tenfold from less than 5 billion to more than $50 billion. However, its expansion also drew scholarly attention, and microcredit has been subject to harsh criticism on several counts.

These critiques of microcredit are first summarized in this chapter. The Akhuwat microcredit model, ostensibly not subject to the same shortcomings, is discussed next as an alternative. Finally, the Akhuwat model is evaluated, based on this author's empirical investigation of the model with Natasha Ansari, and this includes an evaluation of how well the model addresses the conventional critique of microcredit.

Critiques of microcredit: A summary[3]

Critics have charged that both the microcredit organizations and the instruments they use are questionable. The contention is that even nonprofit microcredit organizations pursue their own agenda at the expense of women. Peer group pressure, as a substitute for collateral, was originally designed to tap into and build social capital and ensure the repayment of loans. Critics charged that social capital is cynically used as a mechanism to reduce transaction costs in recovering loans but in the process sets community members against each other since loans become interdependent within peer groups formed to facilitate loan recovery. If the loan to the next person in the peer group is dependent on the repayment of a

DOI: 10.4324/9781003176411-8

loan by another member, it creates the incentive for intrusive monitoring within peer groups, even of each other's consumption patterns. Thus, social capital is systematically undermined given the way incentives are structured. It also creates household discord where by male members, often the ones using the loans, pressure females to secure more loans even if they themselves are responsible for nonpayment of the earlier loans. Finally, it does little to promote genuine entrepreneurship.

A large part of the feminist critique of microcredit is that instead of empowering women, it intensifies their oppression whether or not they use the loans themselves. Field officers capitalize on the lack of female mobility and their "docility", compared to males, to pressure them for repayments. If they pass on the loans to male household members, they are still responsible for repayments and are subject to organizational pressure. If they use the loans themselves, they now have another activity in addition to all the household work since males refuse to do "women's work".

It is further alleged that founders and senior management of the organizations are more concerned with empire-building based on donor funding and organizational growth, including staff size, and this is viewed as a marker of success. Scaling up gets donor attention and more funds but reduces due diligence and hence results in more troubled borrowing. The initial objective of poverty alleviation becomes subordinated to organizational growth impulses and by the organizational concern with recovery rates, even if this means using harsh loan recovery methods.

In addition to organizational growth, financial sustainability is another marker of success, again divorced from the original objective of poverty alleviation. Since peer groups are self-selected and since there is a high premium on avoiding default, the poorest, viewed as poor loan risks, are excluded. Even nonprofit microcredit organizations charge a high interest rate arguing that they need to recover high transaction costs. They also encourage clients to continue to borrow, often inducing them to get onto a debt treadmill. When multiple organizations serve the same area, individuals borrow from one to pay loans secured earlier from another organization.

Finally, critics charge that microcredit has limited value as a true development initiative if economic development is defined as diversifying the economy and moving up the value chain. If fact, it can be antidevelopment in that it draws resources away from medium and large enterprises. It is also perceived as self-defeating as more and more of the same activities are funded for saturated markets.

Akhuwat as an alternative microcredit organization

The Akhuwat model

Akhuwat was founded in Pakistan in 2001 to be consistent with Islamic ethical principles, and it claims to address some of microcredit's shortcomings discussed above. Akhuwat draws contributions from *infaq* (voluntary giving) and in turn gives interest-free *qarz-e-hussn* (literally beautiful loans), hence addressing Muslim objections to *riba* (banned transactions, including interest-based transactions). Charity underlies both the financial sustainability of the organization and its operational principle of interest-free loans.

Akhuwat also applies limited pressure for repayment. If households are found in dire straits, the loan is waived. While group loans tap social capital like other microcredit organizations, it principally relies on imparting to its borrowers the Islamic ethic of responsibility to the community as encompassing worship. Worship involves God consciousness but this is intended to induce right action (based on social solidarity and empathy) that in this case includes charitable giving and repaying loans. The "borrowers to donors" principle has been instituted to this end. Thus, instead of paying fixed interest, beneficiaries are encouraged to donate back in order to assist someone else like themselves. Imparting these ethical principles prior to handing out the loans appear to be effective, and repayment rates are reported to be higher than conventional microcredit (see Appendix 6.1).

Akhuwat tapped into this context-specific value system to build a revolving fund and uses this to provide small loans for enterprises in keeping with Islamic economic philosophy. The return of the loans then recharges the revolving fund, which also continues to grow as knowledge of the good work spreads and the broader community makes donations. Its credit pool has grown enormously with large contributions from the public sector (see Appendix 6.2).

The nature of the public-NGO partnership that Akhuwat engages in enables it to charge a service fee on funds disbursed for the public sector. In principle, this should give it an incentive to disburse at a much higher rate and scale up. Nonetheless, our field investigation showed that it continues to maintain the extremely conservative approach that it started out with when its credit pool was based entirely on private donations and it was free of any incentive to expand. It continues to exercise due diligence in selecting borrowers capable of establishing an owner-operated enterprise. More revenue associated with more indebtedness would violate its underlying philosophy. In this regard, the organization accepts its limitations of not being able to provide an unconditional right to assistance for all who seek it.

Many ex-borrowers become donors when their enterprise succeeds, and the ethic is to graduate from borrowing to donating, when possible, rather than to continue borrowing. Once again, the idea is not to keep borrowers continually engaged by incentivizing more and larger borrowing based on past repayments. Instead, success is premised on enabling borrowers to become independent and not need more loans from the organization. Nevertheless, many respondents we talked to took multiple loans and intended to take future loans as well.

Akhuwat also claims that since their loan is to the household rather than an individual, the responsibility within the household is shared. The loan therefore does not pit household members against each other but emphasizes their unity and common purpose and for the household to work collectively to enhance their own prosperity and meet their community responsibility.

Even though microcredit is a family undertaking, Akhuwat claims the principles of altruism and volunteerism are infused in the execution. Borrowers remind other community members of repayment dates, introduce new borrowers to the program and assist loan officers in explaining the program to potential borrowers. It claims that via "internships" new borrowers are taught bookkeeping, business location (for stores/carts), skills (embroidery/ stitching) and customer management. We were informed that borrowers have also pooled resources for food distribution although we came across no evidence of this in our limited fieldwork.

To mark the simplicity of its ethical philosophy and to emphasize the lack of hierarchy, the lender and borrowers in the Akhuwat branches sit on the floor in an organic setting that facilitates solidarity between the staff and beneficiaries, instead of impersonal exchange. The tight-knit social fabric that is characteristic of these communities is thus preserved, instead of being disrupted by the injection of finance and market principles.

The Akhuwat model of loan delivery encompasses another institutional innovation. Once applications for the loans are reviewed, those who qualify are invited to the community mosque, both men and women. This entails returning the mosque to its original purpose of being a community center but also keeps down transactions cost. The ceremony is not only held at mosques; disbursements are also often conducted at churches and shrines depending on the composition of the borrowing community.

After narrating the values of the organization and emphasizing community responsibility, the checks are handed out by the loan officers or unit managers serving the particular community from which the loan applications were received. The loan officers engage on a personal level with the beneficiaries, serving a community of about 300, and are perceived as friends and advisors rather than as agents of a loan organization. This is an important work ethic instilled and emphasized by Akhuwat's human resource and training procedures for its staff. Staff is rotated and do not serve the community they hail from to prevent conflicts of interest.

Upper management draws on volunteers that serve on an "honorary" basis (Munir, 2012). The organizational culture is infused with the principles of simplicity, égalité, solidarity and community. By adopting a community-oriented approach, Akhuwat intends to be a source of support for its borrowers. Instead of repayment harassment, as many microcredit firms have been accused of, it aims to foster mutual support and self-governance. As indicated above, the organization motivates borrowers to pay back their loans not out of fear of the consequences (harassment) but rather by trying to make them realize their self-worth and self-confidence in their own capacities to engage as involved citizenry of their communities. The organization realizes the operational importance of encouraging the borrower to employ the loan for its intended purpose and to understand that by doing so, and subscribing to the Akhuwat loan methodology, the borrowers are not only serving their own interests but benefit their brethren.

Sermons prior to loan disbursements in religious centers are an important mechanism for this. Akhuwat aims to cultivate a spirit that promotes consciousness in its borrowers by encouraging them to uplift themselves by uplifting their community vis-à-vis timely repayment and donating back to the organization, hence moving beyond competition and enterprise. By adopting this approach, in principle it addresses an important critique of conventional microcredit of eroding community solidarity.

Akhuwat claims that it is not concerned with empire-building and encourages replication by training and mentoring other civil society organizations interested in its approach. According to the chief credit officer (CCO), replications opt for a name of their choosing. Akhuwat provides training, shares its manuals and helps with monitoring, auditing and financial literacy. As of the summer of 2019, 15 organizations had successfully replicated the Akhuwat model (see Appendix 6.3). The Islah Foundation had opened 15 branches and adopted Akhuwat-Islah Foundation as its name. According to the CCO, "Some have even extended the model and are doing better work than us. For instance, Zaadira gives breakfast at disbursements and does not charge any application fee".

The funds collected based on public, private sector, borrower and staff contributions are donated to Akhuwat's credit pool. As Akhuwat's reputation spread by word of mouth, there has been an impressive growth in donations to Akhuwat Financial Services. In nominal terms, these went up about 3,000-fold from 2001-2002 to their peak in 2016-2017 (from Rs. 0.29 million to Rs. 858 million, see Appendix 6.4).

In order to determine eligibility for loans, Akhuwat relies on a social appraisal mechanism as opposed to any kind of collateral. A social appraisal form developed for this process is filled based on a home visit to determine if indeed the household is in need of support and capable of paying back the loan. The criteria used includes details such as whether the house is owned or rented, size of household, forms of income and detailed breakdown of total monthly savings and expenses. If Akhuwat concludes the family should be able to save, the loan could be denied. Similarly, a steady job would generally disqualify a loan applicant. Likewise, the ability to pay back and potential responsible behavior is also gauged by assessing the person's standing in the community through inquiries.

Loans are in principle available to all poor potential entrepreneurs, but Akhuwat selects on the perceived goodness as a community member and personal industry. A household member who is tardy with installments does not necessarily tar the household if they deem another individual in the same household to be worthy. Thus, in one case a son defaulted but the mother's loan application was accepted because the branch office was persuaded that she herself was a responsible person. This enabled the household business (store) to thrive despite the son's loan request having been denied.

Loans are sequential, starting with a small loan without a limit to the number of loans individuals may secure. There is however an upper limit on loan size. The largest size available for an entrepreneurial loan was capped at Rs. 50,000 at the time of our survey.[4] Though a lot of beneficiaries felt the loan size was too small, the underlying philosophy is to gradually build household prosperity, self-sufficiency and independence while minimizing debt burden. Thus, in addition to being interest-free, the small size of the loans along with small repayment installment sizes and an extended repayment period have been institutionalized to maintain payback ease. If they are doing well and want to borrow more to enhance the size of the business, this is encouraged. Prior to each loan, there is a fresh business plan appraisal.

The business plan appraisal is a rough balance sheet filled in by the branch staff based on discussions with the borrower and visits to the site of the enterprise (where relevant) for which the loan is to be utilized or a sighting of the asset like a rickshaw or cart. The idea is to access if the business is running successfully, if it is ongoing, or likely to succeed if it is a new one. The appraisal tallies fixed costs, inventory costs, variable costs and revenue generated.

Findings from a sample survey

Criteria for evaluating success

Success can be assessed at a basic level using statistics on conventional indicators such as the growth of branches, beneficiaries, replications, recovery rates, donations and credit pool. These statistics are reported in Appendices 6.1, 6.2 and 6.4. Imitation in the private sector is often viewed as a marker of business success. The same could be deemed to be the case in the civil society sector. As earlier indicated, many individuals and organizations have in the short period of Akhuwat's existence contacted it to replicate its approach to microcredit and the organization has encouraged such replication with technical assistance. Appendix 6.3 lists organizations that have adopted Akhuwat's lending philosophy and methods. Another criterion of success is how it is being viewed by the competition, and we will report what we were able to glean in this regard during fieldwork.

We think that an important criterion of success is beneficiary perceptions. If those that Akhuwat purports to serve are satisfied on various counts with the service that the organization claims to deliver, then it could indeed be deemed to be a success. Also important in assessing an organization is whether or not it attains its vision and mission as encapsulated in its founding documents. Finally, we use survey responses to evaluate Akhuwat's claims of addressing the critiques and shortcomings of conventional microcredit identified above.

Research method

We relied on both quantitative and qualitative information primarily gathered during our fieldwork. We leaned towards qualitative research methods in order to holistically gauge and understand the organization's role in a context-specific and conceptually in-depth way. Although we relied on other sources, the most critical information was collected from borrowers at the grassroots level based on our sample survey spanning 13 sites across the country and Focus Group Discussions (FGDs) held at each site. Each branch serves the low-income, usually tight-knit, community immediately surrounding it, roughly in a 5-mile radius. The fieldwork was thus conducted in 13 such communities. Eight of our 13 sites were in the Punjab province, two in Khyber-Pakhtunkhwa (KPK), two in Gilgit-Baltistan and one in Sindh. Our fieldwork lasted about five weeks of driving across the country from the plains of Sindh and Punjab provinces in the South to KPK in the Northwest and finally to Skardu, the remote district at the base of the Karakorum Mountain ranges in the North.

The Internal Review Board approval for the fieldwork was obtained through Mount Holyoke College. We initiated all respondent engagements with the recommendation for ethical survey practices of the Internal Review Board, USA, and painstakingly indicated to Akhuwat's borrowers[5] that we were independent researchers, not financially supported by the organization and that we had no influence or say in organizational matters. Further, we assured them of confidentiality and followed appropriate procedures throughout the research to ensure this.

After the initial contact, the field staff left for the duration of the borrower interview as per our insistence to Akhuwat upper management. We used this to signal our independence from the organization and repeated this if we sensed respondents associated us with the organization and also constantly referred to Akhuwat as "they". On one occasion a respondent reproached us saying that "you ask about them as if there might be something wrong with them, and yet they don't even take water from us".

Even so, response biases are inevitable. Ideally, we as independent researchers would have preferred to talk to the borrowers in a setting that established trust and restricted external factors that could potentially influence or confound the responses. However, since we needed Akhuwat field staff to establish first contact with the borrowers, some bias could not be avoided, since the borrowers may have, by association, perceived us to be from the head office despite our best efforts to inform them otherwise. Thus, this is the qualification we must begin with in cases where the beneficiary was a current borrower and intended to get another loan.

We often heard borrowers repeat to us the central messages imparted to them by the organization. The phrases "we give back to Akhuwat, so others can be helped the same way we were helped" and "we want to become givers to society instead of takers" were common responses across sites during our interviews. Whether and how deeply these messages were internalized is impossible to know fully but we were able to glean to some extent from our survey data and discussions.

We also did not know if the unit managers coached respondents prior to our visit to give a positive response. However, when we encountered a disgruntled ex-borrower, whose case was closed, we inquired about the case history to get the organization's perception of the case. We were impressed by a unit manager's humility and his response that the case record should speak for itself.[6] A response bias was also possible because we were unable to secure as much access as we would have liked to ex-borrowers because they were much harder to track.

On the positive side, we were amazed at the completely full access we were given to randomly selected individuals without Akhuwat staff being present during the interviews. In fact, since the perception conveyed to the borrowers was that we were "a checking team", it gave them every opportunity to freely complain in the complete confidence we assured them.

It was quite evident in the field that the daily work routine of the branch office was adversely impacted by our presence and demands and we tried our level best to complete our work as soon as possible. We found the field staff to be very patient and cooperative. Abandoning a car/walk mode of interviewing and embracing motor bikes (riding behind unit managers) to move swiftly into and on narrow city lanes and unpaved village tracks accelerated the survey to mutual benefit. But it bears repeating that this is an organization that freely opened itself to scrutiny with complete confidence that it had nothing to hide.

Research design and sampling

The sampling frame contained 47,914 respondents from 253 branches. This represented the population that we generalized to. We first randomly selected 5 percent of the branches (13 branches out of the 253). Given our budget, we randomly selected 1.5 percent borrowers and ex-borrowers from each branch for a total sample size of 458 respondents, 43 percent females and 57 percent males. Overall, we managed to interview 267 individuals, 78 ex-borrowers, which represented a yield rate of 58.3 percent.[7] As indicated above, we explored and reported when relevant if there was a difference in response by current and ex-borrower. We also explored gender differences in the responses. Of those interviewed, the nonresponse on individual questions was very limited and reported only if notable. The percentages reported are based on those responding.

We did not include a control group for selection bias because Akhuwat deliberately selects on perceived honesty, industry and entrepreneurial skills when reviewing applications and business plans. The point of this exercise is precisely to provide loans to those most likely to succeed and benefit themselves and their communities. This research is therefore not an impact assessment but a broad and qualitative institutional analysis of a particular approach to delivering microcredit.

While our approach is mostly qualitative, we fielded a semi-structured questionnaire to address the research questions identified above.[8] Since our main focus in the analysis was on qualitative responses, we were comfortable with the small sample size selected based on our budget and time constrains. We had the option of hiring a field team for interviews and that would have enabled us to secure many more interviews and hence a larger sample size. However, we thought it better to do the interviews ourselves knowledgeable as we were about the research questions.

Our second instrument was a list of questions we used for FGDs at each of the sites. These questions were also built around the research questions identified above in the assessing success and issues that were flagged during the pretests. In all we held 29 male and female FGDs with individuals not in our sample (three during the pretest). In addition to these two instruments, we extensively interviewed head and field offices personnel for organizational information. The instruments were honed and finalized after two pretests on January 5-7, 2015, and again on May 11, 2015. After finalization of the instruments, the fieldwork began on May 13 in Sukkur, Sindh, and ended on June 12, 2015, in Rawalpindi.

Findings

In a nutshell, we found the organization to be overwhelmingly successful. Loan officers and other staff members informed us that Akhuwat's presence in a locality results in a decline in the business of money lenders, banks and interest-based microfinance organizations that often complain, move out of the area or reduce their interest rate.[9] Beating the competition and enabling replication too could be considered markers of success. However, more important is evaluating Akhuwat's success based on borrower satisfaction and on whether it is attaining its vision and mission successfully and addressing the shortcomings of conventional microcredit as it claims.

We asked respondents to rate their overall level of satisfaction with the organization (1 to 5, with 5 as maximum). A high 87 percent rated the organization as 5, and 7 percent rated it as 4. As expected, the positive evaluation was somewhat higher for current borrowers compared to ex-borrowers. For the former, the high or very high level of satisfaction was expressed by 97 percent of the respondents, while for the latter it was 92 percent.

There was virtually an identical high level of satisfaction expressed with the simplicity of Akhuwat's procedures (89 percent 5 and 8 percent 4) with no difference evident in the responses of current and ex-borrowers. For current borrowers, the responses were 95 percent 5 or 4 (91 percent 5 and 4 percent 4) and for ex-borrowers it was 94 percent 5 or 4 (85 percent 5 and 9 percent 4).

An important question for us is whether Akhuwat is attaining its vision of inducing empathy and social solidarity? Akhuwat advocates that those who have been assisted should help others, even if in a small way, depending on their means. Those who attain self-sufficiency or prosperity should donate more than others. The mechanism for attaining this vision of social solidarity is thus soliciting donations through their "borrowers to donor" advocacy mentioned above.

While these donations are intended to be entirely voluntary, the method employed in receiving donations suggests that staff and peer pressure might be at play.[10] The donations are not anonymous in that they are given publicly in the field office and a receipt is provided for the donation. While the receipt provides some level of assurance of records being maintained and hence that the funds collected are not misused, Islam prefers charitable donations to be anonymous. Many borrowers during interviews and group discussions quoted the common cultural saying in this regard that "the left hand should not know what the right is doing". Others however noted that the receipt ensured their donations reached the organization when they sent them through a group member who collectively submitted their installments.

Ninety-six percent of the respondents donated but more important was the reason why. Over half of the responses (53 percent) suggested the purist form of humanitarian motivation, i.e., they were giving to help others. Over a third (35 percent) gave in the name of God but here too it was because God prescribes giving to help the poor. Several said that giving for God or for others is the same and cast doubt on the validity of our categories. One respondent said we are "vessels for God's work", which means helping others.

At least 9 percent were recorded to have specifically mentioned that they gave to reciprocate, i.e., to "help because they were helped" but this is an overlapping category with the first one, i.e., "to help others". Giving for the mosque (10 percent) is a traditional form of charity. Perhaps one could rule out as altruistic givers the 3 percent of respondents that suggested they were simply following the organization's instructions.

Notwithstanding the generous response from borrowers, 43 percent did not approve of the collection method though 44 percent did and 13 percent were indifferent. Of those who did not approve and indicated why, 97 percent said this was because the collection method was too public. To a direct question on the method of donation collection, 54 percent expressed a preference for anonymous collection.

As stated earlier, for Akhuwat microcredit is a means to an end. The end is social change based on a change in social attitudes. Thus, Akhuwat claims that compared to other microcredit organizations it creates social harmony based on social solidarity. The concept behind giving group loans is that group members should help each other.[11] In the best of circumstances, if one member is unable to muster the resources for an installment, the others should pool resources as a means of temporary support for the member in difficulty. They should also alert each other regarding payments due.

Payments are only accepted for the whole group and not on an individual basis and hence the group is jointly responsible. Therefore, one group member can collectively deposit installments for the entire group, which reduces transaction costs for the borrower in terms of trips to the branch. If there is a delayed payment, the field staff calls the individual who is tardy but also uses the group to apply peer group pressure. Since the group is jointly liable, a delay in payments spoils the collective group record and the worst-case scenario is that the whole group is denied repeat loans. This collective punishment is similar to other microcredit organizations and the outcome can be an erosion of social capital.

There was however a great deal of willingness among respondents across the board to concede that any follow-up on the part of the organization to collect loans was entirely justified since they need to protect their funds for loans to others. Furthermore, there was an acknowledgment, as taught by the organization, that if they repay on time, others got credit on time and that this was part of being good citizens.

We explored the extent to which individuals may have internalized Akhuwat's social philosophy based on responses to several questions. If social solidarity was internalized as a value based on organizational advocacy, most borrowers would have preferred group loans to individual loans. Over nine-tenth of the current borrowers (91 percent) and about four-fifth of ex-borrowers (78 percent) thought the group experience was positive. Females (92 percent) were more likely than males (84 percent) to view group loans as working well for them. Those who found the experience to be positive cited how all the group members were timely and honest and they liked the mutual support.

The main reasons identified for the negative experience of operating in a group was peer group pressure, not finding peers to be responsible or trouble forming a group. As per the organization's rules, a group cannot be formed by members of the same household. However, the group members must also not reside beyond two streets away. This requirement was mentioned as creating difficulty in group formation, especially for borrowers in older branches where most potential borrowers were already in groups.

Notwithstanding the reported positive group experience, more than half (56 percent) said they would prefer an individual to a group loan, 13 percent were indifferent, while only 31 percent said they preferred a group loan. The notable difference between current and ex-borrowers is that while 35 percent of current borrowers preferred the group loan, only 21 percent of ex-borrowers expressed such a preference and so Akhuwat's advocacy might have become more effective over time. Again, notwithstanding the more positive experience of groups claimed by females, 52 percent of them still preferred individual over group loans, while at 58 percent this preference was higher among males.

The main reasons for preferring individual loans were that respondents wanted to avoid the hassle of finding a group, and once found operating in one in terms of establishing trust, coordinating repayments and being held accountable for others. Whether this finding suggests that individualism is the human condition or whether this human trait is created by operating in a market system is difficult to say based on this limited evidence. In any case, Akhuwat has a struggle on its hands in engineering the kind of social solidarity it envisions as a preferred human condition. It has made progress in this regard because those who preferred a group loan, though in a minority, found it to be less burdensome and more convenient to work with others and found the social solidarity to be a blessing.

Akhuwat claims that unlike other microcredit programs criticized for generating household tension, it nurtures household harmony. On a direct question about whether the loan from Akhuwat created any tension in the household, 96 percent of the women and 85 percent of the men said no. Women had particular reason to be satisfied since virtually all reported that they used the funds according to their own wishes. Only one woman reported that the funds were used by her husband against her wishes. In this regard, Akhuwat's ideological predilection of viewing the household as an integrated unit appears well founded.[12]

Household harmony can be created by transparency in the solicitation and use of funds. Akhuwat has introduced an innovation by requiring that all loan agreements need to be signed by a household member in addition to the person soliciting and receiving the loan. Sixty-nine percent of the women but only 57 percent of the men approved of cosigning the loans, while 21 percent of the women and 28 percent of the men opposed the cosigning, while the rest were indifferent.

Most women who opposed cosigning mentioned issues such as the transaction costs associated with obtaining a signature from male family members because it is difficult to convince them to go the branch during working hours, particularly if they work out of town. The reasons cited by men were more patriarchal, with some mentioning that the branch is not a place for women to go to or that it is embarrassing to go and publicly obtain a loan with your wife. Once again, more work is needed to get reluctant borrowers, particularly men, on board to appreciate this practice.

This claim of having low overheads bears out in what we saw in the field and in the numbers. Branch offices have one table with cushions around it on the floor, a file cabinet or a steel cupboard. While area offices have chairs for data entry, they too are simple and austere. Despite being a cash business, they do not hire security guards and had no incidents of theft. Their response to our query in this regard was that they rely on community goodwill.

One of Akhuwat's claims is that unlike other microcredit organizations, its staff conduct is exemplary. Borrowers were asked to rate staff conduct from 1 to 5 with 1 as very poor and 5 as very good. Eighty-nine percent rated staff conduct as very good and another 9 percent rated it as good. Among ex-borrowers, the percentages were 83 percent and 10 percent, respectively. Thus, there is strong support for Akhuwat's claim regarding the polite conduct of its field staff members.

Our field observations and interactions and group discussions also revealed that Akhuwat is indeed exemplary in terms of the gracious, patient, polite behavior of the field staff. As narrated by a unit manager, Dr. Saqib's message is that "it is only the goodness of a person that counts and not their religion, sect, caste, creed, race or gender". As the numbers concerning staff behavior above show, the message regarding treating all people well appears to have been internalized by the staff.[13]

A common expression used to describe the staff behavior was that "they don't even take water when they visit our house", which implies how cognizant the staff is of vulnerable loan-bearing families and the potential burden hospitality can impose. Securing cold water in a hot climate is problematic for those who have no refrigerators. The organization's emphasis and commitment to staff training and careful and context-specific approach was very evident during our fieldwork.

Akhuwat has good reason to claim that it does not put borrowers on a loan treadmill. While it has an incentive to give more and bigger loans since it collects a service charge on public funds that are part of its credit pool, there is no evidence that it acts on that incentive. In fact, the most frequently expressed suggestion from borrowers was that the loan size should be bigger. Akhuwat gradually increases loan size based on demonstrated effective use of the first loan, evidence of continued need and an assessment of sound future business plans to ensure that borrowers are on a path to self-sufficiency and will not have difficulty with repayment of installments. It assesses its success on borrowers graduating and not needing additional loans and this is the antithesis of a business model that hinges on giving more and bigger loans. Finally, it closely monitors the use of funds to ensure appropriate and effective use.

Many microfinance institutions (MFIs) are accused of being agents of neoliberalism such that basic human needs are no longer provided by the state but rather an individual responsibility.[14] Akhuwat certainly believes in self-reliance as part of its mission statement. Initially, its aim was a credit pool for on-lending built entirely on civil society philanthropy and this distinguished it from other donor-funded MFIs. Of late, it can be characterized as a public-private partnership, because on the liability side of its balance sheet the bulk of its credit pool is derived as a contractor from the public sector for enhancing small-scale enterprise employment. It believes that creating livelihoods is the best method of meeting human needs.[15] However, it has moved the discourse beyond neoliberal individualism, or at least attempted to shield communities from intrusive market individualism, by its emphasis on *bhaichara* or brotherhood in its operational practice.

Akhuwat's stated mission is to "alleviate poverty by empowering socially and economically marginalized families through interest-free microfinance and by harnessing entrepreneurial potential, capacity building and social guidance". We also explored in this chapter how successful the organization has been in attaining this mission statement based on survey responses.

We did not use the data we collected on the extent to which the income was enhanced due to the loan. We discerned that the numbers were too rough and ready. The more established businessmen evaded the question and since Akhuwat often supported existing micro businesses, it would be difficult to disassociate the contributions of the individual from that of the loan. Instead, we relied on a host of other questions to gauge the success of the loan and based on the responses found Akhuwat had been successful in attaining its mission statement of promoting self-sufficiency among the poor.

Over nine-tenth (91 percent) responded that the loan had contributed to a substantial increase in household income (same number that responded that the business was still active). There was no variation by gender, but current borrowers were more positive (93 percent) than ex-borrowers (87 percent).

A measure of the operational success of a microcredit organization is their ability to recover loans in a timely manner. Akhuwat encourages borrowers to set Rs. 50 or so aside each day from the business for the repayment of the installment. Many mentioned during fieldwork that this is what they did. The effectiveness of this strategy was evident from the 88 percent who responded that they exclusively paid back the loan from the earnings of their business. Others relied on this source but also drew on other sources of income such as family, friends or a day job.

Twenty-nine percent reported having been late in making payments (58 percent of them were late more than once). Akhuwat's response to tardiness was mostly mild and in one-third of the cases the respondent said they were simply let off without being chastised. In another third of the cases (29 percent), the borrower was given more time. In 14 percent of the cases, the borrower was informed that his record would be negatively impacted and more loans would not be forthcoming, while a tenth were informed that their record had been negatively impacted. Beyond warnings, Akhuwat exercises oversight during the process and 83 percent responded that field staff monitored their use of funds.

Forty-seven percent of the borrowers started the business with the funds procured from Akhuwat in their first loan. The rest supplemented their existing business with the loan. About four-fifth of borrowers responded that they fully attained their objective, while 13 percent said they were somewhat successful. Only 6 percent responded that they failed completely in their objective. The main reason reported for a complete business failure was the lack of a market. The gender distribution indicated that 85 percent of females and 78 percent of the males, respectively, responded that they were fully successful in attaining their objective.

Most of those who responded that they had not fully attained their objective attributed this to the small size of the loan. Fifty-five percent of all respondents thought that the loan size was inadequate. About 77 percent said they would have used a loan of the desired size to expand their business, while 22 percent wanted it to set up a larger business.

The ultimate success for Akhuwat is not only sustained self-employment but also expansion to the point that the micro-business starts creating jobs for others. While Akhuwat strives to support businesses that will thrive and create jobs in the future, at the time of the survey it was mostly supporting self-employment. Two-third of the businesses had no additional family employees, a little more than a quarter had one additional family employee and only 6 percent had two or more additional family employees. Even so, about 18 percent of the businesses had taken on one or more nonfamily members so while modest in scope, some jobs were generated. Over nine-tenth of the businesses (92 percent) expected to expand and almost nine-tenth of current borrowers expected to apply for a new loan from Akhuwat.

One criticism of microcredit pertains to the "fallacy of composition" such that what works for, say, one vendor may not work for many of them collectively (Bateman and Chang, 2012). Perhaps Akhuwat minimizes this impact with its careful review of business plans. In any case, since only 2 percent of borrowers noted the lack of a market as contributing to their inability to attain their objective, there was no evidence to support the fallacy of composition hypothesis in Akhuwat's case.

Summary and conclusions

Based on various criteria identified in this chapter, we view Akhuwat to be a highly successful organization and one that is, for the most part, attaining its vision and mission. In terms of borrower's perceptions, 97 percent of current borrowers and 92 percent of ex-borrowers rated their overall satisfaction with Akhuwat as very good or good. Borrowers viewed it as a great success because it helped the poor or because of how it conducted itself.

Organizationally, we consider its success to be premised on the charisma of the founder and his humility, simplicity and leadership by example. These traits have infused passion and dedication in the field staff that identifies with the Akhuwat vision of building a poverty-free society based on the principles of compassion, empathy, equity and self-reliance. Many viewed the time they spend working for Akhuwat as an opportunity whereby they are being paid to do "good works".

Others who the organization viewed as exceptional for their honesty, hard work and dedication opted for a career path crafted by the organization.

Akhuwat also uses conventional organizational principles to put systems in place to ensure transparency, accountability, fair assessment, efficiency and effectiveness. Akhuwat views itself as a microcredit organization with a difference and also one that has developed a methodology that enables it to avoid the pitfalls of conventional microcredit. This is in addition to its claim that it promotes social solidarity by encouraging altruism. While an impressive percentage of total borrowers give back to help others by contributing to the organization's revolving fund, we were not entirely persuaded that the public method that Akhuwat has developed to promote giving conforms to altruistic giving.

In the past, Akhuwat had posted collection boxes so that the giving could be entirely anonymous. However, the needs of accountability altered the method to giving publicly in the office and issuing a receipt to the donors. This is reassuring to 44 percent of the borrowers who expressed a preference for some accountability. However, 43 percent disapproved of this method of soliciting borrower donations. The main reasons for this disapproval were that the donations were too public and that they were not consistent with a preference for anonymous giving in Islam. Fifty-four percent expressed a preference for anonymous giving.

We also explored the other Akhuwat claims and, overall, we evaluated it to have delivered on its claims on most counts. The organization certainly keeps its overheads very low as it claims by practicing extreme simplicity. The staff was perceived to be helpful, courteous and polite and 89 percent rated them as very good and 9 percent as good. Finally, since Akhuwat does not collect interest but only a modest administrative fee, it claims that it has no incentive to get its borrowers on a loan treadmill. Instead, it takes pride in those who are able to succeed in their business, create jobs and donate so that others can follow in their footsteps. Given its conservative approach to giving loans, despite the service fee it can charge on loans given on public donations to its credit pool, there is evidence to support its claims of preventing indebtedness and creating self-sufficiency.

Akhuwat finesses the feminist critique. Feminist scholars have urged looking within the black box referred to as the household in economics since that is also where gender discrimination and violence against women occur. Akhuwat comes at this issue with an ideological lens insisting that social stability is premised on household unity. This may not hold in practice in male dominated societies and gender oppression cannot be ruled out by wishful thinking. Akhuwat structures incentives to minimize gender conflict by giving the loan to the household rather than an individual. Even though we tried to single out individual beneficiary experience, the responses invariably pertained to the well-being of the household. Ninety-six percent of the women and 88 percent of the men reported no household tension resulted from the loans. Thus, it appears that Akhuwat is able to build on and reinforce household harmony.

Our findings suggest that the organization has so far been successful in attaining its mission of promoting self-enterprise. Nine-tenth of respondents reported a substantial increase in household income due to the loan and four-fifth reported that they paid back their loans exclusively from their earnings. Seventy percent of the borrowers were able to pay back on time. Eighty-five percent said they fully attained the business objective they set out to accomplish and 13 percent said this was somewhat the case. Only 2 percent reported they failed in their objective and the reason cited was the lack of a market. An overwhelming percentage of borrowers expressed satisfaction with what they had accomplished and were very positive about the organization.

Appendix 6.1 Akhuwat's recovery rates since inception (%)

Year	*Recovery rate*
2001-2002	100
2002-2003	99.95
2003-2004	99.9
2004-2005	99.95
2005-2006	99.9
2006-2007	99.5
2007-2008	99.37
2008-2009	99.5
2009-2010	99.85
2010-2011	99.85
2011-2012	99.86
2012-2013	99.87
2013-2014	99.85
2014-2015	99.93
2015-2016	99.93
2016-2017	99.99
2017-2018	99.95
2018-2019	99.92

Source: Akhuwat head office

Appendix 6.2 Akhuwat's expansion since inception

Year	*Loan portfolio*	*Borrowers*	*Branches*
2001-2002	1,895,000	192	1
2002-2003	2,791,300	282	2
2003-2004	8,504,000	832	4
2004-2005	31,811,000	3,124	7
2005-2006	66,020,700	6,264	11
2006-2007	89,935,600	8,674	18
2007-2008	122,445,242	11,388	20
2008-2009	164,226,000	13,821	22
2009-2010	251,808,800	21,073	36
2010-2011	418,211,100	34,194	60
2011-2012	1,137,684,000	67,683	81
2012-2013	2,580,467,000	159,138	169
2013-2014	4,047,109,100	234,883	271
2014-2015	7,310,527,000	367,798	357
2015-2016	11,115,534,694	496,458	500
2016-2017	17,618,984,409	619,396	683
2017-2018	21,607,796,495	731,302	791
2018-2019	19,649,563,816	633,987	813

Source: Akhuwat head office

Appendix 6.3 Akhuwat's replications

Kawish Welfare Trust
Al Nur Umar Welfare Trust
Sojhro
ECI Pakistan
Heral Buniyaad
Decent Welfare, Gujrat
Naimat Foundation
Akhuwat Karachi
Brooke International, Pakistan
Muslim Aid, Pakistan
Rural Development Organization, Dera Ghazi Khan
Din Group
Helping Hands
Islah Foundation
Alkhidmat Foundation

Source: Akhuwat head office

Appendix 6.4 Akhuwat's donated funds since inception (million Rs., current)

2000-2001	Akhuwat	0.29
2001-2002	Akhuwat	0.97
2002-2003	Akhuwat	1.82
2003-2004	Akhuwat	7.14
2004-2005	Akhuwat	10.98
2005-2006	Akhuwat	28.34
2006-2007	Akhuwat	17.72
2007-2008	Akhuwat	21.40
2008-2009	Akhuwat	36.63
2009-2010	Akhuwat	108.06
2010-2011	Akhuwat	127.67
2011-2012	Akhuwat	134.82
2012-13	Akhuwat	119.57
2013-2014	Akhuwat	192.42
2014-2015	Akhuwat	244.89
2015-2016	Akhuwat	352.47
2016-2017	Akhuwat	858.43
2017-2018	Akhuwat Islamic Microfinance	263.11
2018-2019	Akhuwat Islamic Microfinance	225.17

Source: Akhuwat head office

Notes: The chief financial officer speculated that the drop after 2011-2012 might have resulted from bidding for and winning big competitive government grants. This focused management attention toward managing the funds and away from private fund raising for a while. Microfinance operations were legally separated from other projects in 2017-2018 and the numbers for that and the following year represent only donations for microfinance operations. This was the explanation for the decline after the big jump in 2016-2017.

Appendix 6.5 Akhuwat's percentage distribution of loan products

Purpose of loan	*Percentage %*
Enterprise Loan	99.36
Health Loan	0.05
Liberation Loan	0.11
Marriage Loan	0.18
Housing Loan	0.23
Education Loan	0.06
Total	100.00

Source: Akhuwat head office

Notes

1 https://grameenbank.org/, consulted 6/16/2021.

2 Microcredit and microfinance are sometimes used interchangeably. The former is the original financial instrument targeted to the poor, while the latter is a broader term that includes business credit but could also include other financial instruments like consumer credit, saving accounts, insurance, pension provision and remittance services for the same target group. Refer to Flynn (2007) for an account of these products. Refer to Microcredit Summit Campaign for statistics on the spread of microfinance.

3 For a full discussion of these critiques, refer to Khan and Ansari (2018, Chapter 4).

4 One US$ exchanged for 102 Pakistani rupees in mid-2015.

5 One of our key informants at the head office told us that there is a deemphasis by the organization on the term "borrowers" and "beneficiaries" because of the inherent top-down hierarchy the terms imply. Instead, they prefer to use the term "members". This is reflected in official organizational practice as well, since borrower donations to Akhuwat are referred to as member donations. That notwithstanding, Akhuwat has yet to put into place the mechanisms that could turn its borrowers into members and thus at the moment it is not a membership organization in the conventional sense.

6 The unit manager said he did not want to speak ill of anyone and encouraged us to pursue the relevant documentation in the head office.

7 We did not include ten filled-in questionnaires in the analysis and counted them among the nonrespondents. We disqualified two responses in the field since our selection criteria were not met. In four cases, the respondent's ID (identification) card number was not in our sample list. In another four cases, the ID was repeated and we dropped those questionnaires. Strictly speaking, we should have dropped both cases since we could not be sure which of the two questionnaires was valid.

8 Some of the questions we asked involved an ethical judgment. For example, by asking respondents if they are comfortable with giving in public may have made them aware of an issue they might not otherwise have thought of. Thus, we risked changing the social reality by studying it, a well-known dilemma in the sciences. We proceeded because several of these issues were brought up by respondents during our pretest and because we believed ourselves to be benign social researchers who were intent on helping the organization rather than merely intent on critiquing it to score points.

9 Akhuwat at the grassroots level welcomes this and some who would qualify for their loans, based on their stringent criteria, and are carrying interest-based loans are encouraged to use part of the loan to pay off the interest-based loan. If they have recently acquired an interest-based loan, Akhuwat suggests they apply once their loan is paid off so they do not carry the burden of two installment payments a month.

10 We confronted some level of unease with regard to the lack of anonymity in the collection of donations in the pretest, and so for the fieldwork we designed questions to probe this issue further.

11 Akhuwat allows a fair amount of flexibility to the field offices in devising practices that work for them and so there is variation in implementation details though not broad policy. In our sample, about three-fourth of the groups had three borrowers and another two-fifth had four.

12 This view of the household is contradicted by a more nuanced view of household dynamics, such as Sen's (1990) cooperative-conflict model or the feminist literature, for example, Agarwal's conceptualization (1994).

13 The Operations Manual emphasizes the principles of *Muwakat*, including "brotherhood, care, empathy, equity, non-partisanship and sharing". Based on these principles, it emphasizes "responsiveness (to borrower queries)", a "soft language and a gentle tone" and no harassment in soliciting repayments. However, it accepts that social pressures of various kinds in various circumstances may need to be used.

14 Following North's (1990) terminology, MFIs are organizations rather than institutions.

15 Akhuwat accepted a modest grant from a foreign donor (Care International, UK) for the credit pool to be given out on a revolving fund basis. It had initially planned not to accept foreign donor funding. In this case, as in its operating practice, Akhuwat has demonstrated flexibility without compromising ideals.

List of References

Bateman, M. and H.-J. Chang. 2012. "Microfinance and the Illusion of Development: From Hubris to Nemesis in Thirty Years," *World Economic Review*, 1(September 6), 13–36.

Corsi, M. et. al. 2006. "Women and Microfinance in the Mediterranean," *Development*, 49(2), 67–74.

Flynn, P. 2007. "Microfinance: The Newest Financial Technology of the Washington Consensus," *Challenge*, 50(2), 110–121.

Khan, S. R. and Ansari, N. 2018. *A Microcredit Alternative in South Asia: Akhuwat's Experiment* (London: Routeledge).

Munir, K. 2012. "Akhuwat: Making Microfinance Work," *Stanford Social Innovation Review*, 18, February 9.

North, D. C. 1990. *Institutions, Institutional Change and Performance*. Cambridge: Cambridge University Press.

Sen, A. K. 1990. "Gender and Co-Operative Conflicts," in ed., I. Tinker, *Persistent Inequalities: Women and World Development*. New York: Oxford University Press.

Yunus, M. 2002. "Poverty Alleviation: Is Economics Any Help? Lessons from the Grameen Bank Experience," in ed., P. Athukorala, *The Economic Development of South Asia* (Northhampton, MA: Edward Elgar), 487–505.

Part 3: Meso context

Population and the environment

State and civil society partnerships

7 Population planning in Bangladesh[1]

Introduction

Most South Asian countries except Pakistan have managed to reduce their fertility rates dramatically. Bangladesh (formerly East Pakistan) declared its independence from West Pakistan in March 1971. As a province, it had a larger population than West Pakistan but lagged on all economic indicators. Post-independence, all social indicators, and subsequently economic indicators, started to dramatically improve. The drop in its fertility rate in particular excited the attention of social scientists and that is the story narrated in this chapter.

The benefits of the fertility decline on the microlevel and aggregate level are mostly self-evident. Even so, Schultz (2009) and Joshi and Schultz (2013) among others drove home this point. They studied the celebrated Matlab District, Bangladesh, Maternal and Child Health and Family Planning (MCH-FP) program launched in 1977. This was extended to half the villages in the district in 1977.[2] Married women in program villages were provided with home delivery of contraceptive supplies, follow-up services and general advice. Other services were added to the program later such as tetanus toxoid immunization for women, measles immunization for children 9 months to 5 years old, other Expanded Program of Immunization (EPI) for childhood vaccinations, oral rehydration therapy for diarrhea, vitamin A supplements and antenatal care. The control group received normal government services available to all villages.

The recorded fertility in the program villages was 16 percent lower than in control villages for the subsequent two decades until 1996. Women in program villages experienced increased birth spacing, productivity gains, wage increases (for 25–54-year-olds) and enhancement of nutrition, greater use of health inputs and hence improvement of health status. Also, child survival and schooling increased, household physical assets were 25 percent greater (33 percent or more in value terms) per adult than in the control villages and overall capital accumulation increased. Finally, the authors showed that the program effects were sustained over time. Since there were spillover effects of the program on the control villages, the program benefits were, if anything, understated.

DOI: 10.4324/9781003176411-10

We first review some basic demographic concepts and contextualize them with data from South Asia. This also brings into focus Bangladesh's achievement relative to that of Afghanistan and Pakistan. The comparison with Afghanistan and Pakistan is relevant because, like Bangladesh, they are predominantly Muslim countries and the opposition to birth planning on the part of Muslim clerics is sometimes touted as the reason for difficulties in reducing fertility rates in Muslim countries.[3] We turn next to the debate on how Bangladesh successfully attained its fertility decline and subsequently conclude.

Some demographic concepts

The crude birth rate (CBR) is defined by demographers as births per 1,000 population and crude death rate (CDR) as deaths per 1,000 population. In this context, crude represents "average". Given these definitions, the natural rate of population growth is $P_n = (\text{CBR} - \text{CDR})/10$, whereby the division by 10 converts P_n into a percentage. For example, if CBR = 50 and CDR = 30, then $P_n = (50 - 30)/10 =$ 2 percent.

The demographic transition occurs when both the CBR and CDR decline. In HIC, both rates declined, such that P_n declined while in many LICs there was only a partial demographic transition, i.e., CDRs declined but CBRs stayed high. This resulted in a population explosion in many LICs, including in South Asia, that were already poor.

Population dependency ratios measure dependent populations in a household, i.e., those less than 15 or greater than 64 divided by the working population between 16 and 64. This is a crude measure, as is the case for most indicators, since children below 15 work and there is no concept of retirement for the poor, so the elderly keep working until they are not able to in South Asia.

As the demographic transition matures and CBRs decline steadily, the ratio of children (ages 0–14) to adults (ages 15–59) declines, and for several decades the decline in the youth ratio more than offsets the slow increase in the ratio of elderly (ages 60 and older) to adults, i.e., a decrease in dependency ratio. This intermediate stage in the demographic transition is associated with a temporary increase in the share of adults in the population that has been referred to by demographers as the "demographic dividend".

Of course, countries need to make the most of this because the demographic dividend can turn into a demographic nightmare if opportunities, especially for the educated young, do not keep pace and violence and political instability can result. The Arab Spring has partly been explained by explosion of young adults (youth bulge) in the population (Hamanaka, 2017). As Schultz (2009) and Joshi and Schultz (2013) noted (see above), poor Bangladeshi women harvested a demographic dividend with social benefits accruing to the larger society.

The main determinants of CDRs are technologies and knowledge pertaining to public health such as sanitation, pest control and immunization. Since many LICs were assisted via foreign aid in improving their public health, CDRs fell and this was a mixed blessing as CBRs did not simultaneously fall. The determinants of

CBRs are reasonably well known now but are more slow-acting and both demand and supply side factors come into play.

As briefly reviewed by Masih and Masih (1997), there are several theories that may explain fertility declines. Neoclassical economic theory is one among them and it premises the high demand for children among the less well off in L/LMICs on chores, care-giving (girls) and for old age security (boys). Due to high infant mortality rates, high birth rates are a strategy to ensure that the numbers of children desired are attained. This is viewed as demand for children as an "investment good". As household income levels increase, children start being viewed more as a "consumption good" and a quality–quantity trade-off is expected to kick in (Becker and Lewis, 1974).[4] The price of providing quality (schooling, health) is high and so the demand for children drops. Higher female education levels complement this trend if it leads to women entering the labor force. In urban areas, this is likely because two paychecks are often needed to maintain a barely middle-class lifestyle.[5]

It follows from neoclassical theory that incentives can be used for reducing population growth and this has been tried by a number of countries such as with preference in apartment allocations and school admissions for smaller families.[6] Once a reduced demand for children has been achieved, this can be complemented by birth planning programs, a supply side initiative. Female education complements the supply side due to greater receptivity and easier dissemination of birth planning program information on contraception, use and availability.

Ignoring migration and the small impact mortality rates can have, replacement fertility keeps population stationary in a given country and it is viewed as being around 2.1 births per woman. Table 7.1 provides comparative data on fertility rates by decades in South Asian countries since 1970.

In 1970, Bangladesh had a higher fertility rate than Pakistan, but by 2017, it had brought its fertility rate down to the replacement rate like the other non-Muslim majority countries of South Asia. In 2017, Pakistan's fertility rate at 3.6 remained much higher than the replacement rate and was the highest in South Asia, higher even than Afghanistan at 3.5. The Maldives is also a Muslim majority country that brought its fertility rate down to even below the replacement rate,

Table 7.1 South Asian comparative fertility rates, total births per woman

	1970–1979	*1980–1989*	*1990–1999*	*2000–2009*	*2010–2017*	*1970*	*2017*
Afghanistan	7.5	7.5	7.6	6.9	5.3	10.9	3.5
Bangladesh	7.0	5.6	3.9	2.8	2.2	6.9	2.1
Bhutan	Na	6.2	4.6	2.9	2.1	6.6	2.0
India	5.2	4.5	3.7	3.0	2.4	5.6	2.2
Maldives	Na	7.1	7.0	4.5	2.4	7.2	1.9
Nepal	5.8	5.5	4.7	3.2	2.0	5.9	2.0
Pakistan	6.6	6.4	5.7	4.5	3.7	6.6	3.6
Sri Lanka	3.5	2.5	2.2	2.3	2.2	4.3	2.2

Source: World Development Indicators, last updated 12/20/2019.

but it is by comparison a very small and relatively prosperous country with a different dynamic; this chapter therefore focuses on Bangladesh's story.

The natural rate of growth of population is distinguished from P_a or the actual rate of population growth such that $P_a = P_n + m$, where m = net migration and is calculated as $m = (\text{im} - \text{em})/100$, where im = immigration and em = emigration and if im = em, then $P_a = P_n$. For the moment, that is what is assumed. The "rule of 70" applies more broadly, but in particular to population studies in that it is used to estimate how long it takes a population to double in a particular geography. For a long time, both CDRs and CBRs were high but roughly equal globally, so population did not grow much. Between AD 100 and AD 1500, the world population doubled at a P_n of 0.05 percent (70/0.05). After that, it took much less time for the world population to double as CDR gradually declined. If P_n is 2 percent, it would take roughly 35 years for the population to double. The world population between 1950 and 1987 doubled in far less than 140 years due to a fall in CDR relative to CBR and hence the concern in the 1960s and 1970s with a population explosion. Table 7.2 tells the story of South Asia in this broader context.

Population estimates were available from 1971 to 2019. The midpoint, 1995, was arbitrarily chosen to get the first estimate of population growth (between 1971 and 1995) reported in column 4 of Table 7.2. Two countries in South Asia, Pakistan and the Maldives, had more than doubled their populations in only two and a half decades between 1971 and 1995 and both are Muslim countries. The other two Muslim countries in South Asia are Afghanistan and Bangladesh. Afghanistan, despite a very high fertility rate, experienced foreign invasions and bloody civil wars driving out a large percentage of the population as refugees to Pakistan and Iran.

Bangladesh seems to have already started experiencing the impact of supply side policy changes and demand side changes (see next section), so it was not an outlier relative to other South Asian non-Muslim majority countries. Also, Pakistan's population had already outstripped that of Bangladesh by 1995 by a considerable margin even though it had a lower population than Bangladesh in

Table 7.2 South Asian total population in selected years (million)

Country	*1971*	*1995*	*% change 1971–1995*	*2019*	*% change 1995–2019*
Afghanistan	11.47	18.11	57.8	38.04	110.1
Bangladesh	65.53	115.17	75.7	163.04	41.6
Bhutan	0.31	0.53	74.2	0.76	42.7
India	576.87	963.92	69.7	1,366.42	41.8
Maldives	0.12	0.25	113.0	0.53	108.9
Nepal	12.32	21.58	75.1	28.61	32.6
Pakistan	59.73	123.78	107.2	216.57	75.0
Sri Lanka	12.75	18.24	43.1	21.80	19.5

Source: World Development Indicators, last updated 4/26/2021.
Note: Actual numbers, rather than the millions reported above, were used to compute population growth rates.

1971. Sri Lanka was the outlier, on the low side, and its human development achievements discussed in Chapter 4 are part of the explanation.

The changes over the next two and a half decades (between 1995 and 2019) are reported in column 6. Afghanistan and Maldives more than doubled their population in this period but Pakistan seems to finally be on a downward trajectory. Bangladesh continued on a downward trajectory, like the other South Asian non-Muslim majority countries, with Sri Lanka again leading the way. The notable numbers are that Bangladesh had almost 6 million more people than Pakistan in 1971, but almost 54 million less in 2019. What accounted for Bangladesh's success in containing its population growth is the story we turn to next.

Explaining the fertility decline in Bangladesh

Cain and Lieberman (1983) pointed out that at independence, policy commitment to a decline in fertility had to be and was high. The country faced the highest population density in the world and food production was outstripped by population and the 1974 famine brought this starkly to the notice of policy makers. Farm sizes were becoming untenable due to inheritance and the growth of landless labor compounded the existing problem of high rural unemployment in a country that had one of the lowest urbanization rates in the world (about 13 percent).

The First Plan (1973–1978) was expected to reduce fertility via family planning educational activities and delivery of contraceptive services to eligible couples. The Second Plan (1978–1983) unveiled an ambitious family planning program and demographic goals were to be realized through a sharp increase in contraceptive prevalence – from an estimated 14 percent of eligible couples in 1980 to 38 percent in 1985 – and through changes in the mix of contraceptive methods adopted by the population.

While there was likely consensus on the problem, at least initially, there was little consensus on solutions. The debate between Thomas (1993) and Cleland (1993) is illustrative. For Thomas, the poor in Bangladesh faced grave economic insecurity due to human-induced predatory and climatic risks and they lacked social and physical assets to ameliorate them. The cost of meeting children's consumption needs was likely to be prohibitive while children lost their value as insurance in an increasingly hostile environment.[7] This view suggested that poverty itself would reduce fertility, though the better option would be to attain the same outcome by providing entitlements and hence reducing the need for children as insurance.

Cleland (1993) by contrast emphasized that family planning programs even in insecure (and economically unjust) environments can work using the example of Bangladesh. The fertility rate declined in the late 1970s and the decline picked up pace in the 1980s. This happened despite very low female education levels and also low levels of income and growth in income. Since conventional explanations for the demand for contraception use were not in play, the main mechanism for the fertility decline was the use of contraception in marriage. The unmet need for contraception, possibly induced by a higher child survival rate,[8] increased however measured.

Of course, the two stories do not necessarily contradict each other. Thomas may have identified one of the prime causes for a reduced desire for children, while Cleland identified a mechanism via which that was achieved. For Cleland, the main difference between Bangladesh and Pakistan that counted in reducing the fertility rate was the seriousness of commitment to family planning services.[9] This commitment was evident in Bangladesh and it starkly contrasted with the ambivalence in this regard in Pakistan, particularly after the instituting of an "Islamic regime" by a military dictator. The World Fertility Survey in the 1970s identified an almost identical profile of family preference in the two countries.

Cleland et al. (1994) elaborated on the success of family planning programs in Bangladesh in contributing to the fertility decline. While there were program inefficiencies, overall, the success was evident by the attainment of the objective. Elements of the programs that contributed to overall success included a mass communications strategy, outreach such that there was in-house availability of subsidized services in a conservative Muslim country where female mobility was severely restricted, clinical backups, well-advertised and widely accessible non-clinical contraceptive supplies available in pharmacies, widely available surgical contraception, partnership with NGOs that provided up to 20 percent of supplies and partnerships with local religious and secular leaders to contain the cultural resistance to family planning.

Caldwell et al. (1999) contested the conclusions drawn by Cleland et al. (1993) based on their research. They base their findings on secondary and primary (survey) data. The primary data were used to gather general background information about the respondents and also information about their perceptions. Challenging Cleland et al.'s contention that education and social change were nonissues, using secondary data, they reported that there was significant economic and social change since 1971. Between 1973 and 1986, the number of schools and the number of girls attending schools increased by 70 percent and 61 percent, respectively. The gross primary enrollment rate at their time of writing was 122, i.e., Bangladesh had attained universal primary enrollment for both boys and girls. This was reflected in the rise of the Human Development Index (HDI) for Bangladesh between 1960 and 1980 by 45 percent. Between 1990 and 2003, Bangladesh rose 14 places in the HDI ranking.

Other structural economic factors also came into play. The demand for child labor decreased because of the Green Revolution technologies that required less use of child labor. In addition, 10 percent of all women in the 15–29 age group were hired in the textile industry, i.e., the opportunity cost of having children rose. Other relevant socioeconomic changes were the tremendous rise in electrification (which helped studying but also reflected greater work opportunities). Health care access improved (more doctors and nurses per person) that reduced child and infant mortality rates.

To collect primary data, the authors engaged in quasi-anthropological qualitative[10] research in two districts. One of them had below and the other higher than average total fertility rate (TFR). They interviewed 476 women and 379 men in total in the two districts. Their main finding was that TFR was inversely associated with household income and education levels. The authors also recorded and reported the perceptions of the respondents. The general feeling regarding investments in health and education among respondents was that life has become increasingly complex, relative to how things were at the time of their parents, and that the best strategy to prepare for this complexity was to invest in the health and education of the children. This potentially benefited parents, but also prepared children to take advantage of increasing off-farm and urban opportunities that once again were not available during the time they were growing up.

One of the main changes they noted was that land per capita was continuing to shrink with divisions, as per Islamic inheritance laws, and the amount of land available now in most cases was not adequate to support a family. Family planning (FP) in this regard helped because it enabled existing children to stay in school longer. While they made the most of the access they had to FP, only 28 percent thought that the FP program itself had persuaded them. Caldwell et al. concluded that while the supply was important, demand side factors were pivotal.

Thus, to the question: "are family planning programs enough in and of themselves?", they responded in the negative. One additional piece of evidence cited was that of the International Centre for Diarrheal Disease Research, Bangladesh, Matlab rural experimental area had complete contraceptive availability since 1979 and yet it took 20 years for fertility to decline gradually and for contraceptive prevalence rates to rise gradually.[11]

Kabeer (2001) also challenged Cleland et al.'s contention regarding the primacy of supply side factors and did so by examining and citing evidence on the changing economics of family size differentiated by income group. As landlessness increased, the asset that bound poor families and provided leverage for household adults lost its importance. Also, the return from child labor and their insurance value declined, while more children meant lower per capita consumption and inflation added to such woes. Fertility rates were the lowest among those without land, homes and other assets.

Following Kabeer's narrative, also contributing to fertility decline was the change in socioeconomic conditions confronting poor women. They lost their traditional role in food processing and the norm shifted from "bride price" to dowry. Ruthless men saw this as a mechanism of asset accumulation, and wife abandonment and divorce rates increased. An increase in female labor force participation (LFP) became inevitable with the attendant fertility decline.

Such participation among poor women increased via home-based work, in the informal sector, and via opportunities created by the "green revolution" (weeding, transplanting, post-harvest processing), NGO-driven microcredit and other programs and migration to cities. For the affluent, education contributed to the fertility decline and Kabeer noted that the phenomenon of fertility decline was more concentrated at the extremes and differentiated by circumstance.

Kabeer (2000) told a nuanced story taking due account of historical changes, but, like other scholars, concluded that the supply side facilitated fertility decline by addressing the unmet need to reduce family size and by diffusing information about the possibility of doing so and providing the wherewithal. By the turn of the century, this then appears to have become the consensus view and Lush, Cleland, Lee and Walt (2000), stated that the supply side needs to be conditioned by and subordinate to the influence of the demand side (socioeconomic changes).

There is another debate associated with fertility decline in Bangladesh that explicitly introduces gender and female empowerment into the discussion. So far, gender has been, for the most part, implicit in the debates reviewed. Schuller, Hashemi and Riley (1997) utilized a survey conducted in late 1992 of 1,300 randomly sampled married women under age 50, and ethnographic research undertaken in six villages during 1991–1996.[12] They suggested that women's access to credit augmented the use of contraception and was positively associated with the duration of the credit program. Three out of their eight measures of female empowerment – mobility, not dominated in household and independent means – had a positive impact on contraception use. They concluded from their analysis that the two (credit and empowerment) exercised independent effects.

Duvendack and Palmer-Jones (2017) reviewed the literature that suggested that female agency and empowerment and investment in female health and education were prime movers of the fertility decline on the demand side and that the supply side facilitated. NGOs were an important player in this story since they provided the microfinance and other services that empowered women. This they regarded as the consensus view and they regarded other contributions identifying the importance of socioeconomic changes on the demand side (Caldwell et al., 1999, Caldwell and Khuda, 2000, Kabeer, 2001) as not having gained much traction; although this is debatable given, for example, the concessions noted by Lush, Cleland, Lee and Walt (2000; see above).

They in turn used the 1975 World Fertility Survey (WFS) and the 2011 Bangladesh Demographic and Health Survey (BDHS) and contested the "consensus" view. They showed that fertility decline preceded the widespread use of family planning, mother and child health care and microfinance programs. The other interesting findings were that male education was found to be as good a predictor of fertility as female education and that couples who reported that they made decisions jointly were more likely to adopt better reproductive health practices. This then shifted the focus of attention onto the family, much as Akhuwat did for its interest-free microcredit program in Pakistan (Chapter 6). Finally, they found that female membership of microfinance NGOs was not associated with lower fertility.

Perhaps NGOs did not play as big a role in the fertility decline as some scholars claim. However, as evident from the other successful case studies in this book, the government wisely partnered with foreign donors (funding) and development NGOs (implementation) to attempt to attain its objectives. There is evidence that development NGOs leveraged their microcredit programs, which had already attained a high degree of social acceptance, to promote family planning and reproductive health among other social sector services (Amin et al., 2001; Schuller, Hashemi and Riley, 1997, see above). This enabled them to diversify and become multi-program organizations.[13]

Conclusion

There were two notable debates in the earlier literature attempting to conceptually and with empirics explain the remarkable Bangladesh fertility decline. Thomas (1993) and Cleland (1993) were among the first to kick off the debate with others jumping in. One part of Thomas's reasoning was that economic insecurity of the kind the poor in Bangladesh faced reduced the expected benefits of having children while the cost of meeting children's consumption needs had increased. In such circumstances, poverty would reduce fertility and the solution would be enhancing entitlements, further reducing the need for children as insurance. Cleland (1993) by contrast argued that despite very low female education levels and also low levels of income and growth in income, family planning programs facilitated the fertility decline due to an unmet need. The unmet need was perhaps triggered by higher child survival rates via improvements in public health. These stories seem complementary. Thomas identified possible causes for a reduced demand for children and Cleland the availability of supply to facilitate the desired reduction in fertility.

The Cleland et al. (1994) and Cadwell et al. (1999) debate again seemed to be at cross purposes since both sides conceded that the factors highlighted by other scholars were important. Does it matter for policy? Once again, not really since policy makers with a serious commitment to a decline in fertility rates, which improves well-being, need to invest in both human development and population programs and, as the virtuous cycle kicks in, other economic structural changes accompany the economic prosperity that further reduce fertility rates.

The lesson that emerged from this chapter is that Bangladesh policy makers wisely made all the necessary investments (human development, population programs, anti-poverty programs) to attain their objective of reducing the fertility rate. The other lesson that emerged from this chapter pertains to partnerships, the recurring theme of the book. The Bangladeshi state attained its fertility decline objectives by partnering with foreign donors, development NGOs and religious leaders.

Notes

1 Many thanks to Zeba Sathar, an eminent demographer, for extensive and helpful comments on this chapter.
2 While program villages were not randomly assigned, treatment and program areas were shown to have similar characteristics.
3 In this regard, studying Iran's fertility decline is particularly instructive.
4 This theory has been criticized, among other reasons, for ignoring the historical, institutional and cultural contexts.
5 This may not be the case for the affluent who have servants for child care and women do not need to work, particularly in rural areas where working represents a loss of status. Highly educated urban women from affluent backgrounds may choose to work as a lifestyle choice.
6 Singapore experimented with such incentives. Positive monetary and other incentives for having more children are also used in countries (e.g., France, Germany and

Hungary) where population growth rates have slowed and are expected to reduce the size of the future labor force.

7 This theorizing of the high female demand for children as insurance, particularly in the Bangladeshi context, is attributed to the writings of Cain (1977, 1978, 1981). Some of the factors explaining the high female demand for children, other than high child and infant mortality rates, were a large spousal age difference and high adult mortality which resulted in a high probability of widowhood. High divorce rates had the same effect. In addition, weak judicial and law-and-order institutions and restrictions on female movement due to purdah raised the demand for sons for security reasons and for taking over tasks such as commerce or farming. This was vital given the lack of social insurance.

8 Although Caldwell and Khuda (2000) pointed out that the great fertility decline in Bangladesh began when mortality was higher than that recorded in other Asian countries when their fertility rate first began to decline.

9 Lush et. al. (2000) attempted to explain the success of Bangladesh's population policy relative to its failure in Pakistan.

10 There are several studies that have quantitatively identified the determinants of fertility to explain the decline. Among these are Khuda and Hossain (1996) who utilized logistic estimation and Masih and Masih (1997) who utilized time series econometrics to explore the dynamics. Neither of these estimations are likely to capture the complex and interactive dynamics between the institutional supply side and the changing and evolving demand side that can lead to virtuous cycles and a benign snowballing effect as happened in Bangladesh.

11 Caldwell and Khuda (2000) find similar evidence based on a qualitative study of 67 women and this reinforced their message that while the presence of family planning services can make a big difference, the receptivity to these services is driven by socio-economic changes and accompanying changes in household aspirations. Most women interviewed believed that the benefits of having children had decreased and the costs of having children had increased, in no small measure due to providing the kind of education children aspired to, valued and may be grateful for and reward parents for in the future when assistance was needed.

12 The caveat regarding quantitative studies, in studying the phenomenon of fertility decline in Bangladesh, applies once again to the multivariate component of this study and the following study contesting these results.

13 These debates on the cause of the great fertility decline in Bangladesh will no doubt continue. Bora, Saiki and Lutz's (2019) quantitative contributions were that the bulk of the fertility decline can be explained by rising female education.

References

Amin, R., M. St. Pierre, A. Ahmad and R. Haq. 2001. "Integration of an Essential Services Package (ESP) in Child and Reproductive Health and Family Planning with a Micro-credit Program for Poor Women: Experience from a Pilot Project in Rural Bangladesh," *World Development*, 29(9), 1611–1621.

Becker, G. S. and H. G. Lewis. 1974. "Interaction between Quantity and Quality of Children," in ed., T. W. Schultz, *Economics of the Family: Marriage, Children, and Human Capital* (Chicago: University of Chicago Press).

Bora, J. K., N. Saikia and W. Lutz. 2019. "Revisiting the Causes of Fertility Decline in Bangladesh: Family Planning Program or Female Education?," International Institute of Applied Systems Analysis, Working Paper 19-011, Laxenburg, Austria.

Cain, M. and S. S. Lieberman. 1983. "Development Policy and the Prospects for Fertility Decline in Bangladesh," *The Bangladesh Development Studies*, 11(3), 1–38.

Cain, M. 1977. "The Economic Activities of Children in a Village in Bangladesh," *Population and Development Review*, 3(3), 201–227.

Cain, M. 1978. "The Household Life Cycle and Economic Mobility in Rural Bangladesh," *Population and Development Review*, 4(3), 421–438.

Cain, M. 1981. "Risk and Insurance: Perspectives on Fertility and Agrarian Change in India and Bangladesh," *Population and Development Review*, 7(3), 435–474.

Caldwell, B. and B. Khuda. 2000. "The First Generation to Control Family Size: A Microstudy of the Causes of Fertility Decline in a Rural Area of Bangladesh," *Studies in Family Planning*, 31(3), 239–251.

Caldwell, J. C., B. Khuda, B. Caldwell, I. Pieris and P. Caldwell. 1999. "The Bangladesh Fertility Decline," *Population and Development Review*, 25(3), 67–84.

Cleland, J., J. F. Phillips, S. Amin and G. M. Kamal. 1994. *The Determinants of Reproductive Change in Bangladesh: Success in a Challenging Environment* (Washington D. C.: World Bank).

Cleland, J. 1993. "Equity, Security and Fertility: A Reaction to Thomas," *Population Studies*, 47(2), 345–352.

Duvendack, M. and R. Palmer-Jones. 2017. "Micro-Finance, Women's Empowerment and Fertility Decline in Bangladesh: How Important Was Women's Agency?," *The Journal of Development Studies*, 53(5), 664–683.

Hamanaka, S. 2017. "Demographic Change and Its Social and Political Implications in the Middle East," *Asian Journal of Comparative Politics*, 2(1), 70–86.

Joshi, S. and T. P. Schultz. 2013. "Family Planning and Women's and Children's Health: Long-Term Consequences of an Outreach Program in Matlab, Bangladesh," *Demography*, 50(1), 149–180.

Kabeer, N. 2001. "Ideas, Economics, and 'The Sociology of Supply: Explanations for Fertility Decline in Bangladesh," *Journal of Development Studies*, 38(1), 29–70.

Khuda, B. and M. B. Hossain. 1996. "Fertility Decline in Bangladesh: Toward an Understanding of Major Causes," *Health Transition Review*, 6(Supplement), 155–167.

Lush, L., J. Cleland, K. Lee and G. Walt. 2000. "Source Politics and Fertility: A New Approach to Population Policy Analysis," *Population Research and Policy Review*, 19(1), 1–28.

Masih, A. M. M. and R. M. Masih. 1997. "Can Family-Planning Programs "Cause" a Significant Fertility Decline in Countries Characterized by Very Low Levels of Socioeconomic Development? New Evidence from Bangladesh Based on Dynamic Multivariate and Cointegrated Time-Series Techniques, 1965–1991," *Journal of Policy Modeling*, 19(4), 441–468.

Schultz, T. P. 2009. "The Gender and Generational Consequences of the Demographic Transition and Population Policy: An Assessment of the Micro and Macro Linkages," Economic Growth Center Discussion Paper 979, Yale University, New Haven.

Schuller, S. R., S. M. Hashemi and A. P. Riley. 1997. "The Influence of Women's Changing Roles and Status in Bangladesh's Fertility Transition: Evidence from a Study of Credit Programs and Contraceptive Use," *World Development*, 25(4), 563–575.

Thomas, N. 1993. "Economic Security, Culture and Fertility: A Reply to Cleland," *Population Studies*, 47(2), 353–359.

8 Joint Forest Management in India and Nepal

Introduction

This chapter focuses on India and Nepal, the two South Asian countries with the most extensive use of community forestry or in this case co-management. This topic is an application of the participatory development model discussed in Chapter 3 and as such the same conceptual framework applies. It can also be thought of in some cases as a model of co-production in which the state and civil society jointly produce goods and services. In this case, the reference is to forest services. The co-management can pertain to timber or non-timber forest products. Protecting timber forests is exacting in that it requires community silviculture operations such as weeding, pruning, singling, thinning, planting and harvesting.

After briefly establishing the now well-known case for forest preservation and the case for community participation in doing so, this chapter turns to a macro-overview using World Bank forestry data. Following that, the case studies of community forestry in India and Nepal are explored. The institutional details are delineated first and then the evidence of the impact of community participation on forest conservation is reviewed. The chapter ends with a summary.

Case for forest preservation

Ecologists have provided many reasons for preserving forests. Prominent among these is that deforestation raises the risk of flooding and soil degradation which devastates the livelihoods of the most vulnerable. Forest protection and regeneration enhances wildlife, and precipitation raises the water table and increases crop yields. More important, in the current circumstances, the loss of forests results in a reduction in carbon sequestration and hence a rise in global warming.

Forests, sustainably harvested, serve the most vulnerable in various ways. They provide timber for construction and agricultural implements. Non-timber forest products (NTFP) enhance household incomes for the poor in particular (14–60 percent of household income of the poor in Nepal are derived from NTRP). They are a source of energy, food, forest fruits and vegetables, medicinal and aromatic herbs, fodder and bedding for livestock. Veld et al. (2006) found that as forests degrade, there is a switch to using fruit trees for fuelwood.

DOI: 10.4324/9781003176411-11

The case for community participation

Following from Chapter 3, the theory is that locals have better knowledge of local needs, resources and costs. They have the capacity to monitor at the local level and will do so if given the incentive. One part of the incentive is that they have the obvious desire to protect the resources their livelihood depends on. Forest management committees are a vehicle for the local protection and sustainable use of forest and when successful, they represent the reinforcement of social capital that comes into play for other collective action for mutual development.

Macro-overview

Some data are available from the World Bank, World Development Indicators, and these have been processed and tabulated in Table 8.1.

Table 8.1 reports numbers available for forest areas as a percentage of total land area and forest rents as a percentage of GDP. The forest area increased by two percentage points for India between 1990 and 2016, but declined for Nepal by eight percentage points. There was a threefold decline in rent extraction for both countries from 1970 to 2018. The two variables need not move in tandem since the rates of extraction could have changed over time in India despite the increase in the total forested area.

Country studies

India[1]

It was estimated that firewood was used by about four-fifths of rural households in India and about a quarter of energy utilized by rural households was derived from

Table 8.1. Selected forestry indicators for India and Nepal over time

Time	*India*		*Nepal*	
	Forest area (% of land area)	*Forest rents (% of GDP)*	*Forest area (% of land area)*	*Forest rents (% of GDP)*
1970	na	0.4	na	1.5
1970–1979	na	0.8	na	3.2
1980–1989	na	0.5	na	2.0
1990	21.5	–	33.7	–
1990–1999	21.7	0.5	30.8	1.4
2000–2009	22.7	0.3	25.9	1.1
2010–2016	23.8	–	25.4	–
2016	23.7	–	25.4	–
2010–2018	Na	0.3	na	1.1
2018	Na	0.1	na	0.5

Source: World Development Indicators, last updated: 8/18/2020.
Note: – = not relevant
na = not available

biomass. When satellite images became available in the 1980s, they showed that only 11 percent of government-owned land had forest cover. It became evident that command and control mechanisms were not working due to the difficulty in the enforcement of a coercive forest policy. At the same time, the environmental movement was growing and civil society was pressuring government for a solution.

Examples of successful community forest management became evident from practice in West Bengal and Orissa and social movements and donors pushed the central and state governments to take such practice to scale. The National Forest Policy of 1988 and the Government of India Forest Policy of 1990 moved in this direction and State Government policies followed.

These policies formally constituted the launching of Joint Forest Management (JFM) at a national level.[2] By 2000, almost all the Indian States had passed resolutions for setting up Forest Protection Committees (FPCs) and 63,618 JFM groups covered over 18 percent of the forestlands. There was a rapid uptake and Shyamsundar and Ghate (2014, p. 84) reported that within the next decade, this had increased to 84,000 FPCs in 27 states involving 8.4 million households that managed about 17 million hectares (approximately 25 percent) of India's forests.

In broad terms, the co-management works as follows: The Forest Departments (FDs) retained the right to form, register and dissolve user groups or FPCs. The FD is tasked with providing technical assistance (accounting) and ensuring legal rights for communities with a legal framework (for formation and dissolution of FPCs). Thus, it provides a collective choice arena with legal backing to enable collective action and community conflict resolution.

The community's role is to provide labor, monitoring, enforcement (sanctioning, warning, public humiliation, boycotts or more forceful enforcement and court cases), felling at a daily wage with revenue shared with communities (25 percent royalty equally shared) and replanting. FPCs can frame the rules, but the FDs have the final say and reserve the right to intercede in the day-to-day functioning of the committees and in overall management. Villages can share in revenues from timber and NTFP specified by the FDs. In general, this means timber and NTFP could be extracted subject to the approval of the FD.

As indicated below, this devolution of power to the local level via FPCs has met with some success, but there are qualifications. The effective devolution of power is limited since the FDs retain broad managerial authority. Also, generally forests in very poor condition were handed over and regeneration can require the initial closing of specified forest patches to people and animals and monitoring of use as specified by the JFM committees.

Many villages viewed the FPCs as superseding their own governance mechanisms that they perceived to have been effective. Since only one member per household can be represented on the FPC and since they are usually males, the women who are often the collectors and users of forest products get marginalized.

Nepal[3]

As in India, in 2011, firewood was used by about four-fifths of rural households and again a quarter of total energy was derived from biomass by poor rural households. In 1957, all forests were nationalized and this undermined existing local systems of management and led to widespread deforestation as forests started being viewed as state rather than village property.

Nepal responded to this deforestation with various reforms and it is currently viewed as a leader in creating progressive legislation and programs for resource conservation in South Asia. Devolution of authority for forest management began in the 1970s. This included the *Panchayat* Forest Rules of 1978 and the Community Forest Programs of 1980. The devolution of authority to the local level embodied in these reforms was limited. With the onset of democratization, there was fresh legislation that included the Master Plan for the Forestry Sector of 1989, the Forest Act of 1993, including setting up Forest User Groups (FUGs), and the Forest Regulations of 1995.

The objective of these policy measures was to provide incentives to communities to re-forest open and degraded areas, particularly in the hilly regions. FUGs formulated their own constitutions to conserve, use, sell and manage forest products and resources. FUGs receive a set of guidelines describing how to limit extraction from forests under their care. They can ration access to the group's forest and tax anything removed from the forest. Most groups receive funding and assistance to hire guards and build fences around the forestland to make rationing and taxation enforceable.

The devolution allowed for a general body that consisted of all the adult members of the village including women. An executive committee of 9–15 members was elected for day-to-day management with tasks including protection (direct or via hiring guards), rules of use, allocation of benefits, improving condition of vegetation, sanctioning of rule-breakers and the preparation of five-year operational plans for consideration by the FD. Members could bequeath rights to their offspring and hence had a long-term interest in conservation.

While there is full control over commercial profits from forest products, clearing for agricultural use is prohibited. NTFP can be extracted and timber products extracted only subject to the approval of the FD as in India. Revenues are not taxed, but 25 percent is to be spent on collective development activities. Unlike India, Nepal handed over forest patches to communities that were in fairly good shape.

By the mid-2000s, there were about 14,500 FUGs with an outreach affecting 35 percent of the country's population and a quarter of the nation's forests. The rate of formation at the turn of the twentieth century was about 2,000 per year. Once again, the uptake was rapid and Bluffstone et al. (2018, p. 134) reported that as of 2015, Nepal had almost 19,000 registered FUGs representing over 35 percent of the population. Over 2.4 million households managed 1.8 million hectares in the hill districts and over 78 percent of households were FUG members.

By the turn of the twenty-first century, the contribution to household income was 29 percent, fuel wood 19 percent and fodder and leaf litter about 10 percent. About 11.4 percent of the total forest area was covered by FUGs and deforestation appeared to have been reversed. FUGs started forming nationwide federations (like cluster organizations, Chapter 3) to attain lobbying capacity with government, facilitate the dissemination of information and protect existing devolution and lobby for extension.

The devolution was much more far-reaching compared to the JFM of India and the results were much more dramatic, as indicated below, but there were limitations. The government reserved the right to change policy (e.g., a sudden policy change introduced taxation on revenues), there was no provision for the resolution of inter-group problems, leadership succession issues were not addressed and the problem of the presence of patches with no jurisdiction or overlapping jurisdictions was not resolved.

Evidence

As in most social science empirical research, establishing causality is difficult, so many of the results are tentative or suggestive. In this case, problems in empirical research include difficulties of generalization because of different ecological and geographical conditions of assigned forests, different levels of degradation of assigned forests, differences in inherent social capital among FPCs or FUGs, distance to forests, leakage effects (i.e., protect own forests and raid others), jurisdictional holes or overlaps and lack of controls. Most of the studies reviewed understandingly engaged in purposive sampling at some stage in the research design, so quantitatively estimated parameters are suggestive at best.

Shyamsundar and Ghate (2014) point out that the difficulties of getting robust results are inherent to the subject being explored. Forest patches are not randomly assigned but rather degraded forests have typically been turned over to communities. Thus, a comparison with state forests was prone to understating community achievements. The before–after format could work in principle, but it would be enormously expensive because observations would need to be based on a sufficiently long period.

The formation of committees or user groups could be endogenous in that those with a higher level of social capital may also be the ones self-selecting to form the successful village-level institutions. In such cases, village-level characteristics, such as the stock of social capital, may explain both the successful village institutions and forest management. The remoteness of the areas (distance from nearest village) being studied can make the studies expensive and small purposive sampling inevitable.

Another problem is that studies vary a great deal in their research questions. The research question of principal interest for this chapter is the quantitative impact of JFMs or FUGs on the two stated objectives of constituting them, i.e., conservation and poverty alleviation. The quantitative impact of these institutions in attaining these two objectives are the criteria used to select refereed studies for review.[4]

India

To repeat, the expressed purpose of co-management of forests with communities was to attain forest conservation and reduce poverty. To investigate these objectives, Ravi Kumar (2002) collected income stratified randomly selected household (212) data from eight villages (three JFM and two non-JFM) in Jharkhand. Suitable controls were instituted in the study design so that households in villages with JFM could be reasonably compared with households with access to forest resources not under JFM. His main findings were that while the conservation objective was being attained, this occurred at the expense of the poor who disproportionately bore the protection costs and also that the gains of the elites were at the expense of the poor. His pessimistic conclusion was that the elites would resist redistributive institutional redesign mechanisms.

Veld et al. (2006) however found that in villages with JFM women appeared to collect more firewood from the commons and to spend less time doing so compared to villages without JFM.

Based on qualitative case studies, Husain and Bhattacharya (2004) tested the hypothesis that co-management or public–community partnerships are more likely to succeed if via social mobilization community attitudes were first suitably transformed. The study villages in two areas were otherwise ostensibly similar in terms of socioeconomics but showed very different conservation performance. The authors argued that the difference was based on an attitudinal change induced by social mobilization. In Belemath, an awareness of the need to conserve had been created (with intervention of Communist Party of India [Marxist]) but not so in Matha. In Belemath, villages took a long-term view and actually maximized the discounted net present value by moving to conservation and sustainable harvesting rather than cutting. In Matha, all raided resources without any peer pressure and deforestation was the inevitable outcome.

A review of studies in Andhra Pradesh by Reddy et al. (2005) suggested an improvement in the state of forests as a result of JFM when comparing JFM to non-JFM areas. Timber smuggling, illegal cattle grazing, quarrying for sand and stone and encroachments that were degrading forests were all ended. A reduction of felling, fire control and conversion of forest land for agricultural use due to better local protection were some of the other mechanisms resulting in such regeneration. Women participated actively via self-help groups (SHGs) and the forest regeneration improved the well-being of locals. Greater income due to benefit sharing, including via NTFP, resulted in less dependence on moneylenders. The JFM also promoted other collective actions like the building of check dams, water structures, roads and community halls. However, the authors point out that these positives should not be overstated and the negatives mentioned above like elite capture and asymmetric power between the FD and FPCs, gender inequality and interinstitutional conflicts (overlapping mandates of local government, *Punjayat Raj* institutions and FPCs) were endemic.

Mishra, Mandal and Maiti (2006) studied 25 FPCs within nine forest divisions covering five districts of West Bengal. Using standard ecological methods, they computed the density of trees, basal area, distribution of trees and species diversity index. They concluded that tree densities had increased tremendously in the JFM-protected forests and that the enhancement of shrub woody biomass met a lot of biomass needs of the community.

Based on a study of 29 FPCs from seven divisions in Rajasthan, India, Aggarwal et al. (2006) concluded that JFM resulted in an enhancement of species diversity, stem density and species richness. They however cautioned that there was a need for providing alternative income generation options for the most marginalized who relied on the sale of fuelwood and charcoal and were hence pitted against the FPCs.

Sudha, P. et al. (2006) collected data for a purposely selected sample with controls of 59 FPCs from nine forest divisions covering diverse geographic, socioeconomic and vegetation composition of the Eastern Plains and the Western Ghats. Stem density, basal area, species diversity index and biomass were computed using standard ecological methods. The authors found that the JFM areas were characterized by a higher biodiversity index.

Agarwal (2009) engaged in quantitative and qualitative empirical work based on 135 purposely selected FPCs/FUGs; 65 in Gujarat, India, and 70 in Nepal. Development NGOs provided information on the gender composition of the executive committees (EC) of these groups and this information was used for stratification of the groups. The three strata were less than or more than two EC members and the third strata applied only to Nepal where the user group was exclusively female (see findings below). The main hypothesis she tested was that greater representation of women on the EC had a positive impact on improving forest health.

She argued that this is likely to be the case because women have a greater incentive to conserve nearby forests. They have a greater reliance on them for NTFPs and if forests get degraded, they have to go much further afield to harvest those products like fodder and firewood. Substituting lesser quality fuel like dung for firewood has health consequences, particularly when burned indoors as is normally the case.

She contended that women also have more knowledge of forest ecology, i.e., what to plant and when, what to harvest and when. Women are more likely to follow the rules if they are involved in rule formation and also make other women comply, be more active in forest protection (formally and informally via vigilance) and be more capable of challenging female intruders without being charged for harassment.

Her hypothesis was not rejected in that the greater representation of women on ECs did improve forest quality. In the Punchmahal District in Gujarat, India, the probability of forest improvement was 57 percent higher if more than two women were on the EC and the probability that the forest canopy would be thick was 75 percent higher.

Baland, Bardhan and Das (2010) focused on the impact of Van Panchayats (VPs, local forest councils) on forest degradation in Uttaranchal. It is the only Indian state characterized by such a village community management system. VPs were created in 1931 by the colonial authority to contain local protests resulting from attempts to convert forests to state property. VP formation continued to be encouraged after independence. Based on standard ground-level ecological measures of forest quality, conducted by trained local (but outsiders to the village) ecologists, and a stratified random sample of 83 villages (399 forest patches) VP forests were found to be 10 percent (20 percent with controls) less lopped relative to state-protected forests. They were similar on other dimensions such as tree-cutting, timber extraction, forest grazing or encroachment activities.

Nepal

Edmonds (2001) took advantage of household survey data from 1995 to 1996 which was merged with an administrative census of forest groups in the Arun Valley of eastern Nepal. This enabled him to compare resource extraction in areas with and without FUGs over a three-year period. He found that transferring forests to local FUGs was associated with a significant reduction (up to 14 percent) in resource extraction (fuelwood collection). The author used three statistical approaches to test the robustness of the finding given that the FUGs were not randomly placed. Further, the FUGs had the capacity to operate without extensive external oversight.

Adhikari, Di Falcol and Lovett (2004) collected data from eight FUGs from two purposely selected districts in the Nepal mid-hills. After conducting a village census, a stratified random sample of 330 households from three income groups was subsequently chosen. Based on qualitative and quantitative analyses, they concluded that access to community forests was more limited for certain forest products for poor of lower castes compared to the relatively better-off higher caste households. Thus, households with more land and cattle spent more time gathering tree and grass fodder and bedding materials from the forest than did households with little or no land and cattle. The authors recommended a transferable system of property rights over forest products and greater representation of the poor on FUG executive committees as possible steps to ensure equity of resource distribution to poorer households.

Based on the study described above, Agarwal (2009) found that there was a 29 percent greater probability of forest regeneration for all women user groups. All women FUGs made more stringent rules, but this was called for given the more degraded state of forests they received for protection.

Tachibana and Adhikari (2009) used a data set of 101 randomly selected natural forests, stratified by remoteness, in the Middle Hills of Nepal for their analysis. For each sample forest, they conducted a social survey, an aerial-photo interpretation and a forest inventory. They found that user groups that did not receive official support substantially improved forest conditions due to reduced forest fire occurrence. User groups receiving official support, controlling for the possibility of self-selection in applying for support, improved tree regeneration.

Pandit and Bevilacqua (2011) surveyed forest users from eight purposively selected community forests with at least five years of community forestry practice in the Dhading district of Nepal. The selection was based on multiple attributes of forests. They used rating scale–based perception indicators among three social groups: Elite, women and disadvantaged. Irrespective of social grouping, statistical analysis of the summated rating scores suggested that users perceived increased forest products supply and improved environmental conditions at the local level. The overall finding was that community forestry practice brought a positive change in local environmental conditions in the form of increased understory regeneration, reduced incidences of soil erosion and landslides within forests, increased numbers of wildlife in the forests and improved forest greenery (density). Also, respondents noted improved forest products supply.

Poudel, Fuwa and Otsuka (2014) randomly selected 200 FUGs from 447 registered in the District Forest Office of Dang, Nepal, as of 2010. One hundred planted forests which required different management techniques and 20 forests which were registered later than 2005 (not old enough) were excluded. Using econometric techniques, utilizing primary and secondary data, they found that a longer period of community management was associated with a higher density of pole-size trees, indicating that community management facilitated the rehabilitation of timber forests. They also found that population pressure led to deforestation under state management but encouraged better forest management practices and the generation of more revenue per unit area under community management.

Oli, Treue and Smith-Hall (2016) investigated the importance of income from forests under different tenure arrangements (co-management, government-managed and private) for households. They collected data from 304 stratified (by wealth) randomly sampled households within ten villages with FUGs in Tanahun District, Western Nepal. They found that co-management contributed more to forest income (about half) than government-managed forest or private forests. Overall, forest incomes had an income-equalizing effect and served to reduce the prevalence of poverty, the poverty gap as well as the severity of poverty.

The poorest quarter of households derived 17.4 percent of their annual income from forests. The richest quartile derived only 3.8 percent of their annual income from forests, but in absolute terms this was almost 50 percent higher than those of the poorest quartile. The richest derived 74 percent higher incomes than the poorest from community forests, a difference that mainly stemmed from their extraction of almost twice as much fodder. The authors attributed this to elite capture. Incomes from government-managed forests were in absolute terms surprisingly similar across income quartiles. They recommended a modification of rules that govern product extraction at the community FUG level.

Bluffstone et al. (2018) used 620 forest plot measurements taken from a nationally representative sample of 130 Nepal community forests to assess the impact of collective action on forest health. A variety of indicators were used to assess forest health and vitality, including tree and seedling density, crown cover and primary productivity measured as biomass and/or carbon stock, with higher levels indicating higher quality. They used three measures of FUG collective action, including membership in the Nepal Community Forestry Program (CFP). Collective action showed large, positive and statistically significant carbon effects vis-à vis the control group (identified by local forestry officials) of communities exhibiting no evidence of forest collective action. They found that active collective action showed the positive effects rather than just being part of the CFP.

Summary

Based on the quantitative research reviewed, it is evident that involving communities in forest management in India and Nepal has met with reasonable conservation success. There is a need for further clarification of property rights to more accurately demarcate communal boundaries/cover jurisdictional holes, for more local autonomy, particularly in India. In India, FMCs have to be registered to be legal entities and only one-third of the states allow the imposition of sanctions.

The evidence also indicates that co-management of forests works well when there is an investment in social mobilization so that communities are assured that they have a stake in the preservation of resources and are persuaded that participating to conserve will yield more long-term benefits than raiding forest resources.

To meet the associated objective of poverty alleviation and inclusion, studies recommended the blocking of elite capture and benefits of hijacking. This would only be possible if FDs stopped taking the easier and self-interested route of initiating FMC work with elites and meeting established mandates of greater inclusion and empowerment of women.

The exclusive focus on conservation can have a negative social impact. For example, prior to the formation of JFMs, males sided with females if blocked by FD officials when attempting to meet household fuelwood needs. With male household heads becoming enforcers, they were pitted against the women who were left to their own devices to meet such needs. The lack of meaningful poor female representation thus represented a serious omission to the stated goal of JFM marrying conservation with poverty alleviation.

To sum up, the studies reviewed suggest that co-management has had a significant positive impact on conserving forests. Notwithstanding the positive micro-impacts reported for Nepal in the studies reviewed, macro-data reveals a decline in forested area as a percentage of total land area by eight percentage points between 1990 and 2016, the decades over which community forestry was in play. However, the deforestation could have been even worse had co-management not been instituted. The data for India revealed a two percentage points increase over the same period.

While some success has been noted in conservation in the studies reviewed, there has been much less success in attaining the second of the two stated objectives, i.e., attaining poverty alleviation. In this regard, researchers have made several recommendations including transferable property rights for the poor to forestry products and greater representation of women and the poor on executive committees of user groups to ensure the enforcement of these rights. Another recommendation is a modification of rules that govern product extraction.

Notes

1 Institutional details were gleaned from the various papers cited in the evidence section. In particular, refer to Shyamsundar and Ghate (2014) and for broader historical context, refer to Sundar (2000) and Ravi Kumar (2012).

2 Activities that are included in the domain of JFM include coppicing (cut back a tree or shrub to ground level periodically to stimulate growth), shoot cutting, inter-planting, seedling protection, timber harvesting and rotation.

3 Institutional details have been drawn from Edmonds (2001), Poudel, Fuwa and Otsuka (2014) and Shyamsundar and Ghate (2014).

4 Other research, for example, focuses on how to make JFM more effective overall or for specific groups like the poor or women. Persha and Andersson (2014) and Iversen et.a l. (2006) suggest that elite capture is intrinsic to community management and institutional measures could be put into place to mitigate this. Behera (2009), Naidu, (2009), Ray and Bhattacharaya (2011) explore the impact of variables like group heterogeneity on participation. Adhikaria and Di Falcob (2009) explore the impact of caste and participation on the likelihood of being represented on the executive committee of FUGs.

List of References

Adhikaria, B. and S. Di Falcob. 2009. "Social Inequality, Local Leadership and Collective Action: An Empirical Study of Forest Commons," *European Journal of Development Research*, 21(2), 179–194.

Adhikari, B., S. Di Falco and J. C. Lovett. 2004. "Household Characteristics and Forest Dependency: Evidence from Common Property Forest Management in Nepal," *Ecological Economics*, 48(2), 245–257.

Aggarwal, A. et al. 2006. "An Ecological Assessment of Greening of Aravali Mountain Range Through Joint Forest Management in Rajasthan, India," *International Journal of Environment and Sustainable Development*, 5(1), 35–45.

Agarwal, B. 2009. "Gender and Forest Conservation: The Impact of Women's Participation in Community Forest Governance," *Ecological Economics*, 68(11), 2785–2799.

Baland, J., P. Bardhan and S. Das. 2010. "Forests to the People: Decentralization and Forest Degradation in the Indian Himalayas," *World Development*, 38(11), 1642–1656.

Behera, B. 2009. "Explaining the Performance of State–community Joint Forest Management in India," *Ecological Economics*, 69(1), 177–185.

Bluffstone et al. 2018. "Does Collective Action Sequester Carbon? Evidence from the Nepal Community Forestry Program," *World Development*, 101(January), 133–141.

Edmonds, E. V. 2001. "Government-initiated Community Resource Management and Local Resource Extraction from Nepal's Forests," *Journal of Development Economics*, 68(1), 89–115.

Husain, Z. and R. N. Bhattacharya. 2004. "Attitudes and institutions: Contrasting experiences of Joint Forest Management in India," *Environment and Development Economics*, 9(4), 563–577.

Iversen, V. et al. 2006. "High Value Forests, Hidden Economies and Elite Capture: Evidence from Forest User Groups in Nepal's Terai," *Ecological Economics*, 58(1), 93–107.

Kumar, S. 2002. "Does ''Participation'' in Common Pool Resource Management Help the Poor? A Social Cost–Benefit Analysis of Joint Forest Management in Jharkhand, India," *World Development*, 30(5), 763–782.

Mishra, T. K., D. Mandal and S. K. Maiti. 2006. "Evaluation of Regeneration of Shorea Robusta Forests under Joint Forest Management in West Bengal, India," *International Journal of Environment and Sustainable Development*, 5(1), 12–22.

Naidu, S. C. 2009. "Heterogeneity and Collective Management: Evidence from Common Forests in Himachal Pradesh, India," *World Development*, 37(3), 676–686.

Oli, B., N. T. Treue and C. Smith-Hall. 2016. "The Relative Importance of Community Forests, Government Forests, and Private Forests for Household-level Incomes in the Middle Hills of Nepal," *Forest Policy and Economics*, 70(C), 155–163.

Pandit, R. and E. Bevilacqua. 2011. "Forest Users and Environmental Impacts of Community Forestry in the Hills of Nepal," *Forest Policy and Economics*, 13(5), 345–352.

Persha, L. and K. Andersson. 2014. "Elite Capture Risk and Mitigation in Decentralized Forest Governance Regimes," *Global Environmental Change*, 24(January), 265–276.

Poudel, N. J., N. O. Fuwa and K. Otsuka. 2014. "The Impacts of a Community Forestry Program on Forest Conditions, Management Intensity and Revenue Generation in the Dang District of Nepal," *Environment and Development Economics*, 20(2), 259–281.

Ravi Kumar, V. M. 2012. "People's Forestry in the Past and Present--An Analysis of Community Forest Management in South India (AP): Colonial and post-colonial Period," *Journal of Social and Economic Development*, 14(1), 42–64.

Ray, T. and R. N. Bhattacharaya. 2011. "Transaction Costs, Collective Action and Survival of Heterogeneous Co-management Institutions: Case Study of Forest Management Organisations in West Bengal, India," *Journal of Development Studies*, 47(2), 253–273.

Reddy, V. R. et al. 2005. "Participatory Forest Management in Andhra Pradesh: A Review of Its Working," *Journal of Social and Economic Development*, 7(2), 175–199.

Shyamsundar, P. and R. Ghate. 2014. "Rights, Rewards, and Resources: Lessons from Community Forestry in South Asia," *Review of Environmental Economics and Policy*, 8(1), 80–102.

Sudha, P. et al. 2006. "Forest Protection and Regeneration under Joint Forest Planning and Management in Eastern Plains and Western Ghats of Karnataka, India," *International Journal of Environment and Sustainable Development*, 5(1), 70–84.

Sundar, N. 2000. "Unpacking the 'Joint' in Joint Forest Management," *Development and Change*, 31(1), 255–279.

Tachibana, T. and S. Adhikari. 2009. "Does Community-Based Management Improve Natural Resource Condition? Evidence from the Forests in Nepal," *Land Economics*, 85(1), 107–131.

Veld et al. 2006. "India's Firewood Crisis Re-examined," Resources for the Future Discussion Paper 06-25, Washington, D. C.

Part 4: Micro context

State, local capital and foreign capital partnerships

9 Producer cooperatives in Kerala, India

Introduction

Development NGOs induce collective action, often in rural areas, based on latent social capital in groupings that can vaguely be referred to as communities. These development NGOs tap the latent social capital and one mechanism for the collective action are community organizations, a form of constructed social capital (Chapter 3). Another form of collective action, often in urban settings, is producer cooperatives (PCs).[1] The emergence of such cooperatives is often rooted in history whereby worker solidarity results in an attempt to self-deliver livelihoods rather than rely on capital. An example of a livelihood preserving worker takeover and management of firms is the case of Argentina where workers took over firms that were going bankrupt during the economic crisis of late 1990s and early 2000s (Carruth, 2019).

Conte and Jones (2015) theorized on and empirically tested the issue of PC formation in the United States by utilizing a data set spanning over 90 years (1871–1960). They found that PC formation is counter-cyclical (employment preserving) and not pro-cyclical (profit-seeking). Positive factors in PC formation are state support organizations (nonfinancial) and the preexistence of other PCs in a given industry (potential for information sharing). However, there is an inverse association of PC formation in other industries with the clustering of PCs in a particular industry and with the average size of firms in the industry.

The Mondragon producer cooperatives system in the Basque region of Spain, operating in a capitalist market economy, provides a relevant conceptual framework (Whyte, 1999; Campbell, 2011). This model is drawn on to identify some of the relevant theories and hypotheses. The section that follows discusses the evidence regarding the success of PCs. In the final section, the successes of two South Asian PCs are reviewed.

Producer cooperatives: some institutional and conceptual issues[2]

The Mondragon cooperative movement was founded in 1955 by the inspired leadership of a Catholic priest (José María Arizmendiarrieta) in the Basque region of Spain with about 25 workers. It was based on progressive Catholic social doctrine,

DOI: 10.4324/9781003176411-13

including dignity of labor, social solidarity and primacy of labor over capital. Some of the key institutions identified by Whyte (1998) and Campbell (2011) include a General Assembly that meets annually, with all members expected to attend, to discuss the prior year's performance and set the guidelines for future performance.

A Governing Council that workers are voted onto monitors management and ensures consistency with the guidelines. They have the authority to hire and fire a manager or even the whole management team. The Governing Council represents workers as owners and there is a Social Council that represents them as workers.

Social Council members are elected by a group of ten coworkers. Their mandate is to bring worker concerns on issues like occupational health and safety, remuneration and social security to the attention of management. While they are in an advisory capacity, given the cooperative culture, their views are given much weight. As cooperatives proliferated to engage in various economic activities, the Mondragon Corporation Cooperative (MCC) was founded in 1976 with a representative member from each cooperative to share technologies and marketing information.[3]

Various forms of formal and informal trainings acculturate cooperative members into functioning as good cooperative citizens. In particular, the ability to criticize and accept criticism is a central part of cooperative culture. Having to compete with "for profit" entities in a capitalist market economy is a reality that is very much part of cultural awareness. Countering technocratic domination is also part of the culture and one mechanism for attaining this is "skilling-up" workers with motivation, drive and talent to join management. Most producer cooperatives have variations on such institutions to ensure worker control.

Whyte (1999) highlighted that operating and surviving in a capitalist environment is challenging and purists are unhappy about seeming compromises to governing cooperative principles. Discontents include salary differentials, the percentage of wage labor to total members in the complex, concentration of power, the extent of investment in finance and real estate and the extent of joint ventures with private sector firms.

The joint ventures can be explained by the increasing size of capital investment needed to initiate a new enterprise. During the inception of the movement in the 1960s, workers could work on reduced wages to forward funds to a capital investment account and two years of such a concerted effort, with an employment subsidy from the Basque regional government, could produce the desired result. This was no longer possible even three decades later in the 1990s. While the employment subsidy was still available from the regional government, MCC found creating new enterprises, and hence employment, in partnership with private sector capitalist firms a much easier option. Another option to overcome capital scarcity, given the reluctance of private sector banks to lend to PCs, is to form a PC bank. Mondragon successfully initiated its own very successful banks.

To sum up, the defining characteristics of PCs are employee ownership, worker participation in decision making and the primacy of labor which in practice means labor hiring capital rather than the other way round. Since labor rents capital, the risk is borne by labor rather than capital and hence the residual, after expenses, accrues to labor. PCs therefore need to have rules for the sharing of the residual.

For Mondragon, the rules governing the division of the residual are 10 percent for charity, 40 percent for the common good (research and development, job creation, social security, training) and the rest in individual member capital accounts. These accounts are frozen until retirement, but interest accrues on them.[4] Membership can in principle be sold based on the discounted present value of the share of the expected future stream of earnings. However, because of the higher risk, the membership price tends to be below the discounted share of the expected future stream of earnings.

Early theorization based on the experience of worker management in Yugoslavia in the 1950s and neoclassical economics suggested PCs have some characteristics common to both sources (Ward, 1958). While conventional firms are postulated to maximize profits, a PC was expected to maximize net income or value added per employee (VA/L). This theorizing had limitations based on the context and restrictive assumptions and was hence theoretically disputed. For a more general model of PCs operating in a capitalist market economy, new members are generally taken on by a consensus of existing members and so the logic of the neoclassical model suggested that there may be resistance to hiring new members since it would dilute the share of existing members.

This incentive to stay small would militate against market concentration even if the PC becomes very successful economically. Also, on a sociological and psychological level, self-management would be easier in smaller units.

Since workers often live close to their place of work, there is also an incentive to restrict the amount of pollution and to ensure a high standard of occupational health and safety and therefore higher productivity. Worker management could also result in no loss of working days due to labor management conflict. One could also expect turnover to be low and hence the incentive to invest in human capital would be much higher. The latter two features should in principle result in higher productivity compared with conventional firms. Productivity gains may also be forthcoming from greater worker feedback (based on sense of worker ownership) and higher morale.

Basic microeconomic theory would also predict some negatives such as slower decision making due to its collective nature. Since the firm functions in some sense as a club, there may be an incentive to hire from family members and friends and, if so, there would be efficiency losses.

Capital could be perceived as the cheaper factor since incremental labor is paid VA/L. This could create a bias toward greater capital intensity in the long run, depending on the availability of techniques of production. It has been hypothesized that under certain conditions (single input and single output), the supply curve might be negative since higher prices mean greater earnings/income and less incentive to expand. Since shares are generally not tradeable, there is a lack of external inducement to efficiency imposed by the market. Due to an egalitarian wage structure, the more efficient workers in theory have an incentive to leave.

While there may be motivation to work harder out of a sense of participation, there is also a potential free-rider problem since everyone is paid VA/L. Peer-group pressure may partly resolve the free-rider problem. Finally, there could be a horizon problem with different workers having varying preferences regarding current vs. future income. To some extent, rules governing the PC could address this issue.

The evidence (see below), late in coming, nonetheless does not suggest short-run inefficiencies, a negative short-run supply curve, less hiring or disproportionate capital intensity. There is evidence that higher productivity is associated with higher labor participation in decision making. The obvious economist question that follows is that if PCs generate greater private and social benefits than conventional firms (CFs), why do conventional firms continue to be the dominant firm type in market economies?[5]

One obvious answer is risk-aversion. Worker contracts of the traditional kind, particularly with union representation, protect workers against risk with some level of job protection, a guaranteed wage, cost of living adjustments, downward wage rigidity and unemployment insurance.[6] Also, workers in a PC would be investing their human and physical capital in the same enterprise, thus compounding risk (Dow, 2018, p. 79). Capital usually deals with risk by diversifying business portfolios and often can rely on state support. Another reason for the much more limited prevalence of PCs may be that workers have much more limited access to credit than entrepreneurs founding conventional firms. Dow (2018, p. 79) also pointed to the transaction cost and free-rider problems associated with bringing together a group of committed workers to initiate a PC.

Some evidence

Doucouliagos (1995) synthesized the results of 43 published studies to investigate the effects on productivity of various forms of worker participation.[7] Some notable findings for this chapter are that worker management, based on one-member one-vote, was not negatively associated with productivity. Also, in worker-managed firms or PCs, profit-sharing was more positively related to productivity than participation in decision making. The author suggested that since the latter can be assumed to occur in PCs, profits could be expected to be a greater motivator.

The Mondragon complex, the largest cluster of interlinked PCs in the world, has been highly successful in competing with private sector firms. Exporting ability is generally viewed as a marker of success since only products attaining quality can break through into export markets. Whyte (1999, p. 399) documented that in 1976, MCC as a complex exported 10 percent of total production and by 1997 exports as a percentage of total production increased to 46 percent. Market success led to higher worker remuneration even as belt tightening was expected during the tough economic conditions after the oil price increases of the 1970s.

Arnando et al. (2010) documented success in terms of the growth in sales and output compared to comparators. Associated with the increase in sales was the increase in employment. As expected, the group was better able to cope with crises via furloughs, work-sharing, early retirements and wage flexibility. They also documented that by 2008, the Mondragon group comprised about 250 cooperatives, subsidiaries and affiliated organizations, including 73 manufacturing plants overseas; altogether it had almost 100,000 employees (p. 2). Defying mainstream economic predictions, investments per worker have increased steadily, at times even during crises.

The "degeneration" prediction appears to bear out, i.e., the growing share of nonmembers as a percentage of the total labor force.[8] The logic of mainstream economics is that members have an incentive to limit the diffusion of profits. Also, while members are mostly protected in crises, nonmembers and temporary workers face the brunt of adjustments. This defies the principle of social solidarity and the group is addressing this predicted tendency by establishing a member to nonmember ratio limit of 85 percent – one they have managed to come close to attaining.

Pencavel, Pistaferri and Schivardi (2006) found, using data from Italy which has the largest incidence of producer cooperatives in Europe, that employment was somewhat less responsive to product market shocks in PCs than in CFs. This finding is consistent with findings of other studies suggesting that PCs are likely to protect employment. Mutually agreed contributions to a reserve fund are another tactic for surviving economic hard times.

Fakhfakh, Perotin and Gago (2012) compared two representative samples of conventional French firms with 20 or more employees (for comparative reasons) with all PCs in existence in France over a range of industries and years. They found that PCs are as productive as or more than CFs in all industries. Also, capital intensity is often the same in the two groups and they adjust their capital intensity at the same rate.

Burdín and Dean (2009) utilized panel firm-level monthly data comprising monthly wages and employment observations between April 1996 and December 2005 for the entire population of registered PCs and for CFs in 31 industries in Uruguay. They found CFs exhibited an expected negative relationship between wages and employment, while PCs displayed an inverse association. For CFs, the effect of output price changes on employment was significantly positive, whereas no such association was evident for PCs. For both types of firms, a crisis negatively affected both wages and employment, although the employment adjustment was larger in CFs than in PCs. Finally, they found no significant support for the degeneration hypothesis – an association between changes in output prices and changes in the relative employment of hired workers to enable more profit shares for existing members. In another study using the same data set, Burdín and Dean (2012) showed that PCs are concerned with not only net income per worker but also employment.

Using survival analysis on an extended panel (observations over the period April 1996–July 2009), Burdin (2014) showed that the hazard of dissolution was 29 percent lower for PCs than for CFs after controlling for expected differences. This finding is contrary to empirical speculation suggesting on various grounds, including capital market constraints, about the ability of PCs to survive. This result seems to be associated with the greater employment stability in PCs, also identified by the author in a companion study.

Using the same extended panel data, Alves, Burdínb and Dean (2016) found much more stable job dynamics for PCs than CFs, i.e., lower job creation and job destruction. While this could be interpreted as greater dynamism of CFs, during a high growth period, PCs also demonstrated a high level of both job creation and destruction. As expected, in PCs, job creation and destruction rates were very low for members and much higher for nonmembers. Another finding was counter-cyclical job creation by the PC sector. This resulted from new PCs being created during a recession.

While the evidence suggests that there is much that is positive with regard to the functioning of PCs, there can be downsides. Burdın (2016) found that PCs in Uruguay have a more compressed compensation structure than CFs and that high-ability members are more likely than other members to exit. He also found that there was a positive association between the extent of pay compression and the extent of exit. Dean (2019) tested the "degeneration" hypothesis on Uruguayan data, used in the studies reviewed above, to estimate the effect of the success of the firm on PCs' share of employees and did not find evidence of degeneration.

Navarra (2016) explored the role of nonrecoverable asset locks (AL) in producer cooperatives in Italy, where they amount to over 7 percent of total employment. A large percentage (86 percent) of net profits of PCs are devoted to AL. The author hypothesized and empirically confirmed, using two data sets, that AL acts as employment insurance such that profits are accumulated in good times into AL and this enables wages and employment to be stable during hard times. In addition, there is support for findings of other studies which suggested that, if necessary, wages can absorb negative shocks (flexible wage contract) but employment is privileged and sustained. As the AL accumulates, the flexible wage contract is no longer needed and disappears.

Fernandez-Guadano and Lopez-Millan (2018) found, based on a sample of 1,006 Spanish firms (440 CFs and 566 employee-owned – with greater than 51 percent ownership stake), that employee ownership had a positive and significant influence on the distribution of value in favor of the employees but not the other stakeholders (creditors, customers, state and other suppliers). This finding supports Ward's prediction of a PC maximizing value added per worker.

However, Dow (2018, p. 74) summarized the empirical literature and noted three points that do not validate the negative neoclassical theoretical predictions regarding PCs. Contrary to the theorizing, employee-owned firms have been more concerned with employee rather than value per worker maximization. They respond to shocks by stabilizing employment and output while allowing hours worked and wages to absorb the shock. Again, there is no support for the prediction that short-run worker horizons would undermine capital investment. Finally, the predictions of lower productivity (based on free-riding) or lower survival rates are not borne out and, in fact, the evidence suggests that PCs are often more productive and better at surviving than CFs in the same industry. While the causal mechanisms have not been empirically identified, various authors have conjectured that worker participation, higher morale and use of employee knowledge may account for this.

South Asian case studies

Much of the literature on PCs is based on studies done in high- or middle-income countries. This section therefore contributes to the literature by exploring two PCs in a low-middle-income country. There are many examples of PCs from India, Nepal and Sri Lanka, but much less so from Bangladesh and Pakistan. However, there are few examples of successful ones. This section discusses two case studies from Kerala, India. Prima facie, one might expect lower organizational ability and labor self-management in low-middle-come countries, but these case studies demonstrate that it is not necessarily the case.

The Mararikulam Experiment, Kerala, India

The Mararikulam Experiment in Kerala is part of a larger movement for attaining decentralized development in Kerala, India (Issac and Franke, 2002). The progressive Democratic Front government that came to power in 1996 encouraged the People's Campaign for Democratic Development to support the plan to devolve 35–40 percent of the state's Ninth Plan outlay to projects and programs formulated and implemented at the local level. This has been one of the most ambitious devolution exercises across the globe and the Mararikulam Experiment is one part of this ambitious undertaking.

Franke (2003) documented the success of a cooperative soap-making PC in Mararikulam. Kerala has in fact a long tradition of progressive politics and, in keeping with that, high levels of investments in human development. Thus, not surprisingly, even though the poverty rate using the local poverty line showed a headcount poverty of 60 percent in the subject area in the late 1990s, the prevalent literacy rate at the time was over 90 percent.

The main components of the Mararikulam (central coast of Kerala) experiment were 1,500 "neighborhood groups" (NHGs) made up of 20–40 women (one per household) each across eight villages. The group formation started in 1998/1999 with modest public funding based on the state's focus on decentralization. The groups started by initiating savings (regular individual deposits) which were on-lent to those in need by group decision. In a short period of time, the NHGs had accumulated sufficient capital to initiate small businesses by partly drawing on local cooperative banks and State and Central Government assistance. This enabled the transition from credit societies to PCs.

Based on volunteer expertise, two groups in each village (16 in all) were trained in soap-making.[9] The Integrated Rural Technology Center in Kerala, a research institution, provided soap-producing technology kits and training. By May 2002, all 16 units were producing several batches of soap per week. The PC managed to successfully compete with MNCs like Procter & Gamble by keeping prices low and delivering a good product via door-to-door marketing.

By retaining the local market for local production, they induce a larger local multiplier.

Franke viewed soap-making to be a good choice for forming a PC in a low-middle-income country since there is always a local market for soap, the technology is simple, 90 percent of the input (coconut oil) is locally available, the marketing is simple (door to door) and in addition, there are several backward (to oil) and forward linkages to local consumption generated by the income of the PC.

The PC was founded on the practice of sustainable development principles in that the composting is turned into fertilizer for food production. PC members engage in rainwater harvesting, had plans to turn ponds into fish farms and to construct artificial reefs for fish breeding and for protection from sea surges. Thus, the PC collective embodies a high level of ecological consciousness.

Kerala Dinesh Beedi Workers' (KDB) Cooperative Society Ltd.[10]

As Isaac, Franke, and Raghavan (1998) put it, the KDB represents one of the world's largest and most successful experiments in industrial democracy. From a few hundred desperate workers in 1969, among 12,000 who had been locked out by their employers, KDB grew to over 40,000 workers–owners producer cooperative that captured half the total market for beedis (poor people's rolled cigarettes) in Kerala.

On October15, 1968, Mangalore beedi firm owners stopped all their activities, on grounds of labor militancy and a breakdown of law and order, and 12,000 workers were instantly unemployed. The labor unions argued that the real reason for the closings was the threat that the Kerala left government was ready to implement the Beedi and Cigar Workers' Conditions of Employment Act.

Initially, the owners refused to meet the State Government to attempt to resolve the issue. When talks did finally take place, the owner's demands were viewed as completely unacceptable by the left leaning unions. Out of desperation, some workers accepted putting-out work[11] that had partially ignited labor action in the first place, but others turned to militancy. Right-wing unions went along with the putting-out system and the goons of the Rashtriya Swayam Sevak Sangh (RSS) got involved in anti-picketing action. The owner's response to a worker-sympathetic State Government was to move across the border to Karnataka, a more capital-friendly state.

On December 18, 1968, the state government announced the formation of the Kerala Dinesh Beedi Workers' (KDB) Cooperative Society Ltd., with 12 primaries and 1 apex central cooperative. The government asked a team of specialists to formulate the bylaws for the KDB which started production on February 15, 1969. It immediately became the favorite target of right-wing goons of the RSS. However, the KDB cooperative was a State Government initiative and hence able to withstand the pressure. The State Government provided slightly more than half the initial capital contribution, including funds (Rs. 19 of the Rs. 20 per share) to enable workers to buy ownership shares.[12] One wise move of the government was to induct representation from all the political parties, even those that scoffed at the idea of a cooperative, on board positions.

The unions cooperated in following state instructions and provided hands-on experience. By its fifth anniversary, all laid-off workers had been hired back. By the late 1990s, across Malabar (Northern Kerala), in all directions from Kannur, the head office of the KDB, 326 work centers had been established. Workers at these centers produced and packaged for the 22 worker-owned primary cooperatives that made up the company.

The primary cooperatives have 7–12 shopfloors and they elect the board of directors for the primary cooperative from among their own ranks. The focus of the primary board is on shopfloor issues. The primary cooperatives also elect the five worker-directors who serve on the seven-member board of the central or apex cooperative. Issues that concern the financial well-being of the whole cooperative are delegated to the central cooperative which therefore has a major say on primary cooperative decision making. The primary board has limited expenditure authority to improve working conditions. It can resolve disputes not settled at the shopfloor level and also monitor the purchase of raw materials from the central cooperative and the sale of beedis sent back to it for marketing.

Since the State Government continues to own just more than 50 percent of the shares, it appoints the chair of board (President) and one other member (Secretary) as nonvoting members. At the annual general body meetings, workers review the conduct of management and can directly influence its policies. Workers are part of a union and elect local watchdog committees intended to protect them on a day-to-day basis.[13]

While the initial membership was entirely male, by the mid-1990s almost 60 percent of workforce was female. Being new and on average younger, women were not as active as men in the unions and grossly underrepresented in leadership positions. There was awareness of this issue and the situation started to change gradually.

The increase of women in the workforce could be accounted for by the fact that beedi rolling in India is generally home-based work based on a putting-out system by monopsonistic contractors. These operations are highly exploitative of and oppressive to workers who have no alternative livelihood options. Factory rolling instituted by them is no better due to the poor cramped working conditions with no drinking water or latrines. Workers in KDB by contrast have good working conditions in addition to formal sector benefits, including pensions, paid leave, medical allowance, maternity benefits and the ability to borrow interest-free from a thrift fund. The KDB compensation package is worth about three times what is paid by private firms and this constrains worker demands for a greater distribution of the profit surplus by the central cooperative.

Despite its huge output, the management staff of KDB is kept to a minimum and ostentatious spending is carefully avoided. Wages are the equivalent of shopfloor workers and management, including that of the chairman and the secretary who enjoy no perks: The chairman and directors ride to necessary functions in a large van that is put to many other uses as well.

KDB workers work 9-hour days, including lunch and tea breaks. Unlike workers at most other beedi establishments, they sit on bamboo benches with cement backrests at clean, well-lit and well-ventilated work sites. Workers have more free space to move around without bumping into other employees. Outside the work shed are sanitary latrines and facilities for washing up.

The high quality of products, class solidarity and popular sympathy were put to good effect by KDB in its marketing to win share from a fierce and large corporate competitor. From 1969 to 1992, KDB increased its sales from 1 million to 588 million Indian rupees to become the fourth largest beedi firm in India.[14] After the first four years, it continuously clocked positive profits. Based on accumulated profits and other funds, it became financially self-sufficient, so much so that it even provided a loan to the State Government during a period of financial distress.

Issac et al. concluded that an important factor in the success of the KDB is the key role of the apex cooperative in coordinating the activities of the primary cooperatives. It engages in financial management, provides working capital and coordinates production, marketing and quality control. It redistributes surplus as a bonus to the primaries and ensures uniformity of working conditions. The central cooperative also makes decisions regarding wages, improvements in working conditions, investments and diversification.

There is the question of why workers' assured tenure and a uniform wage would perform at a high level. The central society managers hire the foremen who supervise the shopfloor supervisors (*maistries*) hired by the primary cooperative boards. While the supervisors do not have enforcement authority, they can decide on how much raw material can be allocated to workers based on their productivity. Since they are chosen from among the good workers at the primary cooperatives, their decisions have moral authority and are backed by peer pressure given the competition to be among top producers identified at the annual cooperative general body meetings organized by the central cooperative. The supervisors also try to upgrade the skills of workers deemed to be working at sub-par levels. There are also positive incentives at the individual level such that the highest productivity achievers are given special prizes and held up as models for emulation and may also advance to the rank of supervisor and be elected to the board of directors at the primary cooperative and later the central cooperative.

This key role thus enables the central cooperative to look out for the welfare of the whole unit and resolve the degeneration problem that cooperatives can be faced with, as discussed in the literature review above.[15] Not surprisingly, tensions between the apex organization and the primaries often emerge, but they get addressed in the democratic framework governing the PC.[16]

KDB's expansion slowed after the 1990s because it found it difficult to compete with low wages in the rest of the industry. KDB is by contrast a standard bearer of labor standards, eliminated child labor from its operations,[17] tied wages to cost of living increases and provides other benefits and improved working conditions as indicated above. One way of competing with the private sector on costs is maintaining a very thin management structure (the board) with a completely flat compensation package. The lack of corruption facilitates purchase of quality raw materials to enable the delivery of quality output.

Another KDB competitive advantage is happier, healthier and more highly paid workers who are significantly more careful with their rolling of beedis than their counterparts who roll for the private firms. KDB maintains a reputation for producing more high-quality beedis that command a higher market price. This reputation within Kerala has enabled KDB to save on marketing costs compared to private sector competitors. At the same time, economizing on marketing costs, such as not paying distributor inducements, has limited its beedi expansion beyond Kerala or the marketing of high-quality non-beedi products within Kerala.

KDB has faced several challenges over the years other than low-cost competition. Its reputation and public goodwill resulted in counterfeiting which is difficult to stamp out. In addition, taxes are duly paid, unlike evasion by competitors. It faces competition from cheap filtered small cigarettes marketed by multinationals facing hostile conditions in home markets. There is also increasing public awareness about the ills of tobacco smoking in India. Given these challenges, KDB sensibly sought to diversify, including into bottled coconut curry sauce and milk, juices and pickled condiments, although initially they faced worker resistance.

However, as it faced a shrinking market, diversification was inevitable. At its peak in the early 1980s, it directly employed 42,000 workers and this shrank to 12,000 as reported on its website in January 2021.[18] The diversification has continued and it has moved into software development, information-enabled services, education, processed foods, umbrellas, apparels and establishing its own hypermarkets. The state has shown an interest in supporting the diversification. It has maintained its reputation for quality by seeking international certification and this has been acknowledged by its winning national awards for quality. From 2014 to 2018, the Kerala Dinesh BWCCS won the Fair Business Practice Award from the Associated Chamber of Commerce and Industry of India.[19]

Conclusion

The literature review indicates that PCs can coexist with CFs in a capitalist market economy, although doing so is challenging. Even more surprising is finding examples of successful PCs in a low-middle-income country. The Mararikulam Experiment is unique in the literature in that it represents a PC that survived and thrived in a rural context. It is not surprising that both the examples of successful PCs in South Asia reviewed in this chapter are based in Kerala. Both the Mararikulam Experiment and KDB are inspirational. A progressive worker's social movement and an ideologically well-disposed government (in conjunction with a crisis of production in an industry in the case of KDB) gave birth to the PCs. The subsequent success in both cases was the result of the worker efforts.

KDB is also a PC with a difference in the sense that it was initiated by the State Government and therefore the state was initially instrumental in determining the representation on the board. Even after its role declined as its ownership share shrank (remained just above 50 percent), it continued to appoint the chair and one other member (secretary) of the seven-member board of directors.

Another unusual aspect of the KDB is the continued presence of unions. In principle, unions protect worker interests relative to management, so the need for union protection in a worker-owned cooperative should be redundant. The cooperative however evolved with the support of unions and, given this history, union representation remains embedded for day-to-day worker protection in a cooperative complex in which the apex organization has considerable authority over the functioning of the primary cooperatives. In the case of KDB, progressive policies, high worker morale and public support also played a role in its success.

Despite their success, these PCs represent islands in a capitalist sea. In the case of KDB, unless worker remuneration and welfare standards are nationally improved, it is at a competitive disadvantage which caps its ability to increase market share beyond Kerala. KDB faces many other challenges. Among these is retaining a solidaristic consciousness among workers who did not have to struggle for the well-being the cooperative provides them. The human tendency to maximize individual well-being at the expense of the cooperative follows from this.

The cooperative also produces a product that is increasingly vilified and for good reason. KDB's sensible response has been to diversify while bringing its focus on quality to its new ventures. It has won recognition for excellence and while it has had to downsize as the demand for tobacco products shrunk, it remains an inspirational success story for broader replication should favorable conditions present themselves.

Notes

1 Workplace democracy, worker-managed firms, worker cooperatives and employee-owned firms are other terms found in the literature when referring to producer cooperatives. Employee ownership via stock ownership/profit sharing differs from PCs where workers own and essentially govern the firm, even if via hired managers, and this chapter focuses on the latter.
2 Refer to Dow (2018) for a review of theoretical issues based on the experience of PCs in mostly high-income and a few middle-income countries.
3 In 2008, MCC became Mondragon.
4 This in PC terminology is referred to as an asset lock (AL). See evidence of ALs on PC behavior and outcomes in the evidence section.
5 Dow (2018, p. 66) pointed out that PCs amount to about 3–4 percent of total firm, assets and sales.
6 Since the percentage of labor represented by unions has been shrinking, even in high-income countries, workers face much more precarious work conditions as capital becomes more powerful. This should in principle enhance the incentive to form PCs if the opportunity presents itself.
7 The author also provided the various potential shortcomings of meta-analysis, notwithstanding the advantages it can provide as a summary of empirical literature.
8 In this context, degeneration means that PC success will cause them to hire more non-member employees and in due course degenerate or become more like conventional capitalist market firms.

9 Other activities include stitching, weaving, pickle-making, vegetable cultivation (beans, gourds and leafy vegetables) and fish cultivation.
10 The account of KDB is drawn from Issac, Franke and Raghavan (1998) and Gulati, Isaac and Klein (2002).
11 Highly exploitative home-based piece rate work.
12 Shares represent ownership and voting rights. No dividends are paid and workers can recoup the face value of the share on retirement, but they have no claim on the cooperatives assets that are owned collectively.
13 Workers are members of several unions, although the dominant two have accounted for 75–90 percent of worker representation. Union roles differ from conventional ones since workers are the owners. Union activists discuss policy, initiate worker benefits, but also mediate, say, supervisor–worker disputes and short-term management policy suggestions in difficult times such as using paid leave for production closures when there is a stock build up or deferring benefits during a financial crunch. Unions view the cooperative as a major labor success and are vested in its propagation. However, since several unions compete for worker affiliation, union rivalries can be an issue.
14 One $ was equal to 26 Indian rupees in 1992.
15 Another mechanism for avoiding degeneration is the rule that all workers must be members so that problems confronted by PCs like Mondragon, pertaining to the increasing ratio of nonmembers to members, do not occur.
16 There are tensions between the demands of the more productive primary units and the need for maintaining solidarity. For example, the more productive younger workers (often women) can earn more on a piece rate remuneration. This is balanced by an allowance that all who produce a minimum daily amount qualify for it. The younger workers pushed for a higher daily minimum that would disadvantage older workers. The central cooperative resolved the issue privileging egalitarianism and solidarity by containing the daily minimum and allowing older workers to carry work to the next day to attain a minimum, hence losing fewer daily allowances. Another issue is the need for maintaining reserves for investment that the central unit has successfully pushed for vs. demands for profit distribution, particularly by the more productive primary units.
17 Children, because of their delicate fingers, are among the best beedi rollers and the putting-up system utilized them extensively by paying adults for child work at piece rates.
18 https://www.keraladinesh.com/careers.php, accessed 1/10/2021. Reports on current employment vary in different journalist sources to as low as 4,500 (https://www.thenewsminute.com/article/struggling-kerala-dinesh-beedis-sees-spike-sale-due-lockdown-128357, accessed 1/10/2021.
19 https://www.thenewsminute.com/article/struggling-kerala-dinesh-beedis-sees-spike-sale-due-lockdown-128357, accessed 1/10/2021.

References

Alves, G., G. Burdín and A. Dean. 2016. "Workplace Democracy and Job Flows," *Journal of Comparative Economics*, 44(2), 258–271.

Arnando, S., F. Freundlich, M. Gago, D. Jones and T. Kato. 2010. "Assessing Mondragon: Stability and Managed Change in the Face of Globalization," William Davidson Institute Working Paper Number 1003, University of Michigan, Ann Arbor.

Burdín, G. 2016. "Equality under Threat by the Talented: Evidence from Worker-Managed Firms," *The Economic Journal*, 126(594), 1372–1403.

Burdín, G. 2014. "Are Worker-Managed Firms More Likely to Fail than Conventional Enterprises? Evidence from Uraguay," *Industrial Labor Relations Review*, 67(1), 202–238.

Burdín, G. and A. Dean. 2012. "Revisiting the Objectives of Worker-managed Firms: An Empirical Assessment," *Economic Systems*, 36(1), 158–171.

Burdín, G. and A. Dean. 2009. "New Evidence on Wages and Employment in Worker Cooperatives Compared with Capitalist Firms," *Journal of Comparative Economics*, 37(4), 517–533.

Campbell, A. 2011. "The Role of Workers in Management: The Case of Mondragon," *Review of Radical Political Economics*, 43(3), 328–333.

Carruth, P. A. 2019. "Collective Action Spillover and Alternative Organizations: The Influence of Piquetero Protest Activity on Worker-Recuperated Businesses in Argentina, 1998–2007," *Socio-Economic Review*, 17(1), 63–80.

Conte, M. A. and D. C. Jones. 2015. "On the Entry of Employee-Owned Firms: Theory and Evidence from U.S. Manufacturing Industries, 1870–1960," in ed., A. Kauhanen, *Advances in the Economic Analysis of Participatory & Labor-Managed Firms* (Bingley, UK: Emerald Publishing Ltd.), Vol. 16, 1–31.

Dean, A. 2019. "Do Successful Worker-managed Firms Degenerate?," *Journal of Comparative Economics*, 47(2), 317–329.

Doucouliagos, C. 1995. "Worker Participation and Productivity in Labor-Managed and Participatory Capitalist Firms: A Meta-Analysis," *Industrial Labor Relations Review*, 49(1), 58–77.

Dow, G. K. 2018. "The Theory of the Labor-Managed Firm: Past, Present, and Future," *Annals of Public and Cooperative Economics*, 89(1), 65–86.

Fakhfakh, F., V. Perotin and M. Gago. 2012. "Productivity, Capital, and Labor in Labor-Managed and Conventional Firms: An Investigation on French Data," *Industrial Labor Relations Review*, 65(4), 847–879.

Fernandez-Guadano, J. and M. Lopez-Millan. 2018. "Employee-Owned Firms from a Stakeholder Perspective," *Journal of International Development*, 30(6), 1044–1059.

Franke, R. W. 2003 "The Mararikulam Experiment: Women-Owned Cooperatives in Kerala, India," *Grassroots Economic Organizing Newsletter*, 58(May-June), 8–11, http://www.geo.coop, consulted 12/16/2020.

Gulati, G. M., T. M. T. Isaac and W. A. Klein. 2002. "When a Workers' Cooperative Works: The Case of Kerala Dinesh Beedi," *UCLA Law Review*, 49(5), 1417–1454.

Issac, T. M. T. and R. W. Franke. 2000. *Local Democracy and Development: People's Campaign for Decentralized Planning in Kerala* (New Delhi: LeftWord Books).

Issac, T. M. T., R. W. Franke and P. Raghavan. 1998. *Democracy at Work in an Indian Industrial Cooperative: The Story of Kerala Dinesh Beedi* (Ithaca, New York: Cornell University Press).

Navarra, C. 2016. "Employment Stabilization Inside Firms: An Empirical Investigation of Worker Cooperatives," *Annals of Public and Cooperative Economics*, 87(4), 563–585.

Pencavel, J., L. Pistaferri and F. Schivardi. 2006. "Wages, Employment, and Capital in Capitalist and Worker-Owned Firms," *Industrial Labor Relations Review*, 60(1), 23–44.

Ward, B. 1958. "The Firm in Illyria: Market Syndicalism," *American Economic Review*, 48(4), 566–589.

Whyte, W. F. 1999. "The Mondragon Cooperatives in 1976 and 1998," *Industrial and Labor Relations Review*, 52(3), 478–481.

10 Some South Asian export successes

Introduction

Collective action for rural development initiated by civil society or state-supported development NGOs was explored in Chapter 3. In Chapter 9, collective action initiated by unions or progressive state governments for rural development or manufacturing was explored. In this chapter, collective action initiated by entrepreneurs to facilitate production is explored. Clusters embody collective action and, when successful, garner the attention of the state to enhance the impact of the collective action.

This chapter explores four successful South Asian clusters. The first two are the football and surgical goods manufacturing clusters in Sialkot, Pakistan, both of which successfully forged partnerships with foreign companies for their exporting success. This was even more so the case for ready-made garments from Bangladesh. Finally, the information technology clusters in India are explored and the partnership in this case is with the state but also with the Indian diaspora, particularly with the US Silicon Valley cluster, and foreign capital.

All four examples also represent case studies of how low- and low middle-income country (L/LMIC) clusters can insert themselves into global value chains (GVCs) for exporting success. The key theme that emerges from the first three case studies is that such insertion represents an opportunity but also poses threats. This chapter first briefly reviews the concepts of industrial clusters and global value chains, moves on next to the four case studies and then concludes.

Clusters[1]

The obvious question that comes to mind is why firms competing and protecting trade secrets would want to cluster? Obviously, the benefits of clustering must offset the costs for clustering to be observed as it is. Clusters are informal and defined by location and there is no formal registration to be a member of a cluster, though members of a cluster may all be members of the same trade associations. As Nadvi and Schmitz (1994) document, industrial clustering is widespread in L/LMICs, including South Asia.

DOI: 10.4324/9781003176411-14

The explanation of clustering goes back to Alfred Marshall, who observed external (or agglomeration) economies. Negative external economies are "externalities" that normally pertain to the environment such as industrial emissions. This is a market failure in that the social cost of an activity is greater than the private cost and so the world witnesses more than an optimal amount of emissions from the perspective of an environmental economist.[2]

The converse is also possible when the presence of some firms bestows benefits on others in terms of reducing costs of inputs (pecuniary economy) or providing valuable information (technological economy). This again represents a market failure as too little of such activity results because firms conveying the benefit are not able to capture the social benefits.[3] If a tax is the prescribed public action for a negative external economy, a subsidy, or other forms of support, should be the prescribed public action for clusters.

The literature on clusters identifies other forms of passive external economies that firms benefit from by being in a cluster and some benefits could result from joint or collective action of various kinds. Some of the passive benefits include the development of a pool of specialized labor that is drawn to the cluster and which in turn facilitates manufacturing. A successful export cluster also draws a range of ancillary services such as accounting, tax, finance, transportation, marketing (traders/export agents) and office service specialists. The presence of a successful cluster results in both economies of scale and scope for service providers. Input suppliers have several clients within the cluster and so they can benefit from economies of scale and reduce unit costs. Also, the larger the number of firms in the cluster, the more feasible diversification becomes to service particular needs of the final product firms.

The cluster also enables the product to be fragmented with firms specializing in tasks and larger firms subcontracting. The larger firms often internalize key aspects of the production process to ensure quality. However, subcontracting provides lower wage and labor management costs and reduces risks of market fluctuations for the larger firms. Even so, they need to invest in the subcontracting firms via technical support and training to secure the quality of the final product. Small firms might subcontract very labor-intensive processes on piece rates to home-based workers.

There is a rapid diffusion of knowledge and ideas within the cluster via several channels. An input supplier that serves several clients could be a conduit; a repair shop serving several firms; social networks-based links within the cluster; skilled workers changing jobs within the cluster carry information. Since there are many firms in a cluster, there is a greater incentive for government or foreign firms to provide certification services for quality, social or environmental standards. Similarly, enhanced visibility increases market access for all firms in the cluster.

Clustering (as with rural development clusters, Chapter 3) also provides more clout with the government for infrastructure and other needed services. Since the benefits are notably widespread, the state is more willing to engage in public–private partnerships whereby the cluster firms make contributions for self-help and the state pitches in for critical infrastructure such as roads, rail links, dry ports and airports. In addition, the state might establish technical training and technology centers and facilitate credit, quality control, trade fairs and international trade missions.

Flexible specialization and just-in-time production are concepts in industrial organization introduced by Japanese practice. They include market responsive and cost-cutting measures. With the wide number and diversity of service firms operating in clusters, they are ideally suited for adopting both of these practices that enable them to rapidly respond to demand changes and facilitate the final buyers by providing goods as needed.

Collective action of several kinds has been noted in clusters among the final product firms. However, it could also be with buyers, including international buyers, or with suppliers within the cluster. Problems of quality and rapid delivery could involve several firms in a vertical production chain, and there could be a need for joint action for all to succeed.

Horizontal joint action could involve sharing of specialized equipment (bilateral or multilateral), sharing of capacity-depending on demand, product development, information sharing, training and marketing. Joint action to solve a mutual problem invariably results in some free-riding, but there are nonetheless examples such as in the formation of trade associations or holding of industrial fairs to benefit the cluster as a collective. Naturally, some benefit more than others, but individual benefits are high enough to galvanize most of the cluster units.

Researchers have shown that firm behavior can be driven by "trust" and other forms of social capital as is true for interactions within communities. The presence of trust facilitates repeat transactions and hence reduces transaction costs because there is no need for repeated search for new suppliers. Also, being part of the cluster means benefiting from mutual market-based support, which reduces the risk for any given entrepreneur because, until they succeed, they can specialize and operate on a small scale.

Clusters in South Asia are socially embedded in thick networks of ethnic, religious, localness, caste and family relationships. The ability to know of reputations and sanction-deviant behavior is facilitated by such networks, which can also limit free-riding in collective action. Firms are often family-run, and producers know virtually everyone operating in the market, and so production and community overlap and serve each other by reducing transaction costs and facilitating informal credit allocation and information flows.

Clusters in L/MICs often fit into the supply end of global value chains (GVCs)[4] and can be part of a process referred to as off shore outsourcing in high-income countries (HICs).[5] Raikes et al. (2000) traced the origin of GVCs to Wallerstein's (1974) World Systems Theory. Prominent among the contributors to this analytical approach is Gary Gereffi, who has written extensively on GVCs.[6] Value chains have been facilitated by the fragmentation of the production process, improvements in shipping technology (containerization, wide body airplanes, double hull ships), IT (facilitates governance), capital mobility and global improvements in human capital.

Gereffi (2000, pp. 11–12) defined a GVC to include a whole range of related activities involved in the design, production and marketing of a product. Gereffi (1998, p.40) referred to them as rooted in transnational production systems that link economic activities of the clustering firms to technological, organizational and institutional networks utilized to develop, manufacture and market specific commodities. GVCs can be thought of in terms of the location of the various nodes of control in the chain and the system of governance across them instituted generally by lead firms based in HICs.

Some South Asian exporting success stories

Surgical instrument cluster, Sialkot, Pakistan[7]

Despite intense market competition, the Sialkot cluster manufacturing surgical instruments remains a notable exporter at the time of writing (2021).[8] As indicated in Appendix Table 10.1, it has managed to retain a prominent position among world exporters of medical, surgical or dental instruments and appliances (Harmonized System (HS) Code, 901890) between 2003 and 2019. In 2019, it contributed about 2 percent of total Pakistani exports.

A finer distinction to the seven-digit SITC (Standard Industrial Trade Classification) of 8722909 or the ten-digit HS Code of 9018908000 to just surgical instruments would show Pakistan in a more prominent exporting position, but unfortunately these data at a finer disaggregation were not available online from either COMTRADE, the UN's trade data base or World Integrated Trade Solutions (WITS). Even so, between 2003 and 2019, export revenue in the six-digit classification increased threefold in nominal terms.

Sialkot was not a very likely place for the location of any export industry. It is a thousand miles away from the nearest port (Karachi), had no major airport, and was away from the main transportation grids in the country. Yet Sialkot had a concentration of the *Lohar beraderi* (metal working brotherhood) that excelled in the making of swords and daggers during the Mughal period. In the 1890s, they responded to the demand to repair surgical instruments for a local Christian mission hospital. It moved from that to serving the whole subcontinent by the 1920s and then the region by the 1930s. World War II provided a major boost for the industry as the British forces decided to make it a leading supplier for the war effort. At the formation of Pakistan in 1947, it was one of the few operating industries in the country.

Export sales in 2018 were about $221 million, with the United States, Germany, the United Kingdom, France, Italy, UAE, Japan, Brazil, Mexico and Russia as the main export markets. While this amounted to about 1 percent of total Pakistani exports in 2018, Sialkot plays an outsized role in global exports of surgical instruments (it caters to about nine-tenth of global demand).[9] In 2016, the cluster had about 3,000 companies with the labor force ranging from 15 to 450 per unit, of which around 30 could be considered large units, and 150 as medium sized. In addition, there are the ancillary firms serving the final product cluster firms such as steel, chemical and machine parts, and general service.[10]

Firms that tried to base success on locating closer to the port in Karachi were deprived of cluster advantages and did not succeed. The only case of a non-Sialkoti enterprise breaking into this market resulted from their locating in Sialkot. As indicated above, being located in the cluster provides the benefits of external economies or collective efficiencies but also the benefits of collective action.

Two examples of such collective action are noteworthy. In 1987, the quality of steel used in Sialkoti surgical instruments was deemed to be poor and the United States banned imports from Pakistan. The instrument producers successfully pressured and worked with the steel rerolling mills to raise quality via trade bodies. Another challenge resulted from the transaction costs of exporting from an inland site and this resulted in the cluster working together to set up a dry port in Sialkot so that all the formalities and containerization could be handled there at much lower cost.

In 1994, there was a second ban on imports from Sialkot into the United States because the Food and Drug Administration deemed that surgical instrument imports from Pakistan did not meet quality assurance standards. The firms in the cluster organized, contributed and galvanized government financial and diplomatic support. In turn, the government of Pakistan appointed an American company, Medical Quality Systems (MQS), to facilitate the implementation of Good Manufacturing Practice (GMP), the US standards certification, and successfully overcame the crisis. Within two years, 200 local firms were compliant with the US GMP (good management practices) and having attained this, certification to ISO 9000 was easy. This was particularly remarkable since most firms were family-run with little knowledge of modern management practices.

SIMA (Surgical Instruments Manufacturers Association, established in 1958) mediates problems with the state. It also attempts conflict resolution and is supposed to keep abreast of technological developments and quality standards to inform members. It has been lacking in the latter role since individual action is more likely in this case. Other local associations include the Sialkot Chamber of Commerce and Industry and the Metal Industries Development Centre (established by the British in 1943) and the Sialkot Dry Port Trust.

There are limits to collective action, beyond the constraints posed by free-riding. This is because while firms have an incentive to work together to solve collective problems, they are also fierce competitors. Firms responded individually to poor roads (four-wheel drives), communications (cell phones), power (generators) and hotels (guest houses). In fact, personal guest houses are preferred because it enables them to keep foreign contractors away from the competition. While hotels are a business opportunity and the service sector has responded, the state has responded to the poor infrastructure with better roads, a dry port and an airport.

Thus, firms within the cluster have a cooperative–competitive relationship much as Sen (1990) conceptualized for gender relations within the household. While they cooperate to resolve mutual problems, the competition is intense and extends to poaching each other's customers if they can and price undercutting. However, as mentioned above, the cluster is socially embedded in thick networks that include ties based on ethnicity, religion, localness, caste (*beraderi*), family relationships and intermarriages (Nadvi, 1999). This facilitates the ability to know of reputations and sanction-deviant behavior such as free-riding. To repeat, most firms are family-run and know of virtually everyone operating on the market and so production and community overlap and serve each other by reducing transaction costs and facilitating information flows.

The larger firms try to internalize many operations within the firm to internalize trade secrets, that leak anyway, and for quality control. Since almost 95 percent of produce is exported, the interaction with foreign contractors represents an important source of information regarding technological changes, standards and upgrading. They subcontract to medium or small firms and backstop them with technical advice, credit and quality control. They also pick up much information from the subcontractors, so this is a two-way association.

When the Pakistani industry started emerging as a low-cost threat to the German cluster in Tuttlingen, which had been dominating the market in such products, the latter successfully forged a joint venture with firms in the Sialkot cluster. In the 1980s, they sent metallurgical engineers to train partner firms on production engineering and quality control and Sialkot workers were also trained in Tuttlingen. There were regular follow-up visits by teams for technical assistance and inspection (for quality control).

Initially the joint venture meant outsourcing job processing to Sialkot and product finishing, packaging and marketing in Germany. As metal forging improved in Sialkot and they reduced rejection rates from 7 to 3 percent (1 percent in large firms) via cooperation with local agents of large buyers in the United States, many exported independently, and some even went into OBM (original brand manufacturing). However, in this regard the cluster is sorely lacking and a leading daily lamented that the inability to develop brands means that Sialkot, despite being a leading producer, captures a very small amount of the global value of surgical instruments trading which was worth about $17 billion in 2016.[11]

Establishing brands is something the large firms will have to attain on their own and is the obvious next step. Being content to be an outsourcing destination and have their products re-exported with high markups by foreign brands is a mugs game. The state has an industrial policy role to play and, in this regard, has not entirely failed in supporting the cluster. It has provided needed infrastructure, support for standards certification, leased land for the dry port, fiscal incentives[12] and credit. However, the state also needs to up its game; the Metal Industry Development Center that is supposed to assist the cluster via metal testing, quality upgrading, training and technological development seems to be unable to keep abreast of technological developments (Nadvi, 2008).

Football cluster, Sialkot, Pakistan[13]

The focus in this section is on footballs (soccer balls), which are a subset of the broader sport goods cluster. Appendix Table 10.1 presents data on inflatable balls

(HS Code, 950662) between 2003 and 2019. Most of the inflatable balls in this HS category are likely to be footballs and Pakistan has maintained its position as the second most important exporter after China. Pakistan's football exports amounted to about 1 percent of total Pakistani exports in 2019. The country has had the distinction of providing high-quality hand-stitched football for all the world cups from 1990 to 2010 and earned this distinction again in 2018. Another marker of success is that export revenue increased by 51 percent between 2003 and 2019, and so, despite the intense competition, the Sialkot cluster is so far managing to hold its own in the football product line.

In the period in question, Pakistan has been steadily losing market share to China. In 2003, Pakistan's value of exports amounted to 64 percent of China's, while this percentage declined to 29 in 2019. While both China and Pakistan produce the full range of footballs, China specializes in the machine-stitched thermo-molded, footballs,[14] while Sialkot specializes in the high-quality hand-stitched balls, which to date have been the preferred option in professional football. However, machine-stitched thermo-molded balls are gaining increasing currency in this regard, and hence China has represented a growing threat to Pakistan's top-end professional football market share.

Stitching is done in several thousand small- and medium-scale centers, and other works, such as lamination, cutting panels, screen printing, quality control and packing, are done in several hundred factories.[15] Factory work is part of the formal sector with higher wages and benefits, including social insurance, health, pension and unemployment. Factory work however is an exclusively male domain.

As in the surgical goods sector, poor infrastructure, including power shortages, represents a problem in the broader local environment. The key external challenge was the alleged use of child labor in the industry in the home-based work subcontracting on piece rates. In fact, child labor became the principal challenge for football exporters in Sialkot just as quality standards became the challenge for the surgical goods exporters.

Nadvi (2008) documented that international media reports highlighted the presence of child workers in stitching subcontracting to home workers in Sialkot in 1996. These revelations led to demands from Western consumer groups, trade unions and NGOs for a boycott of Sialkot-manufactured footballs. By 1997, there was a concerted attempt to address the issue that involved the Sialkot Chamber of Commerce and Industry (SCCI), Government of Pakistan, ILO, UNICEF, the World Federation of Sports Goods Industries and the International Federation of Football Associations with the support and coordination of the US government to produce the "Atlanta Agreement" that included support for schooling.

To facilitate monitoring, home-based work began to give way to production in designated stitching centers. In due course, local institutions, including NGOs, took over the monitoring and it appeared that the issue had been resolved. Yet, in 2006, NIKE boycotted the purchase of footballs from one of the largest manufacturers of footballs in the cluster. It subsequently contracted with other suppliers, but nonetheless the decision sent shock waves through the cluster.

Khan and Boje (2009) took a dim view of the process of imposing standards on the cluster. The authors considered the whole episode as a corporation spin by Nike to demonstrate it was engaging in Corporate Social Responsibility. Nike was subject to pressure from consumers, stock holders, child advocacy groups, religious groups, labor and, most important, the media that picks up and plays stories, particularly when there is a large constituency. CBS broke the story "Children at Work" on April 6, 1995, and, in modern parlance, it went viral.[16] The International Labor Rights Federation coordinated the campaign, and it was called "Foul Ball".

Villagers whose livelihoods were going to be impacted were blindsided. The Human Rights Commission, Pakistan, conceded that the piece rates were exploitative, but that there was no bonded labor involved or any other form of mistreatment. In fact, piece rates were standard for balls of a particular quality, no matter who did the work.[17]

Nike, accused of running sweatshops in East Asia in the early 1970s, has been dogged by this issue since and so was sensitive about being involved in another scandal. Its initial response was that stopping production would throw the children out onto the street but subsequently muted these responses and came onboard with the broad campaign to eliminate child labor. Its partner in Pakistan, Saga Sports, responded by building stitching centers that could be monitored and certified child labor-free and provided associated health centers and other facilities at its own expense, but this was not deemed adequate.

The US Department of Labor coordinated the campaign with international and Pakistani agencies in 1997, as mentioned above. UNICEF helped with starting nonformal schools (one to three rooms) that would bring the children up to the fifth grade level so that they could join government secondary schools. Stitching centers were established with the help of the Sialkot Chamber of Commerce and Industry for women and ILO was to monitor and certify that there was no child labor involved. The agencies subcontracted to development NGOs to implement the project. Microcredit and vocational training were to be provided as social support to households for the loss of income. This Atlanta Agreement got a ringing endorsement from President Clinton, who declared the campaign to be a success.

Khan (2009) pointed out that such campaigns rarely take into account the concerned voices at the grassroots level. The campaign (Atlanta Agreement) resulted in collateral damage, which could have been avoided if the "subjects" had been consulted. Khan (2008, p. 507) discovered from his fieldwork that stitching is considered a low status occupation with a stigma attached and that the very poorest engage in it. Doing this work in the privacy of the home provided flexibility and saved women from the public humiliation that they were subjected to when going to and from the stitching centers. They were also open to verbal abuse, harassment and even rape at some centers. They estimated that only about 20 percent of the women persisted with the stitching, and the others dropped out citing as reasons the blow to their self-respect and dignity, lack of flexibility and the inability to simultaneously tend to home work and the opposition of males in the household.

In the long term, the campaign could not be considered a success for other reasons also. The schooling program was not sustained and few actually got the microcredit or vocational training (Khan, 2008, p. 506). Some got a higher wage to draw them into stitching centers, but this was at the expense of an independent source of income for women and average household income declined. As the numbers in Appendix Table 10.1 show, manufacturing in Sialkot survived and is thriving for now and Nike has subcontracted with other manufacturers.

Garment exports, Bangladesh

The best way to glean how successful Bangladesh has been in exporting textiles as a broad category is to compare it with Pakistan. East Pakistan (now Bangladesh) gained independence from West Pakistan (now Pakistan) in 1971, and at that time much of the Pakistani textile industry was based in West Pakistan, which grew the cotton and therefore developed a textile industry based on that.

In 2019, the top two exports for Bangladesh in the textile and clothing category were, respectively, knit or crochet clothing, accessories ($ 20.3 billion) and clothing, accessories, not knit or crochet ($19.4 billion). In these categories, its exports were second only to China globally. The top three exports for Pakistan in the same broad category were miscellaneous textiles, worn clothing ($4.2 billion), clothing, accessories, not knit or crochet ($3.5 billion) and knit or crochet clothing, accessories ($3.3 billion). Pakistan was however the fourth highest global exporter of cotton at $1.8 billion. Thus, in the textile and clothing category, Bangladesh exported 3.5 times more than Pakistan even though it is not a significant cotton grower; in fact, cotton was its second largest import in 2019 after machinery.[18]

Another yardstick of Bangladesh's success as an exporter of textile and clothing is that the sector thrived even after the phasing out of the Multi-Fiber Agreement on January 1, 2005, as part of the Uruguay Round Agreements. HICs had attempted to protect their textile and clothing industries by imposing orderly trade via a quota regime negotiated within the GATT called the Multi-fiber Agreement (MFA). Many had expected that without quotas, and hence protected MFA trade, Bangladesh's exports would be completely dominated by China and some even feared a collapse in exports. Bangladesh's clothing and textile exports in 2004, the year before the MFA ended, were $5.4 billion. Thus, in nominal terms, they had increased more than sevenfold by 2019, and this makes clear that Bangladesh continued to be a serious competitor and did not need the quotas to succeed.

Rhee (1990), who documented the origin of the textile and clothing industry in Bangladesh, proposed the catalyst model as an explanation. As some MICs, like Korea, filled up their quota, they "quota-hopped" by relocating production in cheap labor countries that had not fulfilled their quotas. Sewing could not be automated because of the limp nature of cloth and so relocation was the preferred option. Daewoo, a Korean conglomerate, was constrained by the garment quota on exports to the US market. It was also looking for markets for its machinery. Desh was run by a prominent Bangladeshi industrialist and well-connected in the government. Desh and Daewoo signed a five-year collaboration agreement.

The terms of this agreement were that Daewoo would provide six months of training for Bangladeshi managers, production supervisors and production workers in a garment plant in Korea at Daewoo's expense (4 managers, 94 production supervisors and 29 production workers, including 14 women). The training was on machinery installation, start-up and production. In turn, Desh agreed to a royalty of 3 percent of sales and an additional 5 percent of sales for marketing and other consulting advice.

The collaboration proved to be highly successful because of the extensive and effective hands-on training that was extended by a month. Knowledge about management, production and marketing was successfully imparted but the trainees also learned about Daewoo's corporate culture and picked up tacit knowledge by observation, which is as important, if not more, as the specific skills imparted by the training. The Bangladeshi team returned ready to produce and shortly after exported its first batch of garments. Daewoo sent 15 experts to Desh for follow-up training in the local context with a focus on quality control.

Initially, there was a triangular relationship such that Daewoo was subcontracting to Desh, since the former had the international credibility and marketing networks. However, Desh soon picked up marketing skills and contracted independently. Out of the 127 personnel provided training, 115 set up their own export businesses and so the skills started getting diffused widely in a growing sector.

The outbreak of civil war in Sri Lanka in the early 1980s was a turning point in Bangladesh's ready-made garment (RMG) sector growth because a lot of orders moved to Bangladesh. Sri Lankan experts also came to Bangladesh to train workers as part of Sri Lankan foreign direct investment in Bangladesh (Khan, 2009) – a South–South partnership.

While the catalyst model is a good explanation for the origin of the garment industry in Bangladesh, its continued success is based on the ability of the industry to insert itself effectively into the retail GVCs. Most of the well-known US and European brands outsource to garment factories in Bangladesh.

Another key factor in the success of the venture was that it became incorporated into Bangladesh's Industrial Policy of 1982 that offered incentives for export-oriented manufacturing, including trade financing and tariff-free imports needed for production. The government also supported a back-to-back letter of credit (L/C) scheme that minimized credit risk and provided liquidity, and the creation of bonded warehouses (for duty free imports). It provided a generous cash compensation scheme (CCS – equivalent of 10 percent of value added) on exports of garments made from domestically produced fabric and yarn (World Bank, 2006).

The growth of the RMG sector was accompanied by a rapid growth in backward linkages to industries supplying fabrics, yarns, accessories and packaging materials. Supporting service industries such as transportation, banking, shipping and insurance also proliferated to keep pace with the demands of the RMG sector. World Bank (2006) estimated the number of people indirectly dependent on the RMG sector to be 10 million at the turn of the twentieth century.

As in the Sialkot clusters, there were also horizontal linkages between firms (Khan, 2009, Chapter 3). At times, firms with a large order subcontracted to competing firms within their known circle. RMG manufacturers also lent machinery to each other when a piece of equipment was needed for a special order.

Khan (2009, Chapter 3) documented that the emergence of a huge influx of women into the labor force enhanced their disposable incomes. Among other goods, this raised the demand for domestic cosmetics and clothing. Television channels are greatly reliant on the advertising revenue generated from the sales of these products. More important of course was the social change ushered in by the massive rise of women in the workforce (Kabeer, 2000).

However, as mentioned earlier, the phenomenal growth of the RMG sector is mainly a story of successful local–foreign partnerships and then of successful insertions into GVCs. The Desh–Daewoo collaboration in 1979 was mentioned earlier, and there was also a notable successful collaboration between Youngones Corporation of South Korea and Trexim Ltd. of Bangladesh in 1980.[19] Insertion into retail GVCs, such as with Walmart, meant being subject to their code of conduct on labor, environmental and other standards imposed by the brands and retailers.

Just as quality standards and child labor, respectively, were challenges for the Sialkot surgical instruments and football exporters, social standards became a key challenge for Bangladeshi RMG exporters. Owners were taking shortcuts in terms of compliance with the code of conduct standards imposed by the buyers. There were several incidents of deaths resulting from fires due to a lack of proper safety measures in construction and training. Matters came to a head on April 24, 2013, due to the collapse of the Rana Plaza building in Dhaka, Bangladesh, which housed five garment factories. The collapse resulted in the death of at least 1,132 people and more than 2,500 workers were injured. This created a global uproar and RMG brands provided assurance of lasting change.

The ILO[20] reported that accidents continued apace despite the May 15, 2013, establishment of the Accord on Building and Fire Safety in Bangladesh, which was signed by the majority of Western retailers and brands. The news cycle moved on and, unlike Sialkot, Bangladesh experienced little impact on the pace of exports. However, the ILO has stayed involved to put into place a tripartite agreement (its normal modus operandi) including it, the government, and garment exporters to institute a comprehensive employment injury insurance.

Information technology (IT), India[21]

The success of the Indian IT sector[22] is well known. Sharma (2015) documented that Indian IT exports in 1981 were $31 million. By 2018, computer and information exports were reported by UN COMTRADE to have reached $204 billion.[23] Similarly, its contribution to Indian GDP increased from 1.7 percent in 2000 to 5.8 percent in 2013, more than a threefold increase in about a decade (Bhat and Bhatia, 2016, p. 75). Rao and Balasubrahmanya (2017) documented that this percentage had increased to 9.5 percent by 2015. They also indicated that India at that time was the leading global sourcing destination for IT services with a 55 percent market share.

India's IT exporting success represents a partnership of the private sector with the government in the form of an educational and industrial policy as well as a partnership with foreign firms. It also represents the success of clusters that benefit from external economies as in the other case studies above. However, the success of Indian IT exports is also the result of a unique partnership of this industry with the Indian diaspora, particularly in the US Silicon Valley cluster. Finally, India has a language and scale advantage – the enormous numbers of engineering and technical graduates produced each year with English language skills available at very competitive rates.

Bhatnaghar (2006) told the story of the origin and development of the IT industry in India.[24] For Bhatnagar, the opportunity for India's IT sector resulted from the shortage of technical personnel in the West in the 1970s, at a time when India was experiencing an oversupply. The Indian diaspora, many originally trained in Indian Institutes of Technology (IITs), aware of this imbalance, mediated consulting contracts for onsite software development in India. The big break for the Indian IT industry came with the large number of Y2K-related projects[25] that the Indian diaspora was able to deliver to the home country in the late 1990s.[26] The Indian government took full advantage of the opportunity and provided support to facilitate such contracting as did the National Association of Service and Software Companies (NASSCOM). This gave the Indian software engineers and technicians an opportunity to demonstrate their capacity and competence in delivering quality in a timely and cost-effective manner and hence build a base for future contracts. Language skills, technical and engineering talent, low start-up costs (most assets could be leased or acquired) and quick returns to investment made this a particularly suitable activity for India.

By 2000, 972 Silicon Valley companies were headed by Indians. The networks built by the Indian Diaspora in the Silicon Valley were put at the service of Indian exporters. Bangalore, known as India's Silicon Valley, had extensive links with overseas IT market via migrants. Return migrants and expatriates set up shop in Bangalore and brought in knowledge, technology and capital. At the turn of the twentieth century, the Bangalore cluster was ranked fourth globally as a technological hub for innovation behind San Francisco, Austin and Taipei (Ramchandran and Ray, 2005, p. 153).

Once the industry took off, it attracted foreign venture capital. While the downside was that multinational companies (MNCs) drew away local expertise, the upside was that, despite protection of source codes, knowledge spillovers occurred. This was indicated by the very high labor turnover (20 to 30 percent). Many locals decided to set up their own shop having learned modern management methods and software production skills from foreign firms. There was a virtuous cycle in that the growth in the industry attracted more expatriates and accelerated knowledge transfer. Many firms moved up the value chain from low-cost programming to comprehensive software development and from "time and material" contracts to "fixed price" contracts that were more lucrative.

The Indian government invested heavily in higher and technical education from the inception of independence,[27] and this positioned it to take advantage of opportunities resulting from the bottleneck in the West mentioned above. This was in fact against the advice of the World Bank that suggested a focus on primary education based on a conceptually and methodologically flawed calculation of social rates of returns to education.[28] Following its own lights, India invested in world class and highly selective Indian Institutes of Technology (23 in 2021)[29] modeled on the MIT. In addition, there are numerous Indian Institutes of Science,[30] 20 Indian Institutes of Management[31] and numerous regional engineering colleges.

Caniels and Romijn (2003) and van Dijk (2003) pointed out that Bangalore had a formidable science and technology infrastructure, which included 4 universities, 14 colleges and 47 polytechnics.[32] Bangalore benefited from the construction of a modern airport, a technology park and reliable power and communications. The senior most state government officials (including the Chief Minister) marketed what Bangalore had to offer when abroad.[33]

The government also encouraged the creation and expansion of computer science departments. By the1990s, there were 660 engineering colleges producing 300,000 engineering graduates. The private sector was training about one million employees for the IT sector and the government invested heavily in standards certification to assure buyers. Supply kept pace with demand and so the wage advantage did not erode fast. Even as technical education was privatized, the government ensured quality control.

By the late 1990s, four task forces were established and most of the recommendations of these task forces to encourage the IT sector in India were accepted and policy changes instituted. The government helped build high-speed satellite data links to facilitate outsourcing.[34] This was a cross-ministerial effort and so, for example, the Ministry of Commerce granted blanket approval of needed imports from export earnings (see below). Special economic zones (SEZ), Software Technology Parks (STPI) and Electronics Hardware Technology Parks (EHTP) were created by the central and state governments with many incentives, including dry port facilities and a single window instituted for clearances.

Public sector procurement policies provided robust demand for local hardware and software companies. Facilitating and extending rural IT access was another mechanism to boost demand. The government provided an enabling legal framework, including copyright laws. It also facilitated access to capital, technology, land, utilities, training and marketing, and provided incentives via tax exemptions on profit, income, sales, excise and imports. It batted for the industry in enhancing opportunities and work visas in the United States and Europe.

NASSCOM lobbied very successfully on behalf of the industry on various issues pertaining to foreign exchange, infrastructure bottlenecks and deregulation. Incentive packages and concessions and provision of space provided by state and local governments for IT firms could partly be viewed as a result of its efforts. Its membership rose from 38 in 1988 to 1,000 in 2005 to 2,760 in 2018.[35]

There is a common perception that India was highly protectionist. However, even by the early 1970s, companies were permitted hardware imports duty free if they promised to export twice the value in software and services. In the 1980s, the Software Export Promotion Council was formed and imports liberalized. There was zero duty on IT products, and duty, tariffs and taxes were rationalized by the Ministry of Finance; the Reserve Bank of India instituted favorable foreign exchange rules and the Ministry of Education encouraged private engineering colleges and instituted mechanisms for quality control.

A landmark event occurred in 1978 when IBM, which had an association with India since 1951 and completely dominated the Indian computer market as a virtual monopoly (80 percent market share), decided to leave rather than be subject to controls.[36] However, once domestic firms were able to compete, foreign firms were welcomed back in the 1990s to benefit from their technology and marketing networks. IBM returned in 1992 in a joint venture with the Tata Group and by 2014 had 100,000 employees in India and was represented in all components of the IT industry.

As in the case of the clusters discussed above, firms in IT clusters, such as the one in Bangalore, benefited from collective efficiencies by attracting skilled labor and ancillary services. Firms were able to source software, hardware and human and financial capital within the cluster. The cluster also makes it advantageous for foreign buyers to invest in wholly owned concerns or to shop for potential vendors and contractors and to start joint ventures. It enabled ambitious and talented individuals to spot bottlenecks and seize opportunities with start-ups. However, the IT industry seems not to lend itself to the same kind of horizontal linkages experiences by firms in, say, conventional product clusters such as footballs, surgical instruments or textiles discussed above.[37]

Conclusion

When embarking on their economic development journey, most L/LMICs need to boost exports to earn scarce foreign exchange to fund current economic development goals. The examples in this chapter suggest that public policy has a low-cost way of doing this. Instead of across-the-board incentives, they might do well to utilize young hard-working interns to explore foreign trade data to identify hidden surprises.

In Pakistan's case, they would have found surgical goods and sports goods as surprising success stories if they had explored the data some decades ago. Moreover, a little more exploration would have uncovered that many of the world beating firms are located in clusters that have resolved many of their own constraints, often with joint action with other competitors in the cluster. Since many of the advantages of clustering can flow from external economies, there is an additional economic case for public intervention to make the successful clusters more successful.

The lesson for public policy from this chapter is to invest in exploration and then build on existing successes by responding to collective calls for public action. In pursuing such a course, discovery of constraints is left to those needing the support as it should be rather than foreign consultants or scholars. This in essence is the most parsimonious and cost-effective way of engaging in public policy.

The Pakistani state has provided considerable support to the surgical instruments and football clusters as part of its industrial policy. Over the decades it has improved infrastructure such as roads, provided an airport, eased the electricity supply constraint, facilitated a dry port and supported the meeting of standards for both clusters: quality control for surgical goods and social standards for footballs. In addition, as Atkin et al. (2016) pointed out, the government has encouraged exports by subsidizing land (sold at 50 percent of market value) and provided tax incentives for exports (rebates for customs duties, sales tax and excise duties paid on raw materials).

The introduction mentioned that insertion into GVCs presents opportunities but also poses threats. The obvious opportunities for the two clusters in Sialkot, Pakistan, and garment manufacturers in Bangladesh are access to markets in the West and hence exporting success. The threats in all three cases came in the form of an imposition of standards by the GVC governance mechanisms. This took the shape of quality standards for surgical instrument producers and social standards for football producers in Sialkot (eradicating child labor) and social standards for garment exporters in Bangladesh (improving labor working conditions).

In fact, conforming to the standards by following the code of conduct of the lead firms in the GVC could also be seen as an opportunity. Improved quality, social and environmental standards are a win–win in that they improve the product, and work conditions and assurances to importing countries stakeholders (shareholders, consumers) secures markets for the future.

However, another challenge posed by being part of a GVC is more insidious. Having secured market access, the L/LMIC producers could become complacent and engage in satisficing behavior – hence locked into remaining subordinates and dependents. To secure more of the value they create, they need to take the next steps to develop recognized brands. Here they are engaged in a zero-sum game since the lead firms in GVCs have no incentive to enable them to do so.

The IT sector in India is unique in this regard. It has managed to establish well-recognized brands such as Tata Communications, Infosys and Wipro. IT clusters in India also differ from the other clusters with their much more intense partnership with the Indian diaspora. Both these factors have enabled Indian IT clusters to have a more equal partnership with foreign IT giants, many of which have established offices in India. The sector has escaped scandals and standards impositions, as have the other clusters. The Indian IT sector has wisely invested in quality control standards with support from the state.

State support for IT clusters as a form of industrial policy is a commonality it shares with the other clusters discussed in this chapter. A prior commitment to higher education in science and technology created the technical and engineering skills that India was able to draw on when the opportunity presented itself. This opportunity was created partly by the presence of the Indian diaspora in the US Silicon Valley. When the shortage of needed skills in the West became evident, the Indian diaspora was able to point to and tap the abundance of these skills in India. The state used Industrial policy to support the IT clusters via infrastructure and incentives. Partnerships with multinationals abroad and those located in the IT clusters gave the industry another boost via direct investment and diffusion of knowledge and skills. As is true for the other case studies in this book, success is a story of partnerships.

Appendix Table 10.1 Pakistani surgical instruments and ball exports

Year	*Medical, surgical or dental instruments and appliances, HS Code, 901890*			*Balls; inflatable, HS Code, 950662*		
	Exports ('000, US nominal $s)	*Rank in value of exports*	*Quantity ('000)*	*Exports ('000, US nominal $s)*	*Rank in value of exports*	*Quantity ('000)*
2003	132,230.61	23	98,584	112,530.51	2	37,107
2004	125,371.98	25	92,993	157,081.16	2	51,311
2005	169,139.04	21	123,727	185,640.90	2	35,153
2006	155,759.02	26	110,950	225,909.79	2	73,586
2007	219,249.48	22	151,987	161,149.25	2	51,350
2008	258,882.59	21	161,373	160,492.00	2	48,219
2009	232,997.96	23	153,584	118,425.01	2	37,294
2010	219,000.08	26	115,459	157,540.09	2	48,949
2011	271,752.00	23	157,703	148,496.12	2	39,068
2012	291,384.25	24	211,245	149,250.64	2	37,684
2013	296,808.41	24	222,742	155,796.11	2	39,266
2014	319,525.78	25	237,591	195,557.50	2	49,339
2015	332,641.94	25	219,666	168,833.00	2	39,247
2016	326,028.48	24	208,758	163,573.92	2	38,169
2018	373,181.61	24	175,672	163,353.69	2	42,658
2019	404,317.65	21	203,382	170,377.57	2	43,312

Source: Constructed by author based on World Integrated Trade Solutions data set, https://wits.worldbank.org/trade/comtrade/en/country/ALL/year/2019/tradeflow/Exports/partner/WLD/product/901890, Consulted, 1/24/2021.

Notes

1 This section draws on Nadvi and Schmitz (1994) and Schmitz (1999). For a review of cluster research and its evolution, refer to Lazzeretti, Sedita and Caloffi(2014).
2 The optimum emissions for an ecologist are likely to be zero in the current global climate change scenario.
3 Schmitz (1999) pointed out that the firms in a cluster passing off positive externalities are also recipients; hence the incentive to continue to locate in a cluster. Nonetheless, in net terms the presence of external economics makes a public policy case for supporting the cluster.
4 Also referred to as global supply chains.
5 Humphrey and Schmitz (2002) discuss the overlap and indicate how insertion of cluster producers into GVCs can be a boon in winning export markets. However, it can also be a hindrance due to power asymmetries when the lead HIC firms are threatened from technological upgrading of supplier firms in L/MIC clusters and act to block it. Also refer to Naqvi and Halder (2005).
6 The pioneering work is Gerrefi (1994, 1998, and 1999). Sturgeon (2001) is a starting point for researchers in this field and there are many references on the Institute of Development Studies, University of Sussex, website.
7 This section draws on a government of Punjab, Pakistan report, http://www.irispunjab.gov.pk/StatisticalReport/Manufacturing%20Industry%20Data/Surgical%20Instruments%20Industry.pdf, consulted 1/23/21, Nadvi and Haldar (2005) and Chaudhry (2011).

8 According to the government of Punjab report cited above, industry experts claim that Sialkot is capable of manufacturing about 10,000 of the 40,000 or so different kinds of surgical instruments used to carry out numerous medical procedures.
9 https://www.dawn.com/news/1279191#:~:text=Pakistan%20is%20the%20leading%20exporter,is%20lost%20to%20outsourcing%20importers, consulted 1/22/2021.
10 Ibid.
11 Ibid.
12 Since, almost 95 percent of surgical instrument production is exported, and since the product is classified as high value added, the industry pays very nominal taxes.
13 Footballs started being produced in Sialkot in the late nineteenth century. For the historical origins of the cluster, refer to Khan (2008) and Atkin et al. (2016).
14 Their use in the 2010 World Cup in South Africa came in for some criticism by players for unpredictable flight (Nadvi, 2011). This source also distinguishes between various kinds of footballs, including the top-quality match, training (various qualities), promotional, laminated (not stitched) and toy.
15 The processes involved in manufacturing footballs is described in Atkin et al. (2017). Briefly, this includes cutting out rectangular imported high-quality rexine (leather substitute) sheets from long rolls of rexine and then gluing layers of cloth (cotton or polyester) to the back of the rexine sheet using a latex-based adhesive to add bounciness and durability. This laminated rexine is cut into pieces (20 hexagonal and 12 pentagonal), designs and logos are printed onto the cut pieces as specified using durable ink or paint and finally the bladder and valve inserted after the stitching and before the inspection for quality assurance and packaging.
16 Khan (2008, p. 501) pointed out that the initial story was factually incorrect on several counts and when picked up and rereported "further embellished and distorted".
17 Since the higher quality match balls have thicker leather, which is more difficult to stitch, men usually stitch those and get paid a higher piece rate.
18 Daniel Workman, http://www.worldstopexports.com/bangladeshs-top-10-exports/; http://www.worldstopexports.com/pakistans-top-10-exports/, consulted 2/1/2021.
19 http://banglapedia.search.com.bd/HT/G_0041.htm.
20 https://www.ilo.org/global/topics/geip/WCMS_614394/lang--en/index.htm, consulted 2/2/21.
21 Following Singh (2003), IT, also referred to as Information and Communication Technology (ICT), is understood here to mean digital processing, storage and communication of information. It includes many different kinds of data processing and voice interactions that use some IT infrastructure like the internet. The various components of IT include hardware, research, business process outsourcing, consulting and software. Software production includes design, coding, testing, installation, maintenance and support. IT-enabled services include customer call centers, accounting services and other business process outsourcing, Geographical Information Systems and engineering services, R&D and knowledge process outsourcing. Services were provided to foreign airline, banking and finance, pharmacy, auto, accounting and health care among other outfits. At the turn of the twentieth century, there were about 2,500 software exporters from India with TCS, Infosys, Wipro, Satyam and HCL recognized as global brands. Notwithstanding India's IT successes, Sharma (2016, pp. 2016–2017) points out that the quality of education beyond the elite institutions will be a challenge for continued success going forward.
22 Industry and sector are often used interchangeably though industry is probably more appropriate since the classical sectors are industry, agriculture and services. One could think of the various components of IT identified in the endnote above as an industry while recognizing that IT as a general-purpose technology is widely diffused and hence broader than a traditional industry in that it impacts the functioning of all sectors much as power does. Data on IT, such as by COMTRADE and its compendium listed in the

endnote below, report IT statistics as part of the services and hence exclude hardware and peripherals.

23 *International Trade Statistical Yearbook 2019*, Vol. 1, p. 172.

24 Refer to Sharma (2015) for a much fuller book-length account, including origin stories for star Indian IT multinational companies like Wipro, Infosys and Tata Consultancy Services (TCS). He also documented in great detail how members of the Indian diaspora created opportunities and linkages with IT businesses in India for offshore work such as in coding, debugging, data conversion and software writing. This source has been drawn on to tell the Indian IT story.

25 Y2K refers to the coding glitch pertaining to dates, inherited by much software for historic reasons, which would have resulted in a shutdown of many systems in the year 2000 when 00 appeared in the date field.

26 Another opportunity that Indian programmers took timely advantage of was the European currency conversion problem also occurring in Y2K, https://www.cfo.com/banking-capital-markets/1998/04/much-ado-about-the-euro/, consulted 2/14/2021.

27 Few would question that Jawaharlal Nehru's (India's first prime minister) faith in science and technology, as the key to catch up growth, had much to do with India's investments in science and technology and higher education.

28 One telling criticism is that since all levels of education are interrelated, the notion that returns can be calculated for levels separately is flawed.

29 https://www.vedantu.com/iit-jee/iit-colleges-in-india, consulted 11/17/2021.

30 https://www.google.com/search?q=how+many+Indian+Institute+of+science+are+there%3F&source=hp&ei=0Q2VYcDLKJnJtQbq0obwAw&iflsig=ALs-wAMAAAAAYZUb4f2WYp88PYQlz0RD2I89H3kmNXRu&oq=how+many+Indian+Institute+of+science+are+there%3F&gs_lcp=Cgdnd3Mtd2l6EAMyBQgAEIAEMgUIABCGAzIFCAAQhgM6DgguEIAEELEDEMcBEKMCOgsILhCABBDHARCjAjoICAAQgAQQsQM6CwgAEIAEELEDEIMBOggILhCxAxCDAToECAAQQzoRCC4QgAQQsQMQgwEQxwEQowI6CwguEIAEELEDEIMBOgUIABCRAjoICC4QgAQQsQM6CAgAEIAEEMkDOgYIABAWEB46CAgAEBYQChAeOgQIABANOgcIABDJAxANOgQIABAKOgcIABCABBAKUABYgnpgkX1oBnAAeACAAaoBiAGwIZIBBDQ2LjWYAQCgAQE&sclient=gws-wiz&ved=0ahUKEwiA-PGQyp_0AhWZZM0KHWqpAT4Q4dUDCAk&uact=5m, consulted 11/17/21.

31 https://www.careerlauncher.com/cat-mba/List-of-iims-in-india.html#:~:text=into%20an%20IIM%3F-,There%20are%2020%20IIMs%20in%20the%20list%20of%20IIMs%20in,on%20their%202021%20NIRF%20rankings, consulted 11/17/2021.

32 Some of the prominent organizations included the Indian Institute of Science, Indian Space Research Organization, Regional Remote Sensing Service Center, National Aerospace Laboratory, Defense Research and Development Organization and the Indian Institute of Astrophysics, National Law School, National Institute of Advanced Studies and the University of Agricultural Science.

33 Khomiakova (2007) documented that many other Indian states successfully developed their own clusters with a large IT company like WIPRO or TCS playing an anchor and catalytic role. Apart from Bangalore, the other big seven include the National Capital Region (Delhi and suburbs: Noida and Gurgaon), Chennai, Hyderabad, Pune, Mumbai and Kolkata as the other big six metropolitan (Tier I) center clusters engaged, like Bangalore, in hardware design and manufacturing, IT services, software, research and development and IT-enabled services for business process offshoring. In 2005–2006, the big seven clusters accounted for 98 percent of all software exports. However, several Tier II and Tier III cities are engaging in IT activities. Also refer to Rao and Balasubrahmanya (2017) for an account of these seven IT clusters. Ramchandran and Ray (2005, pp. 158–159) provide an account of how the entrepreneurial chief minister of Hyderabad, Chandrababu Naidu, used several industrial policy initiatives to form the Hyderabad cluster to make it more attractive than Bangalore.

34 The satellite data links facilitated the move from "body shopping" (identifying and hiring individuals) to outsourcing contracts to software firms in India.
35 https://nasscom.in/membership-landing, consulted 2/5/2021.
36 Sharma (2015, Chapter 3). IBM was being viewed by the Indian government as profiteering based on importing dated computers and conditioning use on lease and maintenance contracts, transfer pricing, tax avoidance and several other such predatory practices. The sticking point in negotiations was IBM decided against diluting its equity share and losing control.
37 Even so, Kite (2014) argued that IT in India generates many backward and forward linkages with the rest of the economy contrary to what is commonly asserted. Once linkages have been accounted for, he estimated that the total contribution to GDP was about 10.1 percent in 2005–2006, which was more than twice the direct contribution of 4.6 percent. Also, each IT worker contributed about two workers to the rest of the economy, including in the informal sector.

List of References

Atkin et. al. 2016. "On the Origins and Development of Pakistan's Soccer-Ball Cluster," *The World Bank Economic Review*, 30(Supplement_1), S34– S41.

Atkin et. al. 2017. "Organizational Barriers to Technology Adoption: Evidence from Soccer-Ball Producers in Pakistan," *The Quarterly Journal of Economics*, 132(3), 1101–1164.

Bhat, N. A. and S. K. Bhatia. 2016. "Indian Software Industry: Performance and Efficiency," *The Journal of Income and Wealth*, 38(1), 73–86.

Bhatnagar, S. 2006. "India's Software Industry," in eds., V. Chandra and S. Kolavalli, *Technology, Adaptation, and Exports – How Some Developing Countries Got It Right* (Washington, D. C.: World Bank).

Boje, D. M. and F. R. Khan. 2009. "Story-Branding by Empire Entrepreneurs: Nike, Child Labor, and Pakistan's Soccer Ball Industry," *Journal of Small Business and Entrepreneurship*, 22(1), 9–24.

Caniels, M. C. and H. A. Romijn. 2003. "Dynamic Clusters in Developing Countries: Collective Efficiency and Beyond," *Oxford Development Studies*, 31(3), 275–292.

Chaudhry, T. T. 2011. "Contracting and Efficiency in the Surgical Goods Cluster of Sialkot, Pakistan," *South Asia Economic Journal*, 12(1), 91 –115.

Gereffi, G. 1994. "The Organization of Buyer Driven Global Commodity Chains: How U. S. Retailers Shape Overseas Production Networks," in eds., G. Gereffi and M. Korzeniewicz, *Commodity Chains and Global Capitalism* (Westport, Connecticut: Praeger Publishers), 95–122.

Gereffi, G. 1998. "Beyond the Developmental State: East Asia's Political Economies Reconsidered," in eds., S. Chan, C. Clark and D. Lam, *More than the Market, More than the State: Global Commodity Chains and Industrial Upgrading in East Asia* (New York: St. Martin's Press), 38–59.

Gereffi, G. 1999. "International Trade and Industrial Upgrading in the Apparel Commodity Chain," *Journal of International Economics*, 48(1), 37–70.

Gereffi, G. 2000. "Beyond the Producer-Driven / Buyer – Driven Dichotomy: An Expanded Typology of Global Value Chains, With Special Reference to the Internet," Duke University, draft.

Humphrey, J. and H. Schmitz. 2002."How Does Insertion in Global Value Chains Affect Upgrading in Industrial Clusters?," *Regional Studies*, 36(9), 1017–1027.

Kabeer, N. 2000. *The Power to Choose: Bangladeshi Women and Labour Market Decisions in London and Dhaka* (London: Verso).

Khan, F. R. 2008. "Hard Times Recalled: The Child Labor Controversy in Pakistan's Soccer Ball Industry," in ed., K. E. Meyer, *Multinational Enterprises and Host Economies*, Elgar Reference Collection. Globalization of the World Economy Series, (Cheltenham, U.K.: Elgar.), Vol. 21, 492–515.

Khan, S. R. et. al. 2009. *Export Success and Industrial Linkages: The Case of Garment Production in South Asia* (New York: Palgrave/Macmillan).

Khomiakova, T. 2007. "Information Technology Clusters in India," *Transition Studies Review*, 14(2), 355–378.

Kite, G. 2014. "Linked-in? Software and Information Technology Services in India's Economic Development," *Journal of South Asian Development*, 9(2), 99–119.

Lazzeretti, L., S. R. Sedita and A. Caloffi. 2014. "Founders and Disseminators of Cluster Research," *Journal of Economic Geography*, 14(1), 21–43.

Nadvi, K. 1999. "Shifting Ties: Social Networks in the Surgical Instrument Cluster of Sialkot, Pakistan," *Development and Change*, 30(1), 141–175.

Nadvi, K. 2008. "Global Standards, Global Governance and the Organization of Global Value Chains," *Journal of Economic Geography*, 8(3), 323–343.

Nadvi, K. 2011. "Labour Standards and Technological Upgrading: Competitive Challenges in the Global Football Industry," *International Journal of Technological Learning, Innovation and Development*, 4(1/2/3), 235–257.

Nadvi, K. and G. Halder. 2005. "Local Clusters in Global Value Chains: Exploring Dynamic Linkages Between Germany and Pakistan," *Entrepreneurship and Regional Development*, 17(5), 339–363.

Nadvi, K. and H. Schmitz. 1994. "Industrial Clusters in Less Developed Countries: Review of Experiences and Research Agenda," IDS Discussion Paper 339, Institute of Development Studies, University of Sussex, Brighton.

Raikes, P., M. F. Jensen and S. Ponte. 2000. "Global Commodity Chain Analysis and the French Filière Approach: Comparison and Critique," *Economy and Society*, 29(3), 390–417.

Ramchandran, K. and S. Ray. 2005. "Creating Information Technology Industrial Clusters: Learning from Strategies of Early and Late Movers", in eds., T. Thatchenkery and R. R. Stough, *Information Communication Technology and Economic Development: Learning from the Indian Experience* (Northampton, Mass.: Edward Elgar), 149–166.

Rao, P. M. and M. H. Balasubrahmanya. 2017. "The Rise of IT Services Clusters in India: A Case of Growth by Replication," *Telecommunications Policy*, 41(2), 90–105.

Rhee, Y. W. 1990. "The Catalyst Model of Development: Lessons from Bangladesh's Success with Garment Exports," *World Development*, 18(2), 333–346.

Schmitz, H. 1999. "Collective Efficiency and Increasing Returns," *Cambridge Journal of Economics*, 23(4), 465–483.

Sen, A. K. 1990. "Gender and Co-Operative Conflicts," in ed., I. Tinker, *Persistent Inequalities: Women and World Development* (New York: Oxford University Press).

Sharma, D. C. 2015. *The Outsourcer: The Story of India's IT Revolution* (Cambridge, MA: The MIT Press).

Singh, N. 2003. "India's Information Technology Sector: What Contribution to Broader Economic Development?" OECD Development Center Working Paper No. 207, Paris.

Sturgeon, T. J. 2001. "How Do We Define Value Chains and Production Networks?," *Institute of Development Studies Bulletin*, 32(3), 9–18.

Van Dijk, M. P. 2003. "Government Policies with Respect to an Information Technology Cluster in Bangalore, India," *European Journal of Development Research*, 15(2), 93–108.

Wallerstein, I. 1974. *The Modern World System* (New York: Academic Press).

World Bank. 2006. "Bangladesh End of MFA Quotas: Key Issues and Strategic Options for Bangladesh Readymade Garment Industry," Poverty Reduction and Economic Management Sector Unit, South Asian Region, Washington, D. C.

11 India's automobile industry

Partnering with foreign capital

As indicated in the Preface, the Indian vehicle and accessory (parts and components) industry is a success story that belies the neoliberal (structural reform/deregulation – liberalization) vs. developmentalist (industrial policy) dichotomy much as the information technology success story did in Chapter 10. Also, as indicated in Chapter 10, exports are widely considered a measure of success,[1] since they represent a quality indicator, and by that criteria India's vehicles and accessory industry is certainly a success story. It is also a story of partnership between foreign (MNCs) and local capital or buisnesses.

This chapter will start by exploring some foreign direct investment (FDI) concepts as asymmetrical partnerships. These partnerships are between multinational companies (MNC) based in High Income Countries (HICs) and local firms in low- and middle-income countries (L/MICs). The section following provides evidence for the contention that the Indian vehicle and accessory industry is a success story. The literature is drawn on after that to argue that this success is derived from both developmentalist (industrial policy) and neoliberal (structural reforms) policies. The final section concludes.

Asymmetrical capital partnerships: a threat and an opportunity[2]

Associations between MNCs based in HICs and local businesses in L/MICs are obviously asymmetrical given the size and technology advantage of MNCs from HICs that drive the partnership. Heterodox scholars of the neo-Marxist and dependency approaches (Khan, 2014, Chapters 3 and 4) have viewed MNCs with suspicion and a vehicle for the transfer of surplus from L/LMICs to HICs. Recent historical experience indicates that asymmetrical partnerships with foreign capital based in HICs can represent an opportunity that L/LMICs can capitalize on with the right policies and local business dynamism.

Radical political economists have also cited many reasons to be wary of MNCs. To begin with, they warned that the latter are likely to displace local labor-intensive small-scale manufacturing and hence raise unemployment. They also drive out local competition with their access to better technology, risk-taking capacity and scale economies, and hence attain market power to the detriment of local

DOI: 10.4324/9781003176411-15

consumers. Even if they do not completely drive domestic producers out of the market, they force them to produce at a higher point on their average cost curves by capturing market share. FDI is also associated with a rise in inequality since it is mostly elites that benefit via patronage jobs and kickbacks.[3]

MNC products are often viewed as inappropriate for the local market; a notorious example was Nestles milk formula. Women dressed like nurses, and hence as authority figures touted the benefits of formula in advertisements. The problem is that formula requires sterilized bottles in villages where getting potable water is a major chore. Often mother's milk would dry up after the free samples were used up and ill-prepared formula with dirty unboiled water did more harm than good. Meanwhile, the infants were deprived of immunities that come with mother's milk.[4]

Perhaps the most pernicious practice is transfer pricing. This is a form of tax evasion that results from buying inputs from a subsidiary in another country at inflated prices and selling the final product at a low price to show low profits in the host country. Internal accounting can thus show profits where it suits the MNC, generally in tax havens such as the Bahamas or Panama. Since an increasing amount of world trade is inter-MNC, reference prices are not easily available to tax authorities to offset these practices even if they had the capacity to do so.[5] Since MNCs internally source most of their inputs, they have limited linkages with the rest of the economy. A local brain drain also results from their ability to offer better salaries and career prospects.

Overall, critics argued that high royalties, high interest on loans, licensing fees, transfer of dividends and profits mean a massive resource outflow. MNCs jealously guard their technology and are not interested in building local R&D capacity. So, for all the resource outflows, the contention is that L/LMICs get back little in exchange. In fact, with their higher credit ratings, MNCs can tap local credit markets and crowd out local firms instead of bringing in funds.

Studwell (2013) argued that Southeast Asian countries like Malaysia, Thailand, Indonesia and the Philippines engaged extensively with MNCs but got locked into assembly and hence stayed stuck at the lower rungs of the value chain. MNCs have no interest in engineering L/LMIC export success since the fewer the competitors the better.

As indicated above, most MNCs have revenues that dwarf host country GDP and this gives them bargaining power with both the host and home country. For example, they are able to influence home country aid allocations to suit their purposes such as for selective infrastructure development. Size also enables MNCs to engage in questionable political activities to protect their interests. A notorious case is that of International Telephone and Telegraph (ITT) Corporation funding a political campaign against candidate Allende's socialist party in Chile and then funding activities and soliciting US government support to destabilize and overthrow the successful socialist government once it won office via democratic elections.[6]

Notwithstanding the critique above, L/LMICs actively solicit FDI. A cynical view is that political elites gain through kickbacks and jobs for themselves and their offspring, while society loses. It is nonetheless possible that political elites are accountable, even if only through the imperfect mechanisms of elections or social discontent that constrains them to act at least partially for the social good. A more charitable view is that policy makers are also driven by patriotism and they also seek potential gain from soliciting FDI.

They might solicit FDI to benefit from the transfer of technology, marketing knowledge, managerial skills, including quality control procedures, funds inflow, exports (to stabilize the balance of payments), tax revenues and employment. While the critique above suggests that for various reasons none of these objectives are likely to be achieved, the Indian vehicle and accessory case study narrated in this chapter represents a counter example as did the case studies of garment exports from Bangladesh and information technology exports from India.

For successfully gaining from the asymmetrical partnership, developmentalist scholars argue that L/LMICs need to create absorption capacity (Lall and Narula, 2004). Sound institutions and governance, infrastructure and financial development create absorption capacity and that is what makes the difference with regard to benefiting from FDI. The argument then is that MNCs build on host country strengths because this is what also determines their profitability.

Industrial policy in conjunction with investment, technology, competition and trade policies can help in building these capacities. They argue that a completely hands-off neoliberal approach is meaningless. Linkages and spillover effects in the non-natural resource sectors (backward, horizontal, forward) cannot be taken for granted if host country capacity is not there.[7] In fact, in this case FDI can be detrimental because there can be crowding out of domestic investment.

L/LMICs can insert themselves into value chains and this can help with industrialization so long as they view such insertion as a stepping-stone to building full production capacity and going on to OBM (own brand manufacturing) as the Indian vehicle and accessory industry has successfully managed to do. The next section provides evidence that India got it right in partnering with Japanese and Western capital, while Pakistan is still struggling.

Evidence on the success of the Indian vehicle and accessory industry

Appendix Table 11.1 compares Indian vehicle and accessory exports with Pakistan, which is another large country[8] with a partnership with Japanese capital. The predetermined criteria for export item selection for comparison were those where either country ranked as a top 20 exporter in the vehicle and accessory six-digit harmonized system (HS) classification.

Appendix Table 11.1 presents a broad picture of India's success in the vehicle and accessory industry. Of the 80 products in this broad category, India was among the top 20 world exporters in 39 products and a top 10 world exporters in 10 products. By comparison, Pakistan ranked 20th in only one product. The growth rates in units exported for India are astronomical, but these have not been computed and reported because of the small base for the year the reported exports began.

India's rank in Appendix Table 11.1 is understated by one or two positions because world rankings include individual European countries and the EU as separate entities and also a combined category of Other Asia that sometimes outranks India. Thus, India is referred to as a top 20 exporter even with a rank of 21 or sometimes 22. There are also several products in which India is not yet a top 20 exporter but quantitatively a significant player. These products do not show up in Appendix Table 11.1 based on the adopted selection criteria.

Other than bicycle parts, in which it consistently ranked as a top ten exporter country in 2019, it ranked second as an exporter of motorcycles (>50 cc but <250 cc). Other products in which it is a top ten exporter include track laying tractors and tractors, automobiles up to 1,000 cc, dump trucks, chassis (fitted with engine), motorcycles (>250 cc but <500 cc and >500 cc but <800 cc), motor cycle parts and non-mechanical invalid carriages.

The two base years selected to show the increase in exports are 1988 and 1991, though in some cases data on these base years are not available. The data in most cases extend back to 1988. The year 1991 has been selected as an alternative base year to demonstrate that the explosive growth in vehicle and accessory exports occurred mostly after the 1991 reforms (Chapter 2). In almost all cases, exports in 1988 and 1991 were miniscule compared to 2019.

The two exceptions are the decline in exports of motor vehicle bodies and bicycle parts relative to 1988 and 1991, and this is interesting in that it reflects India's move up the value chain. Thus, even though India still ranks as a top ten exporter in all bicycle parts and in motorcycle parts, its exports of these products in a majority of the products (except brakes, pedals and crank gears and parts) are in rapid decline relative to the base years, while the exports of bicycles and motorcycles have rapidly picked up. While it does not have a presence in the top 20 in mechanically propelled larger vehicles like trailers and semitrailers and tankers, it has also established a presence in these markets.

While1988 is the earliest year for which World Integrated Trade Solutions (WITS) export data are available for India, even so, it is possible to glean some information from data using 1988 as the base year and 1991 as the terminal year. It appears that for 15 out of 39 products, the export momentum was well underway prior to 1991. However, for another 15 products, there was actually a decline in exports between 1988 and 1991, which subsequently picked up. This may reflect the crisis period in the Indian economy prior to the 1991 reforms, exacerbated by the import intensity of production due to collaboration with Japanese capital and the appreciation of the yen and foreign exchange scarcity (D'Costa, 1995). It is not possible from such descriptive analysis to attribute causality to reforms, but there is little question that in all cases, other than the exceptions noted above, there was explosive export growth subsequent to the 1991 reforms.[9]

Particularly interesting in this comparison are the exports of automobiles in which the partnership with Japanese and Western capital is particularly evident. India has managed to make it to the top 10 export list in the <1,000 cc passenger car category and in the top 20 in the >1,000 cc and <1,500 cc passenger car categories. In addition, it has a top 10 ranking in dump trucks and a top 20 ranking in two diesel engine vehicles.

Unlike India, Pakistan has not been able to capitalize on the opportunity the partnership with Japanese capital provided. In comparison to India's superlative performance, Pakistan's export ranking is very low and in six cases it had no ranking at all, as indicated in Appendix Table 11.1. It has barely got its foot in the door as an exporter. It ranked in the top 20 and matched India's export share in only one product (mobile drilling derricks).

Pakistan lost market share relative to its base year for 8 out of the 30 products; it has some, albeit tiny, market share. It faced a decline in the little market share it had of diesel engine vehicle bumpers, drive-axles and steering wheels, bicycles, bicycle frames and parts, hubs and sprocket wheels and saddles. It also lost market share for non-mechanically propelled trailers, semitrailers and other vehicle parts. The base year for Pakistan shows it has been late getting into the game, and while there has been notable growth relative to the base period in about half the products it has an export presence in, the magnitudes and the changes are dwarfed by India's performance.

Explaining success

There are two main explanations for export success in the development economics literature. The mainstream neoliberal view is that deregulation of an industry and liberalizations, such as of the exchange rate, trade and FDI make an industry competitive and attain the potential for export success. Deregulation reduces production barriers, transaction costs and covert expenses. Trade liberalization reduces import costs, making raw materials and intermediate inputs cheaper, and competitive pressures force an industry to be competitive. FDI brings in technology and managerial and marketing skills, among other advantages mentioned above, and thus provides a potential fillip to local industry.

The developmentalist industrial policy (IP) explanation is an alternative and could be interpreted to be one of sequencing. The argument is that industry needs to be shielded and nurtured to ensure its survival from competitive pressures of large global players (MNCs based in HICs), and that is the only way to ensure the creation and survival of an industry. However, IP advocates are not opposed to neoliberal structural reforms per se, but the issue is one of sequencing and timing. While the latter is more an art than a science, it appears that India's structural reforms fortuitously came at the right time since import substitution industrialization (ISI) had established a base for the vehicle and accessory industry. Similarly, developmentalists are not opposed to FDI per se. However, they argue that L/MICs need to be selective and cautious to ensure that they are furthering the local agenda rather than resulting in L/LMIC industries becoming cogs in the global MNC agenda.

The growing middle class in India made it attractive for foreign capital, particular the Japanese with their specialization in small cars. D'Costa (1995) argued that despite the 1991 liberalization and deregulation reforms, the Indian state remained involved in trying to build the auto industry. For example, it strictly enforced local content rules and fostered Maruti Udyog Limited (MUL), a joint venture between Suzuki Motors and the Government of India. By the mid-1990s, MUL had a 60 percent market share of passenger cars. Older less efficient companies responded with partnerships with other foreign companies such as Toyota, Mitsubishi, Nissan and Mazda. The success of MUL specifically, and the inroads of Japanese capital, also attracted US and Western European capital-seeking joint ventures with Indian capital. However, the older firms initially found it difficult to replicate MUL's success.

D'Costa (1995) made several important points. He documented that the deregulation, doing away with production controls, had begun with the Industrial Policy Statements of 1977 and 1980[10] and that the focus on 1991 as the turning point is in this sense misplaced since the transformation of the Indian vehicle industry began in the 1980s. The focus on fuel efficiency due to heavy import bills and foreign exchange scarcity encouraged the small passenger car market.

In this regard, the largest Japanese multinational partnership with Suzuki (MUL) was with state (Central) rather than private capital and the state protected this venture via exclusion (licensing) policies in the initial stage. The established Indian vehicle companies remained the largest players in the commercial vehicle and parts markets, in which there was no state sector presence. These large private companies often engaged with Japanese and Western capital in technology-buying joint ventures. Indian capital understood the intricacies of operating in the complex Indian market and facilitated foreign capital such that both could benefit. These points underscore that the Indian vehicle success story is not a straightforward neoliberal story following the 1991 reforms.

Nonetheless, it is also clear that the 1991 and subsequent reforms in early noughties, to become consistent with WTO mandates, further unleashed the production potential of the Indian vehicle and parts industry.[11] One consequence of these sets of reforms was that FDI took off, including in the vehicle and accessory industry (D'Costa, 2004), particularly with the removal of foreign ownership ceilings in 2000. Simultaneously, partnership with the state continued to be important. For example, D'Costa (2004) documented how the Automotive Component Manufacturing Association (ACMA) in partnership with MUL (based in New Delhi) were able to lobby for facilitative policy changes.

D'Costa (2004) also pointed out that other factors in the success of the industry were a partnership with labor. For example, MUL also adopted Japanese labor management institutions like company unions, worker participation, quality circles, worker bonuses for suggestions, continual improvement and cost cutting (kaizen), cellularization of the production process, job security and higher wages associated with quality and higher productivity to ensure labor management harmony rather a conflictual relationship.

Partnerships among firms in accessory clusters, led and facilitated by MUL, also played a key role in removing small firm uncertainty (Chapter 10). MUL engaged in equity partnerships, selectively introduced new product technology and licensed technology as needed. Knowledge transfers via technical advice both in Japan and on location enhanced productivity.

MUL invested in building the skill levels of its supply chain via vendor rating, requiring standards certification (IS0 9000), and awards. It also built vendor capacity via training, domestically and in Japan, technical advice and trouble-shooting and problem-solving. The emphasis was "on improving quality and reducing rejections, waste, and costs" (Okada, 2004, p. 1275). Interfirm cooperation in the clustering and technology transfer also eased MUL's manufacturing supply constraints and enabled a diffusion of technology, and several Indian firms became original equipment manufacturers of automobile components. Interfirm partnerships in clusters also enabled the institutionalization in MUL of successful Japanese management practices such as flexible production and "just in time" delivery (Chapter 10).

Other joint ventures in commercial vehicles between Japanese capital and local legacy capital initially did not meet with MUL's success. The joint ventures that relied on imports rather than local content also suffered from a yen appreciation and the turnkey nature of the projects discouraged indigenization. By contrast, wholly Indian-owned Tata Engineering and Locomotive Company (TELCO) was able to replicate MUL's practices in producing commercial vehicles and met with similar success. D'Costa (2004) concluded from this that success did not necessarily follow from a partnership of foreign and local capital per se but from business and managerial practices. These were pioneered by MUL for passenger cars and accessories and TELCO replicated them initially for commercial vehicles.

TELCO was also able to rely on cordial labor relations and established and created networks to address supply issues and produce at scale that the joint ventures were unable to do in a fragmented market. Skilled and semiskilled worker arrangements between TELCO and other producers like Bajaj Autos reduced labor costs and diffused skills and quality consciousness (Okada, 2004). TELCO's success in commercial vehicle production enabled it to make inroads into the passenger car market.

Foreign firms used partnerships with Indian capital for importing completely knockdown kits for local assembly (Park, 2004). This inherently limits the positive externalities the Indian state would hope in encouraging the engagement with foreign capital. Local firms were initially mostly involved as suppliers of parts and components (Athukorala and Veeramani, 2019). Nonetheless, local conglomerates demonstrated the capacity to become independent global players and strategically partnered with foreign capital and terminated partnerships as suited their needs. Tata Motors has become an exporting powerhouse, and after-sales service was a key facilitator in this regard. Its takeover of Jaguar and Rover in 2008, with the conglomerate's cash reserves, was a strategic decision to enhance technological catchup and marketing and to strengthen its brand (Richet and Ruet, 2008). The export growth record in Appendix Table 11.1 speaks for itself.

Apart from its strategic, pioneering and leadership role in partnering with Suzuki and creating MUL, the central and state governments took a back seat and facilitated diversified private sector conglomerates like Tata, Mahindra & Mahindra and Ashok Leyland. For example, the state of Karnataka attracted Toyota via its joint venture partner Kirloskar (Richet and Ruet, 2008, p. 449). Also, the central government gradually reduced and then completely divested (retaining one managing director) its ownership stake in MUL from the initial 80 percent. However, the state's presence was felt until complete deregulation[12] in 1995 and assemblers/producers and accessory suppliers responded to the state's demand for localization, technology transfer and indigenization of productive capacity via local content rules (D'Costa, 2009).

Summary and conclusions

This chapter argues that just as the ISI vs. EP was a false dichotomy in the development economics literature, so is the current structural reform vs. industrial policy debate. The success of the Indian vehicle and accessory industry represents a success of both policies. Industrial policy built the base of this industry and structural reforms (liberalization, deregulation) unleashed the productive potential of that base but with continued state support.

The chapter also argues that an asymmetrical partnership with foreign capital represents both a threat and an opportunity. Countries can get locked into assembly and hence stay stuck at the lower rungs of the value chain that serves the MNC agenda. Foreign capital has no intrinsic interest in engineering the success of an industry in a L/LMIC since a successful junior partner can win market share from the senior partner. This is precisely what India managed to do with sensible policies, competitive practices, adoption and adaptation of MNC management practices and technology and technology diffusion.

By contrast, judging by export performance, the Pakistani vehicle and accessory industry appears to have fallen into the classic trap of getting locked into assembly and getting stuck in the lower rungs of the value chain. Sialkot (Chapter 10) with its competitive and dynamic business ethos has shown the way and clusters serving conglomerates in a competitive environment could be a solution for Pakistan's lagging vehicle and accessory industry. Based on impressionistic evidence and interviews, Pakistan seems to have adopted an alternative route where crony capitalist firms seek rents in a predatory mutually enriching (companies, bureaucrats and politicians) patronage system that bankrupts the state by emptying the coffers and the country by undermining wealth creation.

A competitive environment could be oligopolistic as has been the case for Indian conglomerates. This model of competition policy was perfected by the Japanese and the South Koreans after them (Khan, 2010). The point is the quid pro quo. Firms are facilitated and get incentives but have to deliver results in terms of productivity, profits, tax revenues and primarily exports, as a marker of quality, or face being left out in the cold. Indian exporting success is once again a success of partnerships; this time that of the state, local and foreign capital and labor.

Appendix Table 11.1 Indian and Pakistani vehicle and accessory exports (HS-87)

Export item	*Rank in world exports in 2019*	*Total value of exports in 2019 (million $)*	*Quantity of exports in 2019*	*Quantity units*	*Quantity of exports in base years*
Tractors; pedestrian controlled (HS-870110)					
India	11	3.27	387	Item	16 (1993)
Pakistan	38	0.23	9,472	Item	1 (2003)
Tractors; road, for semitrailers (HS-870120)					
India	18	40.36	3,738	Item	6 (1992)
Pakistan	30	10.20	2,033	Item	227 (2003)
Tractors; track-laying (HS-870130)					
India	6	47.10	3,742	Item	241 (1988) 2 (1991)
Pakistan	29	0.94	218	Item	55 (2003)
Tractors (HS-870190)					
India	9	762.16	72,128	Item	44 (1988) 67 (1991)
Pakistan	37	12.46	2,525	Item	850 (2003)
Compression ignition vehicles; public transport type (10 persons or more) (HS-870210)					
India	16	197.36	6,599	Item	3 (1988) 2,004 (1991)
Pakistan	83	0.23	4 (2018)	Item	5 (2003)
Vehicles (up to 1,000 cc) (HS-870321)					
India	9	1,554.91	608,344	Item	357 (1988) 17,362 (1991)
Pakistan	59	0.58	3,533 (2017)	Item	2 (2003)
Vehicles (> 1,000 cc but < 1,500 cc) (HS-870322)					
India	16	3,178.16	410,619	Item	275 (1988) 135 (1991)
Pakistan	78	0.18	34	Item	2 (2003)
Dumpers for off highway use designed for goods transport (HS-870410)					
India	7	362.81	730	Item	510 (1988) 85 (1991)

(*Continued*)

Appendix Table 11.1 (Continued)

Export item	*Rank in world exports in 2019*	*Total value of exports in 2019 (million $)*	*Quantity of exports in 2019*	*Quantity units*	*Quantity of exports in base years*
Pakistan	Not ranked				
Diesel engine vehicles for goods transport, < 5 tonnes (HS-870421)					
India	21	219.29	38,299	Item	1,214 (1988) 123 (1991)
Pakistan	106	0.005	5	Item	20 (2003)
Diesel engine vehicles for goods transport, > 5 tonnes but < 20 tonnes (HS-870422)					
India	14	247.79	17,165	Item	16 (1993)
Pakistan	91	0.007	2	Item	63 (2005)
Diesel engine vehicles for goods transport, > 20 tonnes (HS-870423)					
India	17	155.78	5,285	Item	36 (1993)
Pakistan	48	3.29	79	Item	1 (2005)
Mobile drilling derricks (HS-870520)					
India	21	0.92	15	Item	1 (1994)
Pakistan	22	0.70	21	Item	2 (2007)
Concrete mixer lorries (HS-870540)					
India	13	6.50	170	Item	3 (1999)
Pakistan	44	0.43	7	Item	5 (2007)
Chassis, fitted with engine (HS-870600)					
India	4	380.64	125,943 (2016)	Item	1,654 (1988) 4,029 (1991)
Pakistan	Not ranked				
Motor vehicle bodies (HS-870710)					
India	19	9.80	425 (216)	Item	507,306 (1988) 41,826 (1991)
Pakistan	59	.02	2	Item	2 (2003)
Bumpers and related parts (HS-870810)					
India	22	90.83	14,491,600	Kg	3,695,280 (1988) 6,073,590 (1991)

(*Continued*)

Appendix Table 11.1 (Continued)

Export item	*Rank in world exports in 2019*	*Total value of exports in 2019 (million $)*	*Quantity of exports in 2019*	*Quantity units*	*Quantity of exports in base years*
Pakistan	57	0.35	155,511	Kg	734,774 (1988)
Safety belts (870821)					
India	13	52.77	6,283,350	Kg	6,383 (1988) 2,214 (1991)
Pakistan	79	0.01	300	Kg	195 (2003)
Brakes and parts (870839)					
India	16	491.81	75,561,900	Kg	305,650 (1988) 88,488 (1991)
Pakistan	79	0.08	25,798	Kg	1,305 (2004)
Gear boxes (HS-870840)					
India	22	416.02	46,094,000	Kg	33,102 (1988) 343,187 (1991)
Pakistan	47	6.77	2,062,650	Kg	21,639 (2003)
Drive axles (HS-870850)					
India	17	388.90	66,433,00	Kg	41,976 (1988) 485,609 (1991)
Pakistan	67	0.16	2,260 (2018)	Kg	30,691 (2004)
Silencers and exhaust pipes (HS-870892)					
India	20	138.22	18,612,100	Kg	4,000 (1988) 1,875 (1991)
Pakistan	63	2.33	109,058	Kg	902 (2004)
Steering wheels (HS-870894)					
India	20	197.21	18,746,200	Kg	44,183 (1988) 35,478 (1991)
Pakistan	69	0.71	4,105	Kg	11,820 (2007)
Parts and accessories (HS-870899)					

(Continued)

Appendix Table 11.1 (Continued)

Export item	*Rank in world exports in 2019*	*Total value of exports in 2019 (million $)*	*Quantity of exports in 2019*	*Quantity units*	*Quantity of exports in base years*
India	12	2,678.62	427,976,000	Kg	16,359,800 (1988) 23,282,000 (1991)
Pakistan	65	7.16	662,559	Kg	4,779,140 (1988)
Motorcycles (< 50 cc) (HS-871110)					
India	14	12.65	11,629	Item	1,264 (1988) 9,755 (1991)
Pakistan	52	0.02	16 (2018)	Item	1 (2003)
Motorcycles > 50 cc but < 250 cc (HS-871120)					
India	2	1,870.13	3,049,240	Item	11,141 (1988) 9,755 (1991)
Pakistan	46	8.59	1,905	Item	70 (2003)
Motorcycles > 250 cc but < 500 cc (HS-871130)					
India	7	139.54	64,304	Item	1,224 (1988) 2,388 (1991)
Pakistan	60	0.07	161	Item	7 (2003)
Motorcycles > 500 cc but < 800 cc (HS-871140)					
India	9	69.29	21,099	Item	457 (1988) 452 (1991)
Pakistan	Not ranked				
Bicycles (HS-871200)					
India	23	47.17	1,237,330	Item	172,530 (1988) 601,704 (1991)
Pakistan	76	0.02	136	Item	6,717 (2003)
Non mechanical invalid carriages (HS-871310)					
India	8	23.73	173,855	Item	120 (1995)
Pakistan	Not ranked				
Motorcycle parts (not saddles) (HS-871419)					

(*Continued*)

Appendix Table 11.1 (Continued)

Export item	*Rank in world exports in 2019*	*Total value of exports in 2019 (million $)*	*Quantity of exports in 2019*	*Quantity units*	*Quantity of exports in base years*
India	9	349.96	75,213,200	Kg	1,019,270 (1988) 1,704,980 (1991)
Pakistan	60	0.36	106,962	Kg	32,067 (2003)
Non mechanical invalid carriage parts (HS-871420)					
India	15	13.63	2,047,420	Kg	207,032 (1988) 340,496 (1991)
Pakistan	Not ranked				
Cycle frames and forks (HS-871491)					
India	7	57.78	395,630	Kg	426,980 (1988) 2,374,980 (1991)
Pakistan	72	0.08	800	Kg	32,067 (2003)
Cycle rims and spokes (HS-871492)					
India	9	15.85	719,192	Kg	8,147,654 (1988) 16,840,600 (1991)
Pakistan	Not ranked				
Cycle hubs and sprocket wheels (HS-871493)					
India	9	25.02	12,281,400	Kg	18,907,200 (1998) 34,493,900 (1991)
Pakistan	55	0.05	2,000	Kg	204,517 (2003)
Cycle breaks (HS-871494)					
India	8	34.59	9,874,130	Kg	377,377 (1988) 274,287 (1991)

(*Continued*)

Appendix Table 11.1 (Continued)

Export item	*Rank in world exports in 2019*	*Total value of exports in 2019 (million $)*	*Quantity of exports in 2019*	*Quantity units*	*Quantity of exports in base years*
Pakistan	Not ranked				
Cycle saddles (HS-871494) – 2018					
India	10	4.76	138,034	Item	1,153,030 (1988) 2,168,520 (1991)
Pakistan	Not ranked				
Cycle pedals and crank gears and parts thereof (HS-871495)					
India	12	21.09	11,804,400	Kg	1,061,860 (1988) 1,011,050 (1991)
Pakistan	65	0.01	300	Kg	627 (2007)
Other cycle parts (HS-871496)					
India	10	96.70	28,516,500	Kg	14,066,500 (1988) 15,951,000 (1991)
Pakistan	64	0.10	33,921	Kg	200 (2003)
Nonmechanically propelled trailers, semitrailers and other vehicle parts (HS-871690)					
India	18	100.62	26,826,600	Kg	1,352,250 (1988) 161,847 (1991)
Pakistan	71	1.32	32,555	Kg	271,314 (2003)

Source: Constructed by author based on World Integrated Trade Solutions (WITS) data set, https://wits.worldbank.org/trade/comtrade/en/country/ALL/year/2019/tradeflow/Exports/partner/WLD/product/901890, Consulted, 1/24/2021.

Notes

1 In principle, export subsidies rather than quality and price competitiveness could generate exports. However, under the current WTO trade regime, such subsidies are difficult to institute and could draw the attention of competitors and trigger disputes.

2 This section draws on Khan (2020, Chapter 12).

3 Herzer, Hühne and Nunnenkamp (2014) showed using panel data that inequality is positively associated with inflows of FDI in Latin American economies, most likely by enhancing skilled labor wages.
4 https://www.businessinsider.com/nestles-infant-formula-scandal-2012-6#hospitals-were-also-accused-of-pushing-mothers-to-use-formula-7, consulted 3/17/2019.
5 HICs, faced with resource constraints, have in principle come up with a tax deal to ensure MNCs pay a minimum amount of tax of 15 percent in a G-7 meeting. While getting individual country approval and operationalizing the deal is a long way off, if it goes through, L/LMIC also stand to gain from this shift in resources from MNCs to nation states. See, for example, https://www.cnbc.com/2021/06/05/g-7-nations-reach-historic-deal-on-global-tax-reform.html, consulted 6/18/2021.
6 https://www.nytimes.com/1972/07/03/archives/papers-show-itt-urged-us-to-help-oust-allende-suggestions-for.html, consulted 3/17/2019.
7 Few linkages and spillovers are expected in the natural resource industries.
8 Pakistan's population was estimated by the UN to be 224 million in 2021. It is large enough for economies of scale and scope. https://www.worldometers.info/world-population/pakistan-population/#:~:text=The%20current%20population%20of%20Pakistan,the%20latest%20United%20Nations%20data, consulted 4/3/2021.
9 Narayan (2006) and Athukorala and Veeramani (2019) quantitatively estimated the causes of export success using firms and trading partners as the unit of analyses for the period 1980–1981 and 1995–1996 and 1988–2015, respectively.
10 Export incentives introduced in the 1980s were removed with the 1991 liberalizations (Narayan, 2006, p. 450).
11 Refer to Athukorala and Veeramani (2019) for a brief review of policy regimes applicable to the Indian automobile industry. For FDI liberalization pertaining to the 1991 reforms, refer to Park (2004).
12 This included, in principle, the untouchable reservation policy for encouraging small-scale industry that produced accessories and had to respond to the quality demands of assemblers or producers, including with scale economies.

List of References

Athukorala, P.-C. and C. Veeramani. 2019. "From Import Substitution to Integration into Global Production Networks: The Case of the Indian Automobile Industry," *Asian Development Review*, 36(2), 72–99.

D'Costa, A. P. 1995. "The Restructuring of the Indian Automobile Industry: Indian State and Japanese Capital," *World Development*, 23(3), 485–502.

D'Costa, A. P. 2004. "Flexible Practices for Mass Production Goals: Economic Governance in the Indian Automobile Industry," *Industrial and Corporate Change*, 13(2), 335–367.

D'Costa, A. P. 2009. "Economic Nationalism in Motion: Steel, Auto, and Software Industries in India," *Review of International Political Economy*, 16(4), 620–648.

Herzer, D., P. Hühne and P. Nunnenkam. 2014. "FDI and Income Inequality—Evidence from Latin American Economies," *Review of Development Economics*, 18(4), 778–793.

Khan, S. R. 2010. "Towards New Developmentalism: Context, Programs, and Constraints," in eds., S. R. Khan and J. Christiansen, *Market as Means Rather than Master: Towards New Developmentalism* (London: Routledge), 226–252.

Khan, S. R. 2014. *A History of Development Economics Thought: Challenges and Counter-Challenges* (New York: Routledge).

Lall, S. and R. Narula. 2004. "Foreign Direct Investment and its Role in Economic Development: Do We Need a New Agenda?" *The European Journal of Development Research*, 16(3), 447–464.

Narayan, K. 2006. "Technology Acquisition and Export Competitiveness: Evidence from the Indian Automobile Industry," in eds., S. D. Tendulkar et. al., *Industrialization in a Reforming Economy: Essays for K L Krishna* (New Delhi: Academic Foundation), 439–470.

Okada, A. 2004. "Skills Development and Interfirm Learning Linkages under Globalization: Lessons from the Indian Automobile Industry", *World Development*, 32(7), 1265–1288.

Park, J. 2004. "Korean Perspective on FDI in India: Hyundai Motors' Industrial Cluster," *Economic and Political Weekly*, 39(31), 3551–3555.

Richet, X. and J. Ruet. 2008. "The Chinese and Indian Automobile Industry in Perspective: Technology Appropriation, Catching-up and Development," *Transition Studies Review*, 15(3), 447–465.

Studwell, J. 2013. *How Asia Works: Success and Failure in the World's Most Dynamic Region* (New York: Grove).

Part 5

Summary and conclusions

12 Summary and conclusion

Economic development, and development more broadly, are complex processes and the main theme of this book is that there is no simple recipe, but when successes occur, they are often the product of partnerships. The chapters in the four parts of this book explore successes at the macro-, meso- and microlevel. In all cases, these successes depended on partnerships and hence the subtitle of the book: "a story of partnerships".

An overview of South Asian development and economic development is provided in Chapter 1 of Part 1 of this book to provide a context for the book and for Chapter 2 of Part 1. Chapter 2 explores India's impressive economic success that defied the odds to produce spectacular catch-up growth that lasted several decades and hence resulted in a doubling and redoubling of its per capita GDP.

This catch-up growth in India generated an important debate in the development economics literature and Chapter 2 provides an opportunity for reviewing it. It also provides an opportunity to review another theme of this book, which is that economic development defies simplistic dichotomies such as import substitution industrialization (ISI) vs. export promotion (EP) as economic development strategies or neoliberalism vs. developmentalism as broader approaches to economic development.

India devised a set of reforms in the early 1990s in response to a fiscal crisis under the tutelage of an ex-World Bank finance minister. Many development economists view these to be classic neoliberal reforms and the cause of India's subsequent catch-up growth. However, this issue is contested with some development economists timing the catch-up growth to an earlier period of pro-business (rather than pro-market) developmentalist reforms and arguing that India remains interventionist.

Thus, while some economists claimed that market-driven "pro-entry" (neoliberal) reforms explained the Indian takeoff others claimed this to be based on pro-business and pro-incumbent developmentalist policies. Many prominent economists have contributed to this debate and this literature has lessons for South Asia and beyond. Our conclusion from reviewing this literature is that answers and insights lie beyond simple dichotomies.

Turning to the meso-context in Part 2 reviews state and civil society partnerships in various poverty alleviation initiatives. Chapter 3 reviews grassroots

DOI: 10.4324/9781003176411-17

development or participatory approaches that gained prominence in the 1970s. This was also referred to as people-centered development. This approach was a reaction to the mainstream top-down/trickle down approach focusing on capital accumulation and economic growth. Poverty and inequality were viewed to have increased in low- and low-middle-income countries (L/LMICs) and this alternative approach held that to mitigate these problems, one had to engage directly with the so-called subjects of development and empower them to engage in collective action to enhance their own well-being. Development NGOs became the agents of participatory development.

Pakistan developed a novel approach to participatory rural development based on the thinking of two practitioners, Akhtar Hameed Khan and Shoaib Sultan Khan. This has taken the form of a public–civil society partnership whereby a network of Rural Support Programs (RSPs) went to scale in catalyzing the formation of hundreds of thousands of community, village and supra-village organizations across the country based on the principle of mobilizing social capital for collective action.

The basic needs approach of the 1970s and the human development approaches of the 1990s complemented this approach. In fact, one could argue that participation is a mechanism that can be used to make these other approaches more effective. While other South Asian countries like India, Nepal and Sri Lanka (among the first) have extensively used participatory development, this Pakistani RSP initiative is interesting in that the public sector–civil society partnership took this poverty alleviation initiative to a national scale. The partnership included the private sector for input supply, credit and output processing, and donors became highly impressed with the initiative and nurtured it.

Sri Lanka's human development index of .63 in 1970 exceeded what most South Asian countries had attained by 2018 and so investing in humans has been a cornerstone of its development approach. There was debate among economists about whether investing in people (human development) needs to be prioritized, and the more orthodox view is that economic growth should be prioritized and human development follows since there is a high correlation between the two variables. Sri Lanka showed the way in South Asia even prior to the crystallization of this debate. It invested massively in the human development of its population even prior to its independence, mostly based on a state-led initiative, and also was among the first South Asian countries to attain middle-income status.

Another state-led poverty alleviation initiative is the Employment Guarantee Scheme (EGS) in India. It was first implemented in 1979 in Maharashtra for the uplift of the rural poor. Even in 2012, about 70 percent of India's population remained rural. Self-revelation by the poor, which obviates the administrative need for targeting, was among the novel features of the scheme. Other social benefits include increasing social inclusion of lower castes and females into the workforce. The scheme has critics charging administrative incompetence and rent-seeking. Since the scheme has been around for almost four decades in various manifestations, it was possible to review the large empirical literature and, while critics raise important points, the positives appear to outweigh the negatives and addressing shortcomings raised by the critics should strengthen the initiative further. As with the human development interventions in Sri Lanka, one way to make the EGS initiative more effective is via partnerships with civil society.

Mohammed Yunus is widely credited to be the founder of microcredit in 1983 in Bangladesh. However, the popularity of microcredit as a poverty initiative and its rapid diffusion also drew scholarly attention and harsh criticism on several counts. These critiques are explored in Chapter 6 and Akhuwat's interest-free microcredit initiative that presented itself as an alternative model not subject to the same shortcomings is evaluated. Akhuwat is deemed to be a success evaluated on several counts, and its partnership with the state enabled it to attain scale.

Continuing with the meso-context in Part 3, Chapter 7 argues that demography interacts closely with the economy. The phenomenal drop in the fertility rate in Bangladesh excited the attention of demographers for good reason. At the time of independence in 1971, its population exceeded that of Pakistan (then West Pakistan). By 2018, its population at 161.4 million was only three-fourths of Pakistan. Chapter 7 reviews the debate on the decline in fertility rate in Bangladesh with a focus on the effectiveness of policy measures. It concludes that while the state deserves much credit, the success of the Bangladeshi state in containing the fertility rate was enhanced by its partnership with foreign donors and civil society, including development NGOs and the clergy.

Joint Forest Management (JFM) is an experiment in public–private partnership and Nepal is viewed as a front runner in South Asia in this regard with India's success also notable. In Nepal for example, by the mid-2000s, about 4,500 Forest Committees (FCs) were created with an outreach effecting 35 percent of the country's population and a quarter of the nation's forests. The rate of formation of these committees at the turn of the twentieth century was about 2,000 per year. The contribution to household income was estimated to be 29 percent (fuelwood 19 percent and fodder and leaf litter about 10 percent). About 11 percent of the total forest area had been covered by these user groups and deforestation appeared to have been reversed. While India has also had success with JFM, the devolution of power to the FCs (public–private partnership) is considered to be much more far-reaching in Nepal compared to the JFM of India and Nepal's success to date is more dramatic.

Part 4 of this book explores successful business initiatives at the microlevel. While most of these successes are driven by the private sector, one is a unique state sector–driven producer cooperative. This represents an alternative form of organizing production within the market system that privileges labor rather than capital. Some of the characteristics include employee ownership and worker participation in decision making. Employee ownership means that labor procures capital rather than the other way round. Since labor procures capital, the risk is borne by labor rather than capital and hence residual income after expenses accrues to labor. This entails the sharing of the residual income among workers as mutually agreed upon. Among the most famous of producer cooperatives globally is the Mondragon experiment in Spain.

South Asia has also experimented with producer cooperatives and we explore the highly successful rural (hence unique) Mararikulam Experiment in Kerala, India, and the Kerala Dinesh Beedi Workers' (KDB) Cooperative. Both represent a partnership of a progressive worker's social movement and an ideologically well-disposed government. The subsequent success in both cases was the result of worker effort and state support.

The other four success stories are private sector driven but also unconventional and remarkable. All countries in South Asia have exporting success stories. The ones reviewed are based on clusters and the insertion into value chains to gain production and export advantage. Clusters provide many conglomeration advantages of external economies and collective action, but the success ultimately represents a partnership of the state via industrial policy with local and foreign capital.

This is the case for all the case studies including surgical instruments and football exports from Sialkot, Pakistan. With variations, garment exports from Bangladesh are also based on clusters after local production was catalyzed by state support and linkages with foreign capital. Information technology from India is based on the "brain gain" model of harnessing expatriate talent and resources along with a partnership with foreign capital and state support.

Chapter 11 continues with an unusual exporting success from India, i.e., the automobile and accessory industry. Several economists have considered India's catch-up growth model as unusual in that it seemed to have bypassed building a successful industrial base and moving straight to services. The success of the automobile and accessory industry based on a partnership of the state, local, and foreign capital and labor with the former two in the driving seat shows this is not necessarily the case and that India has considerable manufacturing potential that it put to good use in producing this impressive success story.

The exporting success stories in Chapters 10 and 11 again demonstrate that the success stories defy simple ISI vs. EP or neoliberal vs. developmentalist dichotomies and that development pragmatism calls for utilizing all suitable strategies and approaches in the service of catch-up growth. Such pragmatism also requires putting aside hardened ideological positions such as say the opposition to FDI. While MNCs seek advantage as profit-making entities and the asymmetrical power association with L/LMIC gives them a distinct advantage in framing the rules of the game to suit themselves, the case studies in Chapters 10 and 11 demonstrate how foreign capital can be tapped to advantage with state support and smart business strategy.

The role of foreign capital in the form of foreign aid is not as prominent in the success stories documented in this book as proponents of foreign aid suggest to be the case. However, partnership with donors was important in participatory development in Pakistan and to a lesser extent in Joint Forest Management in India and Nepal and in fertility reduction in Bangladesh.

To summarize, this book explores various economic successes in South Asia based on partnerships between the state, civil society and local and foreign capital at the macro-, meso- and microlevels. It also makes a case for development pragmatism and calls for gaining insights from all strategies and approaches and going beyond ossified false dichotomies in strategies and approaches like ISI vs. EP and neoliberalism vs. developmentalism. Finally, another recurring themes of this book is collective action resulting from innovative types of rural (village/community/apex organizations) and urban (producer cooperatives, clusters) partnerships between state, civil society and local and foreign capital.

Index

Note: Page numbers for tables appear in boldface.